Healthcare Analytics for Quality and Performance Improvement

Healthcare Analytics for Quality and Performance Improvement

TREVOR L. STROME

WILEY

Cover image: © iStockphoto.com/pictafolio
Cover design: Andrew Liefer

Published by John Wiley & Sons, Inc., Hoboken, New Jersey.
Published simultaneously in Canada.

Library of Congress Cataloging-in-Publication Data:
Strome, Trevor L., 1972–
Healthcare analytics for quality and performance improvement / Trevor L. Strome.
pages cm
ISBN 978-1-118-51969-1 (cloth) — ISBN 978-1-118-76017-8 (ePDF) — ISBN 978-1-118-76015-4 (ePub) — ISBN 978-1-118-761946-1 (oBook). 1. Health services administration—Data processing. 2. Information storage and retrieval systems—Medical care. 3. Organizational effectiveness. I. Title.
RA971.6.S77 2014
362.1068—dc23

2013023363

Printed in the United States of America

10 9 8 7 6 5 4 3 2 1

Dedicated to
Karen, Isabella, and Hudson—for all your support, understanding, and love

Contents

Preface

Why write a book on healthcare analytics that focuses on quality and performance improvement? Why not focus instead on how healthcare information technology (HIT) and "big data" are revolutionizing healthcare, how quality improvement (QI) methodologies such as Lean and Six Sigma are transforming poorly performing healthcare organizations (HCOs) into best-in-class facilities, or how leadership and vision are the necessary driving factors behind innovation and excellence within HCOs?

The truth is, this book is about all these things. Or, more accurately, this book is about how healthcare organizations need to capitalize on HIT, data from source systems, proven QI methodologies, and a spirit of innovation to achieve the transformation they require. All of these factors are necessary to achieve quality and performance improvement within modern healthcare organizations. However, the professionals working in healthcare IT, quality improvement, management, and on the front lines all speak different languages and see the world from different perspectives—technology, data, leadership, and QI. This gap (a chasm, really) prevents these professionals from effectively working together and limits their capability to perform effective quality and performance improvement activities. This may in fact be lowering the quality of care and decreasing patient safety at a time when doing the opposite is critical.

This book demonstrates how the clinical, business, quality improvement, and technology professionals within HCOs can and must collaborate. After all, these diverse professional groups within healthcare are working together to achieve the same goal: safe, effective, and efficient patient care. Successful quality improvement requires collaboration between these different stakeholders and professional groups; this book provides the common ground of shared knowledge and resources necessary for QI, IT, leadership, and clinical staff to become better coordinated, more integrated, and to work together more effectively to leverage analytics for healthcare transformation.

In this book, I hope to demonstrate that analytics, above all, can and *must* be made accessible throughout the entire HCO in order for the insight and information possible through analytics to actually get used where it is needed. I attempt to dispel the myth that only a select few can be qualified to be working with the data of an HCO. Although the process of generating insight through analytics requires some statistics and mathematics, the output or *result* of analytics must make intuitive sense to all members of the healthcare team. In my experience, if the information and insight produced by business intelligence and analytics is too complex to understand for all but the team that generated it, then that information will contribute very little to healthcare improvement.

In keeping with the theme of accessibility, I have attempted to keep this book very accessible to readers with various backgrounds and experience. The book covers a wide range of topics spanning the information value chain, from information creation and management through to analysis, sharing, and use. As such, it cannot cover each of the topics completely and in depth. But it does cover the areas that I believe are vital in a quality improvement environment driven by analytics. If you work in the area of health IT, data management, or QI, I have attempted to connect the dots in how your professional discipline fits in with the others. I hope that this book can thereby enable technical, analytical, QI, executive, and clinical members of the healthcare team to communicate clearly, better understand one another's needs, and jointly collaborate to improve the efficiency, effectiveness, and quality of healthcare.

I do admit my bias toward the acute-care setting, and emergency departments in particular. The vast majority of my career has been within acute care and emergency, and the writing and examples in this book definitely reflect that bias—although I have tried not to make *every* example an emergency department example! The basic concepts of quality, value, performance, and analytics will translate well to almost any setting, whether it is medicine, surgery, home care, or primary care.

In my opinion, the real value of analytics occurs when the insight generated through analytical tools and techniques can be used directly by quality improvement teams, frontline staff, and other healthcare professionals to improve the quality and efficiency of patient care. To some, this may not be the most glamorous application of analytics, but it is the most important.

Book Overview

After a discussion of the escalating inefficiencies and costs of healthcare (Chapter 1), a high-level overview of the various components of an effective analytics system within an HCO is covered in Chapter 2. Because of the need for strong alignment between the quality and process improvement goals of the organization, the various demands facing healthcare IT departments, and the balancing that analytics must do between these competing interests, Chapter 3 provides an overview of an effective analytics strategy framework that HCOs can use to keep their focus on efforts that achieve the desired improvement results of the organization. Chapter 4 is an overview of the concepts of quality and value, and how these are measured within an HCO. Three quality improvement methodologies (PDSA, Lean, and Six Sigma) are discussed in Chapter 4 as well, and how analytics can provide support to these various types of initiatives.

Chapters 5, 6, and 7 focus on data. Chapter 5 is an overview of data quality and data management, and how to ensure that analytics professionals and stakeholders have access to the high-quality data they need in order to provide information and insight to the organization. Chapter 6 discusses the different types of data, important methods of summarizing and understanding data, and how data type affects the kind of analysis that is possible. Chapter 7 provides tips on how to convert data into metrics and indicators that provide the HCO with a much clearer lens through which to monitor and evaluate performance and quality.

Chapter 8 is about how to meld analytics and quality improvement activities so that QI teams can benefit from the insight and information available throughout all phases of QI projects, regardless of the QI methodology that is chosen. Chapter 9 highlights several of the key statistical and graphical methods for monitoring performance and detecting when in fact a true change in performance or quality has occurred. Chapter 10 talks about usability of analytics from an access and presentation point of view. The advanced analytics discussed in Chapter 11 includes tools such as regression and machine-learning approaches that can be used to identify patterns in healthcare data and predict likely outcomes.

Finally, Chapter 12 discusses achieving analytics excellence within an HCO, including the types of leadership and management required within an HCO to ensure that data and privacy are held secure and that analytics is used appropriately and to its maximum effectiveness.

Acknowledgments

It is impossible to write a book of this scope without tremendous amounts of support and encouragement. I am lucky to be surrounded by people who have been incredibly encouraging and supportive throughout this journey.

First and foremost, I would like to thank my wife and my two wonderful children for your unconditional love and support, and for your inspiration and undying encouragement during the writing of this book. I love you more than you can ever know!

I would like to thank my friends and colleagues at the Winnipeg Regional Health Authority (WRHA) Emergency Program, within other WRHA departments and programs, and in the Department of Emergency Medicine, University of Manitoba. The support, guidance, and feedback you've given me during the writing process were absolutely instrumental in helping me complete this work. I have gained tremendously by working on frontline quality improvement projects with many of the hardest-working and most dedicated clinical personnel in healthcare. To everyone from whom I've drawn the examples and case studies in this book, it is from your experience, efforts, and desire to improve healthcare that I gain confidence that healthcare transformation is truly possible.

I would like to thank Karen Strome, Lori Mitchell, and Ryan McCormack, who provided invaluable assistance by reviewing and commenting on several of the key chapters in this book. Your advice and feedback have made this a much better book than would have been possible on my own.

I would also like to thank Laura Madsen, preeminent healthcare business intelligence expert and author of *Healthcare Business Intelligence: A Guide to Empowering Successful Data Reporting and Analytics*, for inspiring me to write *this* book and for kindly introducing me to her publisher, John Wiley & Sons.

CHAPTER 1

Toward Healthcare Improvement Using Analytics

Innovation is anything but business as usual.

—Anonymous

How sustainable is healthcare in its current state? Most healthcare organizations (HCOs) claim to be undertaking quality improvement (QI) initiatives, but only a few are consistently improving the quality of healthcare in a sustainable fashion. Despite increased spending on healthcare in the United States, there is little evidence that the quality of healthcare can be improved by increasing spending alone. Health information systems is one technology with the potential to transform healthcare because, among its many capabilities, it can deliver the best evidence to the point of care, employs intelligent algorithms to reduce and prevent medical mistakes, and collects detailed information about every patient encounter. Even with growing volumes of data to analyze resulting from the continuing proliferation of computer systems, HCOs are struggling to become or remain competitive, highly functioning enterprises. This chapter will highlight current challenges and pressures facing the healthcare system, identify opportunities for transformation, and discuss the important role that analytics has in driving innovation and achieving healthcare transformation goals.

Healthcare Transformation—Challenges and Opportunities

Healthcare delivery is undergoing a radical transformation. This is occurring as the result of both necessity and opportunity. Change is necessary because, in many ways, the provision of healthcare is less efficient, less safe, and less sustainable than in the past. The opportunity, however, arises from the advancement of technology and its impact on healthcare delivery. Technology now allows increasingly intelligent medical devices and information systems to aid in clinical decision making, healthcare management, and administration. The challenge facing HCOs is to leverage advances in both clinical device technology and information technology (IT) to create and sustain improvements in quality, performance, safety, and efficiency.

Data generated via healthcare information technology (HIT) can help organizations gain significantly deeper insight into their performance than previous technologies (or lack of technology) allowed. HCOs, however, face the very real risk of information overload as nearly every aspect of healthcare becomes in some way computerized and subsequently data-generating. For example, radio frequency identification (RFID) devices can report the location of every patient, staff member, and piece of equipment within a facility; sampled every second, the location data captured from these devices accumulates quickly. Portable diagnostic equipment now captures and stores important patient clinical data, such as vital signs, and can forward that data to electronic medical records (EMRs) or other computerized data stores. Similarly, devices with embedded "labs on a chip" can now perform point-of-care testing for many blood-detectable diseases, and generate enormous volumes of data while doing so.

HCOs must find a way to harness the data at their disposal and take advantage of it to improve clinical and organizational performance. Data analytics is critical to gaining knowledge, insight, and actionable information from these organizations' health data repositories. Analytics consists of the tools and techniques to explore, analyze, and extract value and insight from healthcare data. Without analytics, the information and insight potentially contained within HCOs' databases would be exceedingly difficult to obtain, share, and apply.

But insight without action does not lead to change; data overload can risk impeding, not improving, the decision-making ability of healthcare leaders, managers, and QI teams. In my experience, the true potential of analytics is realized only when analytics tools and techniques are combined with and integrated into a rigorous, structured QI framework. This powerful combination helps to maintain the focus of QI and management teams on achieving the quality and business goals of an organization. Analytics can also be used to explore the available data and possibly identify new opportunities for improvement or suggest innovative ways to address old challenges. When an HCO uses analytics to focus improvement efforts on existing goals and to identify new improvement opportunities, healthcare can become more effective, efficient, safe, and sustainable.

The Current State of Healthcare Costs and Quality

A discussion on the topic of healthcare analytics must first begin with a discussion of healthcare quality. This is because analytics in healthcare exists for the purpose of improving the safety, efficiency, and effectiveness of healthcare delivery. Looking at the current and emerging challenges facing healthcare the way we looked at problems in the past can and will only result in more of the same. And it seems that many people, from healthcare providers who are overworked to patients who must endure unacceptably long waiting lists for relatively common procedures, are extremely dissatisfied with the way things are now.

Despite the seemingly miraculous capabilities of the healthcare system to maintain the health of, and in many cases save the lives of, patients, the system itself is far from infallible. The question of how safe is healthcare delivery must continually be asked. The often-cited Institute of Medicine (IoM) report *To Err Is Human: Building a Safer Health System* declares that a "substantial body of evidence points to medical errors as a leading cause of death and injury."[1] The report cites two studies that estimate between 44,000 and 98,000 patients die every year in hospitals because of medical errors that could have been prevented. These are people who expected the healthcare system to make them well again or keep them healthy and were horribly let down.

According to the IoM report, the types of errors that commonly occur in hospitals include "adverse drug events and improper transfusions, surgical injuries and wrong-site surgery, suicides, restraint-related injuries or death, falls, burns, pressure ulcers, and mistaken patient identities." Not surprisingly, emergency departments, operating rooms, and intensive care units experience the highest error rates and those with the most serious consequences.

Not only do hospital errors result in a staggering yet largely preventable human toll, but they result in a tremendous financial burden as well. It is estimated that the cost to society of these preventable errors ranges between $17 billion and $29 billon in both direct and indirect financial costs. Of course, the majority of these errors are not caused by deliberate malpractice, recklessness, or negligence on the part of healthcare providers. Rather, according to the IoM report, the most common causes of healthcare errors are "due to the convergence of multiple contributing factors" and that "the problem is the system needs to be made safer."[2]

In the near decade and a half that has passed since the release of the 1999 Institute of Medicine report, most of its findings are as relevant today as they were in 1999. Despite dramatic innovations in biomedicine and healthcare technology since the IoM report, many HCOs today still find themselves under immense pressures, some of which include:

- Improving quality and patient safety
- Ensuring patient satisfaction

- Adapting to changes in legislation and regulations
- Adopting new technologies
- Demonstrating improved patient outcomes
- Remaining sustainable and competitive

The challenge facing HCOs today is to balance the need to innovate by adopting new technologies and improving processes while providing the essentials of safe, efficient, and effective patient care. While these two needs are complementary, with improved patient care as the ultimate goal, they both require financial, human, and technical resources that are drawn from a limited, and in some cases shrinking, resource pool.

The Cost of Healthcare

HCOs must endeavor to reduce unnecessary deaths, injuries, and other hardships related to medical errors and other issues stemming from substandard quality. But given that the cost of healthcare delivery seems to be increasing unabatedly, could healthcare be at risk of becoming unsustainable in its current form? Direct and indirect costs attributed to healthcare represent a significant and increasing burden on the economies of countries providing modern healthcare, and may not be sustainable at current growth rates.

Figure 1.1 illustrates the immense cost of healthcare by showing the percentage of healthcare expenditures as a proportion of the gross domestic product (GDP) of selected countries.[3] Of the countries in Figure 1.1, total health expenditure as a share of GDP ranges from 2.4 percent (Indonesia) to 17.4 percent (United States). Of significance is that healthcare expenditures in the United States totaled over 17 percent of its GDP—5 percent more than the next highest country, and almost 8 percent more than the OECD average of 9.6 percent. But not only have expenditures on healthcare increased in the United States from approximately 5 percent of GDP in 1960 to over 15 percent in 2008, they are expected to grow still further, reaching approximately 20 percent of GDP by 2018.

Andy Grove, former chief operating office and chief executive officer of Intel Corporation and a pioneer in the semiconductor industry, once stated, "There is at least one point in the history of any company when you have to change dramatically to rise to the next level of performance. Miss that moment—and you start to decline." Given the numerous pressures and escalating costs facing the healthcare systems of many nations, *now* is the time for HCOs to innovate using available tools and technologies to transform into more sustainable, efficient, effective, and safe providers of care.

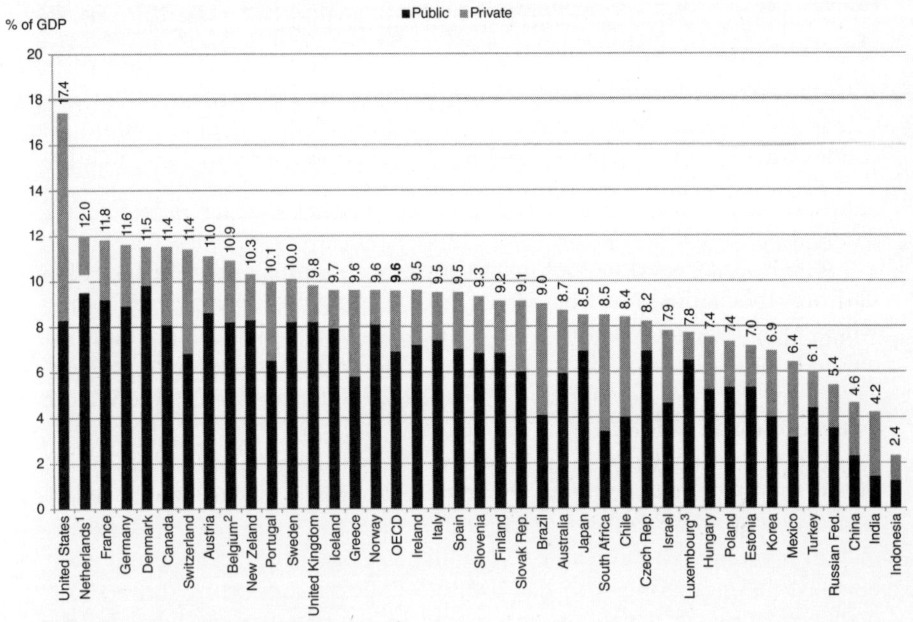

FIGURE 1.1 Total Healthcare Expenditures for Selected Countries as a Share of Gross Domestic Product (2009)

1. In the Netherlands, it is not possible to clearly distinguish the public and private share related to investments.
2. Total expenditure excluding investments.
3. Health expenditure is for the insured population rather than the resident population.

Source: OECD Health Data 2011; WHO Global Health Expenditure Database.

The Analytics Opportunity in Healthcare

The good news is that HCOs can take the necessary action to improve quality of care, increase value to patients, and raise the bottom line. Advances in HIT, and particularly the field of healthcare analytics, are now helping HCOs to reveal and act on opportunities for transformative improvement.

The term "analytics" has been described in myriad ways. For the purposes of this book, I will refer to analytics as the systems, tools, and techniques that help HCOs gain insight into current performance, and guide future actions, by discerning patterns and relationships in data and using that understanding to guide decision making. Analytics enables leaders, managers, and QI teams within HCOs to make better decisions and take more appropriate actions by providing the right information to the right people, at the right time, in the right format, with the right technology.

Healthcare Analytics

Healthcare analytics consists of the systems, tools, and techniques that help HCOs gain insight into current performance, and guide future actions, by discerning patterns and relationships in data and using that understanding to guide decision making.

One doesn't need to look far to observe the impact that analytics has had on other industries. Companies such as Google, Amazon, and others whose very existence depends on users' ease of access to highly targeted, tailored, and user-friendly information demonstrate the realm of the possible—that the tools, techniques, algorithms, and data now exist to drive our analytics-powered world.

The use of analytics in healthcare, however, has lagged behind other industries. Internet search engines make it incredibly easy to enter a search term and almost immediately retrieve a list of web pages that contain information pertaining to the search term ranked in order of relevance and likely usefulness. Yet anyone who has used an EMR or a reporting tool to look up information on a patient, or a group of patients, knows how difficult finding the necessary information can be. And anybody who has tried to get the information they need for a healthcare quality and/or performance improvement project would not be faulted for thinking that obtaining *any* information of value is downright impossible.

WHY QUALITY IMPROVEMENT PROJECTS FAIL HCOs are always working to improve the quality of their care and the efficiency of their business operations. Many HCOs do not see much improvement in quality and performance despite engaging in multiple improvement initiatives. Unfortunately, some HCOs will undertake QI projects without an overall quality strategy or long-term evaluation plan and end up with many disconnected, half-evaluated projects that never seem to achieve their objectives.

Some HCOs focus on improving quality in bursts, with intense activity and enthusiasm that lasts only for a short period of time. Such torrents of QI activity is usually in reaction to some negative event such as a critical incident, or after a "eureka" moment occurs in which an executive member learns something new at a conference, after seeing a product demonstration, or while speaking with a consultant. Once the initial excitement wears off the initiative, the unit, department, program, facility, or entire enterprise may revert back to its initial or some other suboptimal state if a solid quality framework and sustainability plan are not in place.

Even HCOs with QI entrenched in their organizational culture, a proven track record, and well-evolved QI frameworks in place rarely achieve total success and must revisit areas of improvement (often multiple times) to help ensure that improvement results are maintained. This is because achieving change within HCOs is difficult and, much like breaking a bad habit, rarely is sustained after the first try.

> *Health care is the most difficult, chaotic, and complex industry to manage today [and the hospital is] altogether the most complex human organization ever devised.*
>
> —*Peter Drucker*

Making changes to an HCO is difficult because healthcare is a very dynamic environment and in a constant state of flux. Innovations in healthcare technology are ushering in changes at a rapid pace, emerging diseases and changing patient demographics are presenting new treatment challenges to clinical staff, and organizations themselves face an ongoing barrage of new regulations and changes to funding models. What might have been an effective and/or necessary process, workflow, or policy 20 years ago (or even two years ago) may be no longer relevant, or in need of major updating to be made relevant once again.

HCOs must evolve and adapt not merely to maintain and improve quality, performance, and patient safety, but to survive. Of course, the standard principles of providing safe, efficient, and effective patient care will never change—but exactly *how* that is done must *always* evolve.

LEVERAGING INFORMATION TECHNOLOGY Although HIT is one of the largest drivers of healthcare innovation (or disruption, as some healthcare providers would claim), HIT provides the tools required to monitor, evaluate, and improve healthcare quickly and with clarity. In fact, improving quality in a modern HCO to the extent and at the pace necessary *without* the benefit of the information derived from HIT would be an onerous task.

A NOTE ON TERMINOLOGY

I will use the term "healthcare information technology" (HIT) when referring to systems that are mainly clinical in nature such as electronic medical record (EMR), radiology information system (RIS), and other similar systems. I will use the term "information technology" (IT) more generically to include both clinical and nonclinical systems (such as financial, supply chain management, and other such tools).

Despite what some vendors may promise, it takes more than simply adopting HIT to improve quality and performance within an HCO. In fact, it is ironic that a mere decade ago many healthcare improvement efforts were likely stymied due to lack of data. Now it is entirely possible that improvement efforts could be hindered by having *too much* data available without the necessary experience and tools to analyze it and put it to good use.

This is not to say that healthcare improvement cannot occur without the use of IT, but at some point every HCO must use data to monitor and evaluate ongoing changes and fine-tune improvements. I have seen mediocre HCOs become top performers as a result of the intelligent use of information in combination with strong leadership, a clear vision, a culture of innovation, and a drive to succeed. Although technology is never the *only* solution, analytics consists of many tools, technologies, and techniques that HCOs can employ to leverage the data amassed from the increasing number of HIT systems in operation. These innovations in combination with competent, effective leadership enable HCOs to become more efficient and adept at achieving, evaluating, and sustaining improvements in healthcare.

THE ANALYTICS KNOWLEDGE GAP In pursuit of clinical and operational excellence, HCOs are drawing from diverse, nontraditional professions (from a healthcare perspective) to form QI and innovation teams. In addition to nurses, physicians, and administrators, it is not uncommon to see engineers, computer scientists, and other specialist roles working within healthcare. Although having traditional and nontraditional roles working side by side to solve the many problems facing healthcare brings incredible diversity and flexibility, this arrangement also poses some challenges.

Successful healthcare quality and performance improvement initiatives require strong executive sponsorship and support, QI expertise, subject matter expertise, and information management and analysis expertise. Bringing these various disciplines together provides diversity that can lead to the synergistic development of innovations but also exposes significant knowledge gaps between these groups. (See Figure 1.2 for an illustration of this knowledge gap.)

Each professional group brings with it its own particular skill sets, knowledge, and comfort levels working with data and analytics. The analytics knowledge gap may make it seem like nobody is speaking the same language, which can prevent teams from working effectively and cohesively together. To reduce friction and misunderstanding on healthcare quality and leadership teams, it is necessary to bridge the knowledge gap. Bridging the gap enables team members to communicate more effectively, to ask the right questions, and to frame the answers and insights in ways that make sense and are relevant to the improvement challenges at hand.

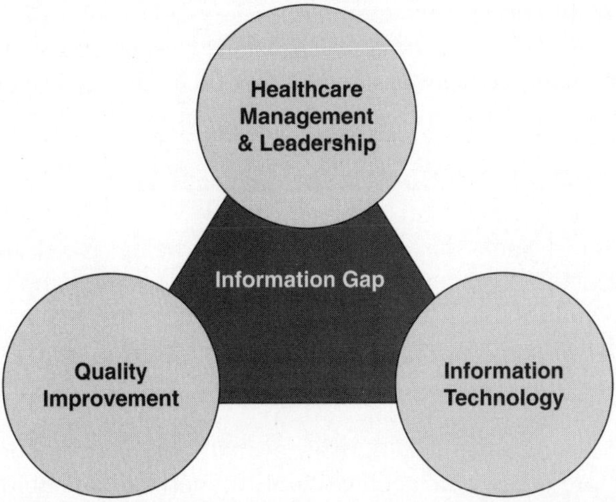

FIGURE 1.2 The Analytics Information Gap between QI, IT, and Healthcare Leadership

Leveraging Information for Healthcare Improvement

As HCOs turn to technological solutions to manage business operations and treat patients, many are literally becoming awash in data. In fact, some estimates are that healthcare data in the United States alone totaled approximately 150 *exabytes* (150×10^{18} bytes) in 2011 for clinical, financial, and administration systems; of course, this number will only continue to grow. In fact, a single large American healthcare provider alone is estimated to have accumulated up to 44 petabytes (a petabyte is 10^{15} bytes) of patient data from electronic health record data (including images and annotations).[4]

As HCOs continue to amass large quantities of data, that data is only of any value if it gets used. Many HCOs are becoming more "data centered," in

"BIG DATA" IS A RELATIVE TERM

Although "big data" is a term commonly used to describe the very large data sets of today, there is no doubt that the anticipated future growth in healthcare data will make today's "big data" seem minuscule. I still remember when having 16 megabytes of random access memory on a computer was a big deal, and a 1-gigabyte hard drive was considered more storage than you'd ever need.

that they are making conscious efforts to make better use of the data available to assist with decision making and QI initiatives. Of course, HCOs vary in the extent and degree of sophistication by which they are leveraging their available data for informed decision making and performance improvement.

TRADITIONAL TOOLS ARE OUTDATED AND INEFFECTIVE As analytical tools become more commonly used in healthcare beyond executive-suite analysts and biostatisticians, the questions that are being asked are increasingly complex. It is becoming clear that traditional reporting approaches are becoming woefully inadequate and outdated—they are unable to deliver information that is accurate and timely enough to drive decision making, and they can only scratch the surface of today's growing healthcare databases.

Healthcare leaders are dealing with a multitude of regulatory, quality, and financial pressures and need accurate, timely, and readily available information to make decisions. In fact, HCOs do not require more reports to achieve desired improvement goals. HCOs require better insight into their own operations, transparency across boundaries, and accountability for their performance. The limiting, conventional views about decision making, data, and reporting must be challenged to allow for creative use of the available data and emerging analytics tools to foster data-based (not gut-based) decision making—in real time and near the point of care.

INFORMING DECISION MAKING It is commonly said that data must be used to "drive decisions" in order to impact quality and performance improvement. What does "drive decisions" really mean, however, and how do we measure and judge how well information is being used? Much information is produced by analysts and other users of healthcare business intelligence (BI) systems, and most of this information is consumed by managers and other healthcare leaders. But how does (or how can) all this information actually drive decision making?

Unfortunately, the default position for many organizations with respect to using information is the same type of reporting on which they have always relied. I am sure that after installing new HIT and healthcare BI solutions, every organization requests the BI and analytics team to develop the exact same reports as before. This discomfort of leaving behind what never really worked anyway means that many HCOs fall into an information rut that inhibits them from truly leveraging the information at their disposal.

It is not my intention to give the term "report" a bad name, as if reports are the root of all that is wrong with the use of healthcare data. The truth is that a report can come in many guises. One example is the old-fashioned monthly multipage report that is distributed throughout an organization but rarely makes it out of the e-mail in-box. (Nobody distributes *printed* reports anymore, do they?) Dashboards, of course, are also reports, but good dashboards present up-to-date indicators, consisting of relevant metrics with targets to maintain accountability, that truly assist with making decisions.

In fact, the usefulness of information has absolutely *nothing* to do with the medium in which it is presented. A graphical, interactive dashboard can be just as disadvantageous as a stale, printed multi-page report in tabular format if the information contained within does not help answer the pressing business problems facing an HCO.

> **Tip**
>
> The usefulness of information has absolutely nothing to do with the medium in which it is presented.

Rather than getting caught up in which medium information is presented, I believe that analytics professionals need to focus on ensuring that the information that is being used for decision making and QI has most (if not all) of the following attributes, which will be described later in this book. It is:

- Accurate
- Timely
- Relevant (to the questions being asked)
- Directed (at the right individual or stakeholders)
- Analyzed (appropriately given the types of data and questions being asked)
- Visualized (in a way that makes sense to the stakeholder)

Beginning the Analytics Journey in Healthcare

QI is often considered to be a "journey" in healthcare because of the constant evolution the HCO undergoes, because of the constant learning required to adapt to a changing environment, and because quality is a moving target. An HCO should never strive for good enough, but should always be improving.

The use of analytics within an HCO to improve quality and performance is a journey in much the same way. Analytics must be developed in an agile manner to keep pace with the changing needs of quality and performance improvement initiatives. Analytics specialists must keep their professional knowledge up to date and relevant because the technology that enables analytics is always changing as are the analytic techniques (such as algorithms and statistical models) that are used to gain insight into healthcare data. Analytics is very much a moving target—what is sufficient (and even leading-edge) in today's healthcare environment most likely will not be five years from now.

The role of analytics professionals in healthcare will continue to grow both in scope and in importance. I believe that for analytics to become a true game changer, analytics professionals must no longer be relegated to the back rooms of IT shops simply building reports and fulfilling endless data requests. Analytics must be brought to the front lines, where the innovative and transformational QI work takes place. Analytics professionals must be willing and prepared to engage with frontline QI teams and clinical staff directly, participate on quality initiatives, and experience what information is needed and how analytics is, and has the potential to be, used on the front lines. Information served up on a "report development request" basis *cannot* play a transformational role in healthcare improvement; transformation is possible only with embedded, agile, and motivated analytics teams working side by side with other QI team members to achieve the quality and performance goals and objectives of the organization.

It is incumbent on healthcare leaders to enable QI, IT, and analytics teams to work together with frontline staff to support analytics-driven evidence- and data-informed quality and performance improvement initiatives. In order for that to happen, there must be some common understanding around the topics of technology, data, and QI so that professionals in these different disciplines can communicate effectively within a team-based project environment.

Unfortunately, many QI professionals and QI team members have limited knowledge of the technology involved in healthcare analytics, what data is available, or even what analyses, visualizations, and other aspects of analytics can even be requested. Technology experts in IT who develop the code to transfer data from source systems to data warehouses (or other data stores) may not know the best format in which to make data available to BI and analytics tools, and so they may choose default data types based on how the data "looks" rather than on contextual knowledge of what the data means and how it will be used. Finally, analytics professionals who are building dashboards and other analytics for QI teams may not know the terminology around Six Sigma or Lean, and may not be familiar with the specific types of visualizations (e.g., statistical process control charts) or other analyses common with such methodologies.

Despite where your HCO is on its analytics journey, remember that although the tools and technology of analytics will likely change at a rapid pace, the *people* are the most important component of healthcare analytics. The future of healthcare analytics will involve professionals from many

A NOTE ABOUT TERMINOLOGY

It has been an enigma throughout the writing of this book how to name analytics professionals within the HCO. It is challenging to attach a label to a group of professionals who come from such diverse backgrounds, bring such an amazing range of skills, and play such an important role in bringing data to life within an HCO. As is typical in this book, I have shied away from using the trendy term of the day, and instead have leaned more toward classical or enduring terminology. I have opted to use the term "analytics professional," or sometimes "analytics developer," to be as inclusive as possible. I know that not everyone will agree with this term, and I am ambivalent about it myself, but it is a term I believe is nonetheless both inclusive and descriptive.

disciplines, with a common understanding of how analytics and QI must work together, using information made possible via analytics to create an environment able to provide patients with safe and effective healthcare of the absolute highest quality possible.

Notes

1. Linda T. Kohn, Janet M. Corrigan, and Molla S. Donaldson, eds., *To Err Is Human: Building a Safer Health System* (Washington, DC: National Academy Press, 2000), 26.
2. Ibid, 49.
3. *Health at a Glance 2011: OECD Indicators* (Paris, OECD Publishing, 2011), http://dx.doi.org/10.1787/health_glance-2011-en.
4. Mike Cottle et al., *Transforming Health Care through Big Data: Strategies for Leveraging Big Data in the Health Care Industry* (New York: Institute for Health Technology Transformation, 2013), www.ihealthtran.com/big_data_in_healthcare.html.

CHAPTER 2

Fundamentals of Healthcare Analytics

If you always do what you always did, you will always get what you always got.

—Albert Einstein

Effective healthcare analytics requires more than simply extracting information from a database, applying a statistical model, and pushing the results to various end users. The process of transforming data captured in source systems such as electronic medical records (EMRs) into information that is used by the healthcare organization to improve quality and performance requires specific knowledge, appropriate tools, quality improvement (QI) methodologies, and the commitment of management. This chapter describes the key components of healthcare analytics systems that enables healthcare organizations (HCOs) to be efficient and effective users of information by supporting evidence-informed decisions and, ultimately, making it possible to achieve their quality and performance goals.

How Analytics Can Improve Decision Making

Healthcare transformation efforts require decision makers to use information to understand all aspects of an organization's performance. In addition to knowing what *has* happened, decision makers now require insight into what is likely going to happen, what the improvement priorities of the organization should be, and what the anticipated impacts of process and other improvements will be. Simply proliferating dashboards, reports, and data visualizations drawn from the HCO's repository of health data is not enough to provide the insight that decision makers need. Analytics, on the other hand, can help HCOs achieve understanding and insight of their quality and operational performance by transforming the way information is used and decisions are made throughout the organization.

Analytics is the system of tools and techniques required to generate insight from data. The effective use of analytics within an HCO requires that the necessary tools, methods, and systems have been applied *appropriately* and *consistently*, and that the information and insight generated by analytics is accurate, validated, and trustworthy.

In modern healthcare, substantial quality and performance improvement may be stymied without changes to the way information is used and acted upon. With this in mind, the fundamental objective of healthcare analytics is to "help people to make and execute rational decisions, defined as being data driven, transparent, verifiable and robust":[1]

- **Data driven.** Modern healthcare standards demand that clinical decisions be based on the best possible evidence that is generated from extensive research and data. Yet administrative decisions, process and workflow design, healthcare information technology (such as EMRs), and even some clinical decisions are often not held to these standards. Analytics in healthcare can help ensure that *all* decisions are made based on the best possible evidence derived from accurate and verified sources of information rather than gut instinct or because a process or procedure has always been done in a certain way.
- **Transparent.** Information silos are still a reality in healthcare due to the belief by some that withholding information from other departments or programs best maintains autonomy and control. This belief, however, often has the opposite effect and invariably leads to misunderstandings and a deterioration of trust. A key objective of analytics in healthcare is to promote the sharing of information and to ensure that the resultant insight and information is clearly defined and consistently interpreted throughout the HCO.
- **Verifiable.** Consistent and verifiable decision making involves a validated decision-making model that links the proposed options from which to choose to the decision criteria and associated methodology for selecting the best available option. With this approach, the selected option "can be verified, based on the data, to be as good as or better than other alternatives brought up in the model."[2]
- **Robust.** Because healthcare is a dynamic environment, decisions must often be made quickly and without perfect data on which to base them. Decision-making models must be robust enough to perform in non-optimal conditions. That is, they must accommodate biases that might be introduced as a result of missing data, calculation errors, failure

to consider all available options, and other issues. Robust models can benefit from a feedback loop in which improvements to the model are made based on its observed performance.

> **Analytics and Decisions**
>
> Healthcare analytics improves decision making by replacing gut instinct with data-driven, transparent, verifiable, and robust decision methods.

Analytics, Quality, and Performance

The techniques and technologies of analytics provide insight into how well an HCO is performing. Analytics enables healthcare leaders and QI stakeholders to make evidence-informed decisions through techniques, tools, and systems that:

- Clarify and improve understanding of patterns seen in data.
- Identify when (and why) change has occurred.
- Suggest (and help validate) the next logical steps to achieve desired change.

First and foremost, analytics must help answer questions and drive decision making related to achieving and maintaining safe, effective, and efficient delivery of healthcare. Effective healthcare analytics, however, consists of more than pointing statistical analysis software at large databases and applying algorithms and visualization techniques.

What distinguishes analytics from most currently deployed reports and dashboards are the graphical, mathematical, and statistical tools and techniques to better *understand* quality and performance issues, and more importantly, to identify what possible actions to take. Figure 2.1 illustrates the ways in which information can be used to support decision making for quality and performance improvement initiatives. Most HCOs use reports and dashboards to review past performance (circle 1). Although a solid understanding of past performance is essential in identifying quality issues and monitoring progress toward meeting targets, relying *solely* on retrospective data provides little insight into what an HCO should be doing now or in the future.

Many HCOs are adopting the capability for real-time performance monitoring, which may include real-time (or short-cycle) dashboards that provide a reasonable picture of what is currently happening within the HCO (circle 2). To be effective, real-time monitoring must encompass appropriate

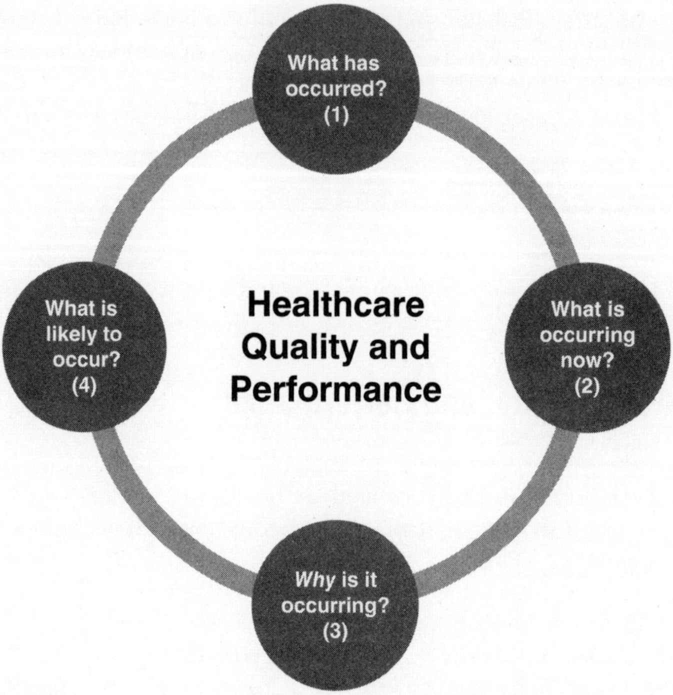

FIGURE 2.1 Reporting and Analytics Capabilities for Quality and Performance Improvement

indicators that are aligned with strategic and/or tactical performance goals and be linked to triggers within business processes that can signal that an action or decision is required.

> **Tip**
>
> To be effective, real-time monitoring must encompass appropriate indicators that are aligned with strategic and/or tactical performance goals and be linked to triggers within business processes that can signal that an action or decision is required.

The reports and dashboards typical of circles 1 and 2 may help highlight what has occurred in the past, or what is currently occurring. But on their own, the information typical of circles 1 and 2 provides little insight into *why* performance is the way it is.

Analytics goes one step further and helps answer questions such as why problems likely are occurring, highlights relationships between events and issues (circle 3), and, given the right models and data, can even begin to anticipate future outcomes and occurrences (circle 4). Analytical approaches (such as regression modeling and data mining techniques, for example) help to highlight relationships between various factors that, to various degrees, may be impacting quality and performance.

For example, within existing reports and dashboards, an HCO might see that there has been a steady hospital-wide drop in patient satisfaction over the last quarter, and that an increase in central line infections has occurred over a similar period. Reports and dashboards may also highlight an increase in emergency department lengths of stay, and an increase in staff absenteeism rates. But most standard methods of reporting are incapable of providing any insight into *why* these issues are arising; charting methods such as basic bar or line graphs would be able to illustrate a trend over time and the amount of change in a measure that has occurred. Analytics tools and techniques go one step further to help provide better insight into why these quality issues are present, determine if they are related, and predict future trends and possible outcomes.

Applications of Healthcare Analytics

One benefit of analytics is to enable healthcare leaders, QI teams, and other decision makers to ensure that the decisions being made are evidence-based, transparent, verifiable, and robust. Most areas of healthcare can benefit from decision making that meets these expectations; a few examples are outlined next.

- **Process and workflow improvement.** Efficient, effective, affordable, and safe patient care begins with processes and workflows that are free of barriers to quality and from which waste is reduced or eliminated. Determining what to improve, and how to improve it, is the responsibility of dedicated multidisciplinary QI teams. The productivity of these QI teams, however, is greatly enhanced when they can leverage analytics to provide detailed insight into the processes and workflows that comprise the management and provision of healthcare.

  QI teams rely on analytics for superior analysis of baseline data to identify bottlenecks and other causes of poor quality and performance. Analysis of baseline performance and quality data helps QI teams to identify and prioritize these causes so that the improvement initiatives selected are the most likely to have an impact and be successful. Analytics is also necessary for monitoring ongoing performance of processes and workflows, after improvements have been made, to ensure that the improvements are sustained in the long term.

- **Clinical decision support (CDS).** Many people incorrectly consider analytics as merely an extension of reporting. But analytics is not just a back-office capability. Analytics in support of clinical decision making can take on many roles, ranging from providing suggestions and evidence regarding the management of a single patient to helping manage an entire unit or department during a surge in patients. CDS is perhaps the ultimate use of healthcare analytics, which is disseminating timely, actionable information and insight to clinical providers at the point of care when that information is required and is the most useful. CDS leverages the information available within the entirety of the enterprise data warehouse (EDW) and clinical source systems to give providers insight into many clinical issues, ranging from possible diagnosis suggestions to predictions for excessive length of stay or adverse outcomes.

  An example of analytics in CDS is computerized provider order entry (CPOE) systems. The best of these systems automatically check the order with medical guidelines and compare ordered medications with other medications a patient is taking to check for the possibility of adverse drug interactions. Benefits of CDS systems are already being realized; one study demonstrated a 40 percent reduction in adverse drug reactions and other critical events in just two months.[3]

  Other examples of analytics in CDS include flagging a patient as being at risk for an extended emergency department visit, or assisting with the triage of multiple patients presenting with an unknown respiratory ailment during influenza season. In the first case, the patient may be placed on special protocols to prevent unnecessarily long stays in the emergency department. In the second, analytics can help fill gaps in patient information and identify which new cases may be high-risk, allowing care providers to take appropriate isolation and infection control precautions.
- **Population health management.** Population health management is "the coordination of care delivery across a population to improve clinical and financial outcomes, through disease management, case management and demand management."[4] Analytics helps HCOs achieve these improvements by identifying patient subpopulations, risk-stratifying the subpopulations (that is, identifying which patients are at highest risk of poor outcomes), and using CDS tools and best evidence to manage patients' and populations' care in the best way possible. Analytics also contributes to the ongoing tracking of patients to determine overall compliance and outcomes.
- **Payer risk analysis and fraud prevention.** One contributing factor to the high cost of healthcare is fraud and other improper billing

to healthcare insurance. Healthcare data analytics is expected "to fundamentally transform medical claims payment systems, resulting in reduced submissions of improper, erroneous or fraudulent claims."[5] This transformation in fraud prevention is possible because computer algorithms are able to analyze healthcare databases, scanning for patterns and other clues in the data that might indicate fraudulent activity and other irregularities. Once a manual, painstaking, and imprecise process, this is now an automated, immensely more efficient process, saving healthcare systems billions of dollars. For example, the Centers for Medicare and Medicaid Services (CMS) achieved $4 billion in recoveries because of the fraud detection abilities possible with data analytics.[6]

In addition to improving understanding within each of these and other components of healthcare, analytics offers the potential to break through traditional barriers and allow understanding across so-called silos.

Components of Healthcare Analytics

Analytics consists of much more than back-office analysts applying computer algorithms to ever-growing volumes of data. Analytics exists in healthcare to enhance the quality and safety of patient care while reducing costs. Patient care is a human-driven endeavor, therefore healthcare analytics requires the *input* of stakeholders to define what is useful and necessary. The *output* that healthcare analytics provides must be utilized by leaders, QI teams, and other decision makers in order to have any effect. Between the initial input and the resultant output, there are many levels and components to an analytics system that make evidence-based decision making possible. Forrester Research, Inc., identifies the "business intelligence [BI] stack"[7] to consist of the following layers:

- Infrastructure
- Performance management
- Supporting applications
- Analytics
- Discovery and integration
- Data
- Infrastructure

The Forrester Research BI stack (and similar models from other organizations) provides a highly detailed summary of the components required to construct a BI infrastructure within a business enterprise (of which healthcare is but one example). The purpose of this book is to focus on the essentials of analytics for healthcare quality and performance improvement, so I have employed a modified stack optimized for healthcare analytics that focuses on business problem identification and insight generation.

Figure 2.2 illustrates this "analytics stack," a representation of what is required of an analytics system within an HCO to provide insight and support evaluation of outcomes. Although not strictly necessary for analytics, a well-developed BI infrastructure will definitely support and enable analytics and decision making throughout the HCO. For an excellent healthcare BI resource, I recommend *Healthcare Business Intelligence: A Guide to Empowering Successful Data Reporting and Analytics*.[8] The analytics stack described here does not focus on the particulars of any one data warehouse model or technology but instead assumes that a mechanism is in place for data to be made available for analytics in a suitable format.

The basic layers of this analytics system for performance and QI are:

- Business context
- Data
- Analytics
- Quality and performance management
- Presentation

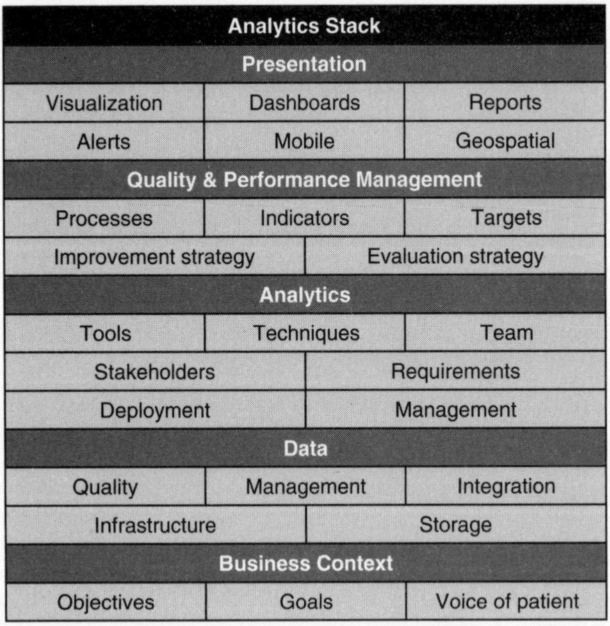
Analytics Stack
Presentation
Visualization
Dashboards
Reports
Alerts
Mobile
Geospatial
Quality & Performance Management
Processes
Indicators
Targets
Improvement strategy
Evaluation strategy
Analytics
Tools
Techniques
Team
Stakeholders
Requirements
Deployment
Management
Data
Quality
Management
Integration
Infrastructure
Storage
Business Context
Objectives
Goals
Voice of patient

FIGURE 2.2 Components of the Healthcare Analytics "Stack"

- **Business context layer.** This layer is the foundation of an analytics system and represents the quality and performance goals and objectives of the HCO. Included in the business context is the "voice of the patient" as a reminder that, above all, the goal of HCOs is to provide value to patients by delivering effective, efficient, and safe medical care. Every organization will have its own set of goals and objectives because of varying circumstances, demographics, and other factors. The goals and objectives of the business, and the strategies the HCOs employ to achieve them, drive requirements at every other level.
- **Data layer.** This layer of the analytics stack represents the quality, management, integration, and storage of data and the associated infrastructure. With the generation and accumulation of healthcare data comes the need to extract and integrate data from source systems such as electronic medical records (EMRs), store the data securely, and make high-quality data available for analytics and BI uses. Aspects of the data layer include:
  - **Data sources.** These are the source systems such as EMRs, plus financial, supply chain, and other operational systems, that providers and other staff utilize in their day-to-day work. By and large, data in source systems is optimized for transactions, not analysis. When more than one data source exists, the data sources must be integrated to achieve true enterprise-wide visibility.
  - **Operational data store.** As part of the integration process of bringing multiple data sources together into a single enterprise view, an HCO may opt for an operational data store (ODS) as an intermediary level of data integration. The ODS forms the basis for additional data operations (such as cleaning and integrity checks).
  - **Enterprise data warehouse.** An EDW is built when available sources of data must be cleaned, transformed, and integrated for analysis and reporting to provide an enterprise-wide view of data. The data warehouse contains key indicators and other performance data pertinent to the quality and performance of multiple domains throughout the HCO.
  - **Analytic sandbox.** The data in the EDW may be stored in a way that is aggregated to allow for faster, more efficient queries and analysis. Analysts may require access to lower-level data (for example, line-level patient data) to test new business rules or to run data-mining algorithms. The analytic sandbox is an area set aside for data for these purposes that does not negatively impact the performance of other operations on the EDW outside the analytics sandbox.
  - **Data marts.** It may not be necessary, or advisable, for somebody to see all the possible data from across the entire enterprise that is available in an EDW. In these cases, data marts are instantiated; data

marts are subsets of data from the data warehouse (or the entire data set when only one source system exists), are usually organized by lines of business or healthcare domain, and represent what somebody within a particular line of business would need to see to best understand the performance of his or her program, department, or unit.

- **Integration.** Combining multiple source systems into a connected EDW is the process of integration. Without proper integration, an EDW would be nothing more than a collection of data points without any clear logic linking them. Integration can occur through a process of Extraction/Transformation/Load (ETL), which, in the most typical scenario, copies data from the source system(s), applies logic to transform it to the analysis needs of the organization, and loads it into an EDW. Other forms of integration, including virtualization, which defines a single interface that links to every point of data in the HCO, are increasingly common as volumes of data expand and new approaches to data management are required.

- **Analytics layer.** This layer is comprised of the tools and techniques that analytics teams use to generate information and actionable insight that drives decision making. Components of this layer include the intellectual knowledge of analytics teams and the computer software tools to apply that know-how. In this layer, analytics helps to identify quality and performance problems, develop analytical models appropriate to the problem, perform statistical analyses, generate insight into problem-solving approaches, and trigger necessary action.

  The analytics layer requires strong involvement from stakeholders, who provide the requirements for analytics that link the strategic-level goals and objectives for the organization to more tactical-level analytics for decision making on the front lines by managers and QI teams. Consideration of how analytics projects and teams are to be managed to ensure a successful deployment is also necessary. There are several key features of the analytics layer:

  - **Online analytical processing (OLAP).** OLAP tools typically accompany data sets that are preaggregated and stored in a multidimensional format (that is, based on dimensions and facts) that allows users to quickly and interactively analyze data from multiple perspectives. OLAP typically consists of three types of operations: drill-down, which allows users to obtain and navigate through additional detail (for example, viewing revenue from each line of business of an HCO), roll-up (the opposite of drill-down, or the consolidation or aggregation of data), and slice-and-dice (with which users can extract a subset of data and view it in multiple dimensions).

  - **Ad hoc analytics.** When more complex analysis is required than is available through OLAP tools, analysts will use more statistical-based or other specialized tools to conduct deeper analysis. This type of analysis usually relies on nonaggregated data, and is often best performed in an analytics sandbox away from other EDW activities.
  - **Text mining.** Text mining involves extracting value (by deriving patterns and trends) from unstructured text data. This is data that is stored in progress notes and wherever else codified data entry is not performed.
  - **Data mining/predictive analytics.** These two disciplines consist of the process of determining patterns and trends in the data, and using the knowledge and understanding of those patterns and trends to make predictions about future performance or occurrences.
- **Quality and performance layer.** This layer aligns analytics to the processes that need to be improved, the indicators by which processes and outcomes will be evaluated, and the performance targets desired by the HCO. The actual improvement strategies and methodologies to be used (such as Lean and Six Sigma) should also be considered in this layer. This is important because improvement projects usually require extensive analysis of baseline performance and typically utilize indicators to evaluate project outcomes in order to sustain improvements in the long term.
  - **Processes.** Data is a by-product of the work that clinical providers and other healthcare workers perform. When these workflows and processes are documented, data can be aligned with them to increase understanding of what the data means.
  - **Indicators.** These are measures of certain aspects of an HCO's performance.
  - **Targets.** These are values that represent what the performance levels of a process or workflow should be, and represent the ideal range of an indicator.
  - **Improvement strategy.** This describes how an HCO intends to address quality and performance issues, and what methodology the organization intends to employ (such as Lean or Six Sigma).
  - **Evaluation strategy.** This is how organizations plan to monitor and evaluate the performance of key processes and indicators within the HCO.
- **Presentation layer.** This layer of the analytics stack can be considered the analytics "user interface." The presentation layer manages the form in which insights and information are delivered to the decision makers. This layer is comprised of elements ranging from traditional reports to contemporary dashboards and can include more specialized tools such as geospatial visualization (or mapping). Although much of the heavy

lifting of healthcare analytics is situated within the data, analytics, and quality management layers, the presentation layer is critical because how well information is communicated will impact its usefulness to decision makers, QI teams, and other stakeholders.

Given the different components that must work in concert to provide meaningful insight to decision makers, the effectiveness of an analytics system for quality and performance improvement will be greatly diminished without an analytics strategy. (See Chapter 3 for further information about developing an analytics strategy.) The purpose of the analytics strategy is to guide the HCO's ability to rapidly respond to the information needs of stakeholders while maintaining a consistent direction in supporting the quality and business goals of the HCO. The analytics strategy provides a guide for sorting through the many and perhaps conflicting analytics needs of the HCO, and ensuring that each of these layers is configured, aligned, and/or developed appropriately to achieve the quality goals of the HCO. The strategy must guide decisions regarding what projects to undertake, what tools to invest in, and how to maximize return on investment in analytics tools. The analytics strategy will align with, or be a component of, the overall BI strategy, since many analytics capabilities will depend on the extent to which a BI infrastructure is in place.

Beyond the layers of data and technology of an analytics system is how the data is used—that is, the problem-solving that spans all of these layers. For example, many dashboards and reports merely reflect what has happened, and provide data in typical, predictable ways. But analytics encourages and assists people to think differently about the data they have and the problems they are solving. Sometimes a simple change such as applying a new visualization or applying a new statistic can help illuminate an existing problem in a whole new light. Other times, more sophisticated analytical techniques will be required to solve a particularly perplexing problem. All components of the analytics stack require careful consideration to ensure that the known questions of today are being addressed, and that an analytics infrastructure is being built that ultimately will address the *unknown* questions of the future.

Notes

1. Rahul Saxena and Anand Srinivasan, *Business Analytics: A Practitioner's Guide, International Series in Operations Research & Management* (New York: Springer Science+Business Media, 2013), 9.
2. Ibid, 10.
3. Mike Cottle et al., *Transforming Health Care through Big Data: Strategies for Leveraging Big Data in the Health Care Industry* (New York: Institute for

Health Technology Transformation, 2013), www.ihealthtran.com/big_data_in_healthcare.html.
4. The Free Dictionary, "population health management," http://medical-dictionary.thefreedictionary.com/population+health+management.
5. Mike Cottle et al., *Transforming Health Care through Big Data*.
6. Ibid.
7. Boris Evelson. *It's Time to Reinvent Your BI Strategy* (Cambridge, MA: Forrester Research, 2007), 4.
8. Laura B. Madsen, *Healthcare Business Intelligence: A Guide to Empowering Successful Data Reporting and Analytics* (Hoboken, NJ: John Wiley & Sons, 2012).

CHAPTER 3

Developing an Analytics Strategy to Drive Change

You've got to think about big things while you're doing small things, so that all the small things go in the right direction.

—Alvin Toffler

An analytics strategy is more than simply a data utilization strategy, a data analysis strategy, a technology strategy, or a quality improvement strategy. In fact, elements of all these are required for an effective analytics strategy. An analytics strategy is necessary to ensure that an organization's analytics capabilities are aligned with its quality and performance improvement needs. This chapter discusses what an analytics strategy is, and will outline the steps necessary to develop an effective analytics strategy. In developing a strategy, the chapter will discuss the components of and inputs to an analytics strategy, stakeholders who must be involved in developing the strategy, communicating the strategy, and how to implement it for maximum success.

Purpose of an Analytics Strategy

The purpose of an analytics strategy is to guide a healthcare organization's (HCO) ability to rapidly respond to the information needs of stakeholders while maintaining a consistent direction in supporting the quality and business goals of the HCO. It provides a guide for sorting through many, perhaps conflicting information and analysis needs, and prevents the HCO from being too swayed by vendor hype and other distractions.

The strategy provides analytics teams with the focus and direction needed to establish analytics and business intelligence (BI) as a strategic resource for healthcare leaders, quality improvement teams, and other decision makers within the HCO. Ultimately, the analytics strategy must aid the HCO to determine:

- What data is most required to address key quality, efficiency, and performance issues facing the HCO;
- What major analytics development projects to undertake and on what tasks to focus the analytics team;
- What skills and knowledge are necessary in the HCO's analytics team;
- What data and integration infrastructure is necessary to support analytics initiatives;
- What analytics software and hardware tools to invest in; and
- How to maximize return on investment in analytics tools, teams, and training by demonstrating value to the HCO.

One definition of strategy is "a bridge that connects a firm's internal environment with its external environment, leveraging its resources to adapt to, and benefit from, changes occurring in its external environment," and as "a decision-making process that transfers a long-term vision into day-to-day tactics to effect the long-term plan."[1] This definition is pertinent to an analytics strategy because the analytics strategy will enable the HCO to leverage its information and analytics resources as it responds to and begins to control the many factors, both internal and external, that impact overall quality and performance. An analytics

ANALYTICS AND BUSINESS INTELLIGENCE

The analytics strategy is a critical adjunct to an HCO's BI strategy, because the hardware, data integration, and data management required for BI also enables the use of analytics. If an HCO is just embarking on the development of a BI infrastructure (perhaps including enterprise data warehouse development), then analytics requirements should be considered during the requirements gathering phase. If a BI infrastructure is already in place, an analytics strategy can help to identify any gaps that exist in BI that might need to be addressed to fully enable the desired analytics requirements of the HCO.

strategy also helps to guide day-to-day decisions regarding systems, people, tools, and techniques, with the long-term goal of enabling analytics to provide information and insight regarding the most pressing problems facing the HCO.

HCOs should develop a strategy for analytics to ensure that the information resources of the organization are aligned with the activities necessary for achieving the HCO's quality and performance goals. Having a strategy cannot guarantee success, but without a strategy, analytics and IT development, team formation, and infrastructure procurement will proceed without the benefit of any clear plan or mandate. This likely will result in an investment of money and time (both resources usually in short supply) in analytics infrastructure, technology, and development projects that *may not* contribute to the fundamental goals of the organization, and may distract the HCO from achieving its goals.

One of the most challenging aspects of working in a healthcare environment is the "emergencies." Not the medical emergencies—those are the domain of the clinicians—but the frequent and urgent need for data and information. These urgent requests range from information required by government agencies, to data for critical incident occurrence reviews, to a quick aggregation of data for a researcher racing to meet a grant deadline. These are a fact of life when working with healthcare data and cannot be avoided, but they should not result in complete and utter chaos within an analytics team.

One struggle for healthcare analytics teams is to maintain sight of "true north," that is, to know where and when to resume work on strategic priorities despite many competing demands. The analytics strategy can help prevent analytics teams from becoming overwhelmed and underproductive by keeping the organizational priorities in focus. Without a strategy that outlines what the analytics priorities are and against which to judge the priority of new and urgent requests, what gets done is usually the request initiated by the person who is the most persuasive, or the problem that seems the most interesting to the analytics team, not necessarily the issue or problem that is the most important to the organization as a whole.

An analytics strategy that aligns with the quality and performance goals of an organization will help the analytics team balance competing requests with strategic priorities and help the team maintain their productivity by reducing the feeling of being overwhelmed. A solid analytics strategy will help enable the analytics team to become a strategic information resource for business improvement and not simply purveyors of reports and data. When analytics teams are primarily occupied fulfilling the data requests of others, the result is that not much time is available for the strategic development of the group.

STRATEGIC DEVELOPMENT VERSUS DEVELOPMENT BY AGGREGATION

I often joke (somewhat ruefully) that analytics tools and capabilities within an HCO are developed through aggregation instead of through design and strategy. For example, whenever an analytics team gets a request for information, they might add the report, dashboard, or other analytics tool to the general analytics or BI repository because "somebody else might need it." The result is a sizable collection of reports and other tools that even the team doesn't remember what they all do. To make matters worse, this causes work to be replicated because one analyst may not be aware of what somebody else has done, or because the original work has been lost in the collection.

Analytics Strategy Framework, with a Focus on Quality/Performance Improvement

In most healthcare information technology (HIT) initiatives, the information technology (IT) department of an HCO is primarily responsible for the implementation and maintenance of the technology itself (that is, the hardware, software, implementation, testing, and maintenance). The primary *users* of HIT, on the other hand, reside within the business side of the organization, and it is also the business side that gains benefit and value from having such tools in place. The partnership between the business side and IT in development of an effective BI and analytics infrastructure may at times be at odds, not because of competing interests necessarily, but because each group may not be aware of or fully understand the interests and priorities of the other.

Building an Analytics Strategy—Templates

To download sample templates and worksheets for developing an analytics strategy within your organization, please visit this book's web site, http://HealthcareAnalyticsBook.com.

Healthcare analytics is not immune to this requirements tug-of-war between IT and the business side of an organization. For example, with clinical applications such as EMRs, the end users are decidedly clinical, whereas IT personnel, who are primarily nonclinical, are responsible for system deployment, support, and maintenance. Analytics development tends to require significant input and participation from both the IT and business side of the organization and should include clinical, data, statistical, application, and technical subject matter experts. With the diversity of skills, knowledge, and people working on analytics for quality improvement and other projects, the analytics strategy helps HCOs:

- Recognize and agree on the quality and performance goals of the HCO;
- Determine the best methods for achieving those goals;
- Identify the analytics required to enable those methods; and
- Assemble the team, build and/or buy the tools, and implement the techniques necessary to make the analytics work.

Figure 3.1 illustrates an analytics strategy framework that incorporates the key components of an effective healthcare analytics system that supports

FIGURE 3.1 Analytics Strategy Framework

quality and performance improvement. The areas that should be considered in a comprehensive analytics strategy include:

- Business and quality context
- Stakeholders and users
- Processes and data
- Tools and techniques
- Team and training
- Technology and infrastructure

These components of an analytics strategy framework are discussed in the following sections.

Business and Quality Context

The business and quality context outlines the business problems facing the HCO, and the quality, financial, and performance goals to which the HCO is committing to address those problems. It is essential to start drafting the analytics strategy with a clear understanding of the needs and requirements of the business; without clear guidance from the needs of the business, analytics may not provide the insight and information required to support the evidence-based decision making necessary to achieve the desired quality and performance goals. To this end, all elements of an analytics environment should be aligned in support of the needs of the business.

The root of every successful analytical venture in which analytics is actively used throughout an HCO by decision makers is a detailed description of the problem being addressed and a clear articulation of why solving that problem is important to the organization. A well-articulated business problem defines a gap between the current (undesirable) state and the future (more desirable) state. Without a clear and concise problem definition, much effort and resources may be focused on addressing mere *symptoms* of a much deeper-rooted problem, or on issues that are not really a priority at all.

There are many types of problems facing HCOs, ranging from financial pressures to regulatory requirements; problem statements identify which are the most pressing for an individual HCO to address at a given time. The types of problems that HCOs need to address will also direct the types of analytics (and supporting data) required. Some problems typical of those experienced and expressed by HCOs include:

- **Clinical quality.** Is the HCO providing the best possible care and diagnostics at the right time, to the right patients, and in the most efficient and safe manner possible?

- **Financial.** Is the HCO making clinical, operational, and administrative decisions that are the most financially sound while still in the best interest of the patients?
- **Patient throughput and value.** Is the HCO providing value to its patients by minimizing the time they must wait for appointments, assessments, treatments, or other services within the organization, and are they satisfied with the performance and care they experience?
- **Human resources.** Is the morale and well-being of the HCO's staff consistent with HR guidelines and, more importantly, consistent with positive patient experiences?

Quality and performance targets are a necessary accompaniment to the problem definition. HCOs cannot possibly improve every process, eliminate every inefficiency, and reduce every risk at once; otherwise, chaos will ensue and *nothing* will improve. Quality and performance targets define what the current priorities of the HCO are, and help to focus the efforts of quality improvement and analytics teams.

The quality goals represent the most pressing problems that have been identified by stakeholders in the organization, highlight what most needs to improve, and indicate the desired or target performance levels. An analytics strategy needs to include the most relevant and important quality goals. This is because an HCO needs to communicate these critical goals to all relevant programs, departments, and units that will be held accountable for their performance.

Stakeholders and Users

From a project management perspective, stakeholders are "individuals and organizations that are actively involved in the project, or whose interests may be positively or negatively affected as a result of project execution" and "may also exert influence over the project and its results."[2] Likewise, an analytics stakeholder is a person or group of persons who are impacted by, will be users of, or otherwise have a concern or interest in the development and deployment of analytical solutions throughout the HCO. In a modern HCO there are few people who are *not* impacted in some way by the use of analytics to improve quality and performance, and there are fewer yet whose roles could not be enhanced through the innovative and effective use of analytics.

When developing an analytics strategy, it is important to elicit and document what each of the stakeholders will require, and develop approaches to ensure that their information needs are being met. There are many stakeholder groups within an HCO; analytics stakeholders typical within an HCO are summarized in Table 3.1.

TABLE 3.1 Summary of Stakeholder Types within an HCO

Stakeholder	Description
Patient	The person whose health and healthcare experience we're trying to improve with the use of analytics.
Sponsor	The person who supports and provides financial resources for the development and implementation of the analytics infrastructure.
Influencer	A person who may not be directly involved in the development or use of analytics within the HCO, but who holds considerable influence (positive *or* negative) over the support of analytics initiatives.
Customer/user	A person within the HCO who accesses analytical tools, or uses the output of analytical tools, to support decision making and to drive action.

Patient. The most important analytics stakeholder within an HCO is the patient. The patient is the reason healthcare exists, and is whom we are trying to care for in safer, more efficient ways through the use of analytics. Most pertinent quality improvement methodologies implore quality improvement practitioners not to lose sight of what is the best for the patient. Although it is possible to forget this fact when not working on the front line, analytics professionals must always remember that they are building analytics to directly support the teams that improve the health and in-hospital experience of the patient.

Sponsor. The sponsor may be one of the most critical stakeholders in the successful implementation and application of analytics within the HCO. The project sponsor is "the individual or group within or external to the performing organization that provides the financial resources, in cash or in kind, for the project."[3] This is the individual (or group of individuals) within the organization at a corporate level who approves, or provides a very strong recommendation to approve, the financial resources necessary to implement a viable analytics infrastructure. In many HCOs, the sponsor may be the same executive who recommends and/or approves funding for other IT initiatives. Keep in mind, though, that analytics efforts cross the boundary between IT and the business so there are likely to be clinical, business, and/or technical sponsors for analytics initiatives.

Customer/user. From a project perspective, the customer is the individual or group that makes use of a project's product.[4] Although the customers and users are often synonymous, within a large organization the customer is often the one who *pays* for the product or work, and the users are the ones who make direct use of the product. The customers and/or users are the individuals within the HCO who require and use the information and insight available with analytics. It is important not only to know *who* these analytics users and customers are, but *how* they intend to interact with the analytics tools and resultant data. For example, will the results of analytics be used to influence clinical decision making, financial planning, quality/process improvement, or for other reasons?

Influencers. Influencers are people who, though not directly involved in the development or use of analytics within an organization, wield significant influence over it. Influencers can be found at almost every layer of an organization. It is important that influencers be informed of and understand the benefits of analytics within an HCO. Without the support of influencers at all levels of the HCO, important analytics initiatives may suffer or even be shut down. Nothing is worse for analytics within an HCO than apathy—the thinking that the "same old" data and information is good enough when it clearly is not.

An obvious subset of customers are the "traditional" users of analytics—the decision makers, analysts, and quality improvement facilitators. It is not uncommon, however, to see more frontline staff, including physicians and nurses, receive information regarding their performance. In addition, analytics tools are making their way to the point of care as they become embedded in clinical applications, which in turn provides critical decision support evidence and insight to frontline providers when and where it is needed most.

Stakeholders classified as users are likely to be the most diverse, and will vary on several important dimensions. Table 3.2 lists several typical customers or users of analytics, as well as a few high-level analytics use cases for each user that are indicative of how analytics will be applied.

TABLE 3.2 Sample Analytics Customers with Analytics Use Cases

Customer	Sample Analytics Use Cases
Physician	Use real-time analytics for improving diagnostic accuracy.
	Use personalized performance report to adjust care practices.
Unit manager	Determine which patients are likely to exceed length-of-stay targets.
Quality improvement team	Identify bottlenecks in patient flow.
	Evaluate outcomes of quality improvement initiatives.
Executive	Evaluate and monitor overall performance of the organization.

Analytics Use Cases

Discuss and document analytics use cases with all stakeholder groups; this information will inform future decision making concerning data, infrastructure, and usability.

When developing the analytics strategy, it is a good idea to document analytics use cases, or how stakeholders intend to use analytics to make decisions and guide quality and performance improvement projects. Analytics use cases, in combination with goals and objectives of the organization, identify what data elements are most important, what indicators will be necessary to calculate, and what types of accessibility and usability factors (such as dashboard design, configuration of automated alerts, and mobile access) need to be considered. Information elicited from stakeholders to develop analytics use cases should include:

- Specific problems being addressed by the HCO.
- Decisions for which analytics insight is required.
- Actions that are triggered by analytics indicators.
- Risks that analytics identifies and/or helps to mitigate.
- What key processes need to be monitored and/or improved.
- What indicators are required to monitor quality and performance.

Obtaining as much information as possible about the possible uses of analytics will help to identify any gaps in analytics capabilities and reduce the likelihood that critical analytics needs will be missed.

Strategies for Working Well with Stakeholders

Analytics initiatives are most likely to succeed when stakeholders are involved throughout all phases of a project. Here are a few strategies for working well with stakeholders.

- Identify key members of each of the stakeholder groups.
- Understand the needs of each stakeholder group, and the needs of members within each stakeholder group.
- Listen to, acknowledge, and act on the input of stakeholders.
- Keep stakeholders informed of progress.
- Deliver on promises made to stakeholders and demonstrate the value of analytics in addressing the stakeholders' needs.

Processes and Data

Accurate, timely, and readily available data is the backbone of all analytics used for decision making, especially in quality and performance improvement projects. Without data, it is impossible to determine baseline performance, use a verifiable decision-making process to decide on improvement opportunities, or evaluate outcomes. Modern computerized clinical systems, such as EMRs, contain dozens if not hundreds of individual data elements; with multiple systems online within HCOs, the potential exists for thousands of possible data items from which to choose. Even if every data item captured from available computerized systems within an HCO is made available via an enterprise data warehouse or other data store, most of this data would require additional processing and analysis to be useful. To make data useful, an analytics strategy must address:

- How to determine which data is most important for quality and performance improvement.
- How the data is managed and its quality assured.
- How the data links back to business processes for necessary context.

See Table 3.3 for a summary of strategy components relating to data and processes.

TABLE 3.3 Strategy Components for Data and Processes

Strategy Component	Issues
Data sources	What are the sources of data available? What data is necessary for the analytics required to address key business issues?
	What data sources (and data elements) are most important to address financial, quality, and performance issues of the organization?
	How is data integrated from source systems?
	How and where is data stored and made accessible to analytics; for example, is there an enterprise data warehouse?
Data quality	How good is the quality of available data?
	Is the data quality "good enough" for analytics?
	What gaps in data exist?
	Does metadata (documentation) exist for the data?

(continued)

TABLE 3.3 *(continued)*

Strategy Component	Issues
Data management and governance	Who is responsible for data management, governance, and stewardship?
	What policies and procedures exist for data governance and management?
Business processes	What business processes and workflows align with important quality and performance issues of the organization?
	What data is available for measuring performance and quality of key processes? If no data exists, what proxy measures are necessary or available?
	What additional processing and analysis is required on available data?

Please see Chapter 5 for a thorough discussion on data quality, management, and governance issues and practice.

DATA QUALITY, MANAGEMENT, AND GOVERNANCE Before any analytics are possible, the relevant and necessary data must be understood and made available. Given the many possible sources of data within an HCO, one challenge is integrating data from these source systems into a manageable and accessible framework from which data can be drawn for analytics. These multiple data sources must all be managed to ensure suitability and usability for analytics purposes.

> **Tip**
>
> Data from source systems must be inventoried, analyzed, documented, and aligned with business processes.

Successful execution of an analytics strategy requires relevant data to be identified, documented, processed, and made available to appropriate analytics users and applications. It may not be possible, feasible, or even necessary to account for every available data source. When initiating, or improving, the use of analytics within an HCO, focus on ensuring access to data that is related to the organization's major quality goals and key business objectives. Trying to encompass too much will only serve to water down the strategy document and risk sullying the insight and information required by stakeholders. Remember that a goal of the analytics strategy is to focus efforts on achieving the most important quality and performance objectives of the HCO. As the organization's priorities evolve, so, too, can the strategy document remain aligned with the priorities of the organization. At this point, new business problems and additional data can, and should, be considered.

> **Tip**
>
> Remember that the goal of the analytics strategy is to focus efforts on achieving the most important quality and performance objectives of the HCO.

The quality of data available and used for analytics impacts what information, insight, and value can be derived from such toolsets. Data stewardship is a critical function in the management of large and complex data sets. Improper management of data can lead to BI producing incorrect information. Because the needs of every organization are different, the analytics strategy will help the HCO determine what data management and governance structures are best suited to the HCO based on the extent of existing and future data sources, IT support, and any existing governance structures already in place.

BUSINESS PROCESSES One of the other data-related challenges facing HCOs is adding context to data. From an analytics perspective, data and processes are inseparable; knowing what a value "is" is almost useless without knowing what it "means." Knowledge of business processes provides essential context to and understanding of what data represents. A business process is the collection of actions taken to transform an input (such as raw material, information, knowledge, commitment, or status) into a desired outcome, product, or result and performed according to established guidelines, policies, procedures, rules, and subject matter expertise.[5]

The business processes are what provides context to the data, and without context, data is almost meaningless. Essentially all quality improvement methodologies require indicators and metrics that examine intervals on the other process measures. This requires a strong alignment between business process components and the data that measures those components. As part of the analytics strategy, you should consider if and how current business processes are documented, and how data items are mapped to these documented business processes.

Tools and Techniques

Once the business problems, quality goals, stakeholder requirements, and available data items have been identified, the necessary tools and techniques, plus their acquisition strategy (build versus buy), need to be outlined in the strategy. Selection of appropriate software, statistics, or models is necessary to ensure that the "right kind" of analytics can be performed to address stakeholder needs and the HCO's business problems. Inappropriate tools and misaligned capabilities can lead to issues as basic as providing an inappropriate summarization to using a predictive model that does not work with the data available or is inappropriate for the use an HCO was intending.

For example, if an HCO is looking to determine its geographic catchment area based on ZIP codes to fine-tune a marketing campaign, that information might be best presented visually using some sort of geographical representation rather than a table of numbers and ZIP codes. Not having the tools to properly visualize data in meaningful ways for decision makers would be a capability gap. Another example relates to advanced analysis; many reporting tools do not include anything other than basic statistics (such as mean, median, etc.). Yet sometimes an analysis needs to look beyond these simple statistics to determine correlation or to implement more complex statistical models.

Because there are many ways in which analytics can be used, there are many different types of analytics tools. Several of the most common types of analytics tools include:

- **Statistical.** Statistical tools are used for deeper statistical analysis that is not available in most "standard" BI or reporting packages, including correlation and regression tests, ANOVA and *t*-tests, nonparametric tests, and statistical process control chart capabilities.
- **Visualization.** Beyond the static charts and graphs typical of almost all spreadsheet and business analysis software, some analytics users are looking for advanced visualization tools that allow them to interact visually with and explore data that is dynamic (that is, the visualizations update as the data is updated).
- **Data profiling and quality.** Because the volume of healthcare data is growing, HCOs are increasingly relying on software to identify and highlight patterns of good and poor data within a data set, and to help fix and prevent instances of poor-quality data.

If an HCO has invested significantly in a BI infrastructure, there may not be much money available for analytics-related capabilities beyond what comes with the BI suite. Adding new and specialized tools to the analytics tool belt can become cost-prohibitive (especially when expensive "value-add" modules of already expensive base software are required). The good news is that there are very good open-source tools such as R (www.r-project.org) that can provide significant analytical horsepower without a prohibitively high price tag.

For More Information on Tools and Techniques

The landscape is constantly changing regarding the available tools for analytics. For an up-to-date summary of the most important tools and most recent developments, please visit this book's companion web site, http://HealthcareAnalyticsBook.com.

Team and Training

Analytics is a very quickly evolving field, and it is impossible for one person to be an expert in all aspects of BI and healthcare analytics. Training and professional development are key to ensuring that a knowledge gap does not become a gap in analytics capability within an organization. Professional development can (and most definitely should) involve both autodidactic and instructor-led instruction on the use of existing tools, the introduction to new tools, and education on new innovations in analytics (e.g., predictive analytics) and related technologies (e.g., new database formats for "big data"). Investing in analytics training is one of the smartest choices an HCO can make from the perspective of using available information to the maximum extent possible to enable evidence-informed decision making and smarter quality and performance improvement activities.

Analytics teams, especially those working closely with quality improvement teams, are not composed solely of "analytics professionals" (that is, expert developers, analysts, and/or statisticians). HCOs are creating more interdisciplinary teams to tackle quality performance improvement issues. For example, it is common to have MBAs and engineers working alongside nurses and physicians to tackle various issues facing an HCO. So, too, are analytics teams becoming more interdisciplinary. In fact, it benefits an entire HCO to ensure that stakeholders who rely on analytics have some degree of knowledge about tools, techniques, and technologies available for analytics. The information gathered in the "stakeholders" section of the strategy document can be used to identify what type of knowledge is required of all analytics users, and to develop a plan to ensure necessary information and/or training is made available.

There are many skills at which a healthcare analytics professional must be proficient. In general, healthcare analytics teams require broad knowledge in several key areas—the business of healthcare (both clinical operations and finance-related); technology (such as data warehouses, BI and analytics systems, and source systems such as EMRs); analytical techniques (including data and statistical modeling); and communications.[6] See Table 3.4 for a summary of the common types of skills required of healthcare analytics professionals.

TABLE 3.4 Sample Skill Sets Useful for Healthcare Analytics Professionals

Skill Set	Description
Communications	Analytics professionals must be effective communicators, both in listening and explaining. They must be able to listen to end users and subject matter experts to understand what information they need and how they intend to use it. They must also be able to explain analytics to those same people in a way that gets the point across. ■ Effective, clear, and accurate writing ■ Data graphing and visualization ■ Requirements elicitation
Technical	Analytics can be a highly technical field, therefore analytics professionals need to be competent in several key areas in which healthcare analytics intersects with other technology disciplines. ■ Intermediate programming and computation skills ■ Database query skills
Clinical	Healthcare analytics professionals must know enough about the business of healthcare, from both a clinical operations and a financial perspective, so that they are aware of the context from which the data used is drawn. ■ Basic healthcare processes ■ Basic healthcare financing models
Quality improvement	One of the primary uses of healthcare analytics is for quality and performance improvement, and therefore healthcare analytics professionals must be familiar with at least the major approaches and methodologies in use within their HCO. They may not need to be Six Sigma Black Belts, but should be able to converse with the practitioners of quality improvement methodologies. ■ Lean, Six Sigma, or other improvement methodology ■ Process mapping ■ Team and group facilitation
Analytical	Needless to say, healthcare analytics professionals must be analytical and curious in nature. The toughest of all challenges in healthcare analytics is identifying the root of a problem—and this requires more than simply going through the motions of applying statistical tests and building data models. ■ Ability to think critically and analytically ■ Data centered; obsession with evidence-based problem resolution ■ Familiarity with and ability to use scientific principles in addressing quality and performance problems

In addition to bringing the right mix of people onto the analytics team, keeping their skills up to date and relevant is another important aspect of managing analytics teams. There are always new tools, approaches, and knowledge in the field of analytics. Regular training is required to keep analytics users' and developers' skills up to date, and they should be encouraged to maintain their own professional development. In this regard, there are certifications available in the field of analytics, and professional organizations, which enable analytics professionals to remain up to date.

It is unlikely that a single person can be proficient at all the necessary skill sets required for effective analytics within an HCO. However, there may be strong generalists who are good at several of the key areas. It is important to recognize what skills are required to develop, implement, and utilize the particular types of analytics your organization requires, what gaps may exist, and what to do to address any gaps.

Finding the Right People

It is absolutely critical to have the right mix of people on an analytics team. Look for people who are naturally analytical, curious, and creative, and who will mesh well within a team environment.

Technology and Infrastructure

Note: HIT infrastructure is a very large and important topic. It is impossible to do it justice in one small section of a book. The purpose of this section is to provide a high-level overview of how business and analytical considerations should drive technical requirements, not to delve deeply into all aspects of technical infrastructure.

Interestingly, technology and infrastructure are often the first stops along the analytics path taken by IT professionals. There are numerous reasons for this. Many analytics professionals reside in the IT departments within HCOs, and IT departments are naturally drawn to think about servers, networks, and other infrastructure requirements.

Analytics must remain very business-focused because of the information and insight needed by healthcare leaders, quality improvement teams, and other decision makers. The technology required to enable analytics, however, can be complex especially in larger organizations with numerous data sources and many stakeholders. Because of the volumes of data that may be available, the variety of sources supplying data, the sophisticated algorithms that can be applied to the data, and the speed at which decisions need to be made, analytics is growing beyond what can be accomplished by a single analyst running statistical software on a stand-alone computer. Instead, a highly connected and reliable communications and data infrastructure to enable the sharing of what information analytics produces is necessary to drive evidence-informed decision making in most modern healthcare environments.

Aligning the Needs of the Business and IT

Ideally, the analytical needs of an organization and the technological requirements to supply those needs figure prominently in the organization's IT infrastructure deployment strategy.

An HCO's data infrastructure is the backbone of analytics. The three key elements of the infrastructure include the *network* (that provides connectivity between all elements of IT infrastructure), *servers* (on which applications are run and data is made available), and *physical storage* (the devices on which data are stored),[7] and now cloud computing (in which case the data used for analytics may not be housed by the HCO at all). All these components are typically managed by an HCO's IT department, and they must be chosen and scaled appropriately to support the many applications and services required by an HCO.

Closely related to these more physical elements of infrastructure is what is sometimes called a *knowledge and discovery layer*. This layer of infrastructure is where integration of various data sources occurs. For example, the data resulting from a hospital visit by a single patient may span multiple source systems, such as admission/discharge/transfer, electronic patient record, lab information system, and radiology information system. For analytics, it is best if this information is integrated into a single view and the knowledge and discovery layer helps to logically link these various independent sources of data into a cohesive, comprehensive, and cross-silo representation of a patient's visit.

Although there are many different applications and tools that fit within this layer of infrastructure, the tools that are most pertinent to analytics and the most common in HCOs include Extraction/Transformation/Load services that copy information from source systems, transform it (into a form suitable for a data warehouse), and load it into a data store so that it is accessible for analytics. Newer approaches to integration include loose coupling of data so that a unified view of data spans multiple sources of data without necessarily needing to copy it all into a completely different data store; in other words, through a modified data schema, a "virtual" database can access data from source systems directly.

One challenge of developing an infrastructure to support analytics is that analytics requirements will undoubtedly expand as more data sources are added, new problems and issues confront the HCO, new analytical capabilities are required, and new hardware and software systems, optimized for analytical performance, emerge on the marketplace. Scalability, which "allows us to maintain a consistent level of performance regardless of changes and growth,"[8] must be built into an analytics infrastructure so that the HCO has spare capacity to grow into as the amount and types of data, as well as analytics needs of stakeholders, continue to evolve and expand.

Although the analytics strategy may not necessarily state what technical infrastructure should be acquired, the strategy should make it clear what the near- and long-term analytics needs of the business are going to be. The decisions made regarding hardware selection and infrastructure design and configuration essentially set the boundaries for what analytics will be capable of within the organization. The analytics strategy can be a very important input to the HCO's overall technical strategy—the sooner that analytical requirements can be incorporated into an HCO's IT development plan, the less likely it is that technology will be purchased that is not appropriate (either insufficient or complete overkill) for the analytical requirements of the organization.

Developing an Analytics Strategy

Developing an analytics strategy is critical to ensuring that the analytical needs of an HCO are being met. Most HCOs will not be starting from square one, however. In all likelihood, there are many pockets of analytical know-how throughout every HCO, suffering through some inadequacy in analytics capabilities and not living up to an analytics potential. For example, some of these analytical pockets may be using outdated or inadequate tools for data management or analysis, some may be reaching the limits of poorly designed data warehouses, and others might simply be so overwhelmed with report requests that they are unable to perform any "real" analytics.

An analytics strategy is the starting point to help organizations achieve maximum benefit from their data. A completed strategy will help an organization identify what it does well, what it needs to do better, where it can consolidate, and where it needs to invest.

The three main steps in creating an analytics strategy are:

1. **Document the current state.** Review the six main components of strategy discussed above, and speak with stakeholders who are current (and potential users) of analytics to identify how analytics is currently used and what capability is required but does not yet exist, as well as what exists now but can be improved.

2. **Identify gaps.** Documentation of the current state will reveal a laundry list of things that are needed. Some of these gaps will be in infrastructure, some will be in software/tools, some will be in knowledge/training of the team, and some will be in knowledge of what is possible with analytics.
3. **Execute strategy.** Once the gaps are identified, identify which gaps are a priority to address and which can be addressed quickly and affordably, and develop a plan to implement the strategy's recommendations.

Many organizations in all industries spend a significant effort on developing a strategy but in the end fail miserably at executing on the strategy and achieving any of the goals and objects that the strategy was to enable. The bottom line is that developing a strategy is a wasted effort without a true intention and/or capability to execute on it. Having a strategy is simply not enough; organizations must find ways to actually execute what is set out in the strategy, otherwise it will become another piece of "shelfware."

An analytics strategy is not set in stone; it needs to evolve as the analytics needs of the organization and its stakeholders evolve, as technology becomes better and/or less expensive, and as the state of the art in analytics itself changes. An organization should not be afraid to revisit the strategy frequently to ensure that it is up to date and that its execution is successfully meeting all stated requirements.

Developing and Implementing an Analytics Strategy

For a full analytics strategy template that you can use to create and implement a detailed analytics strategy for your organization, please visit the companion web site to this book, http://HealthcareAnalyticsBook.com.

Notes

1. Steven Stralser, *MBA in a Day: What You Would Learn at Top-Tier Business Schools (If You Only Had the Time!)* (Hoboken, NJ: John Wiley & Sons, 2004), 153.
2. Project Management Institute, *A Guide to the Project Management Body of Knowledge (PMBOK Guide) 2000 Edition* (Newton Square, PA: Project Management Institute, 2000), 208.
3. Ibid, 16.
4. Ibid.

5. Roger T. Burlton, *Business Process Management: Profiting from Process* (Indianapolis, IN: Sams Publishing), 72.
6. Steve Miller, "BI, Analytics and Statistical Science," Information-Management.com, April 19, 2010, www.information-management.com/blogs/business_intelligence_analytics_statistical_science_bi-10017679-1.html.
7. Boris Evelson, *It's Time to Reinvent Your BI Strategy* (Cambridge, MA: Forrester Research, 2007), 4.
8. Laura B. Madsen, *Healthcare Business Intelligence: A Guide to Empowering Successful Data Reporting and Analytics* (Hoboken, NJ: John Wiley & Sons, 2012), 106.

CHAPTER 4

Defining Healthcare Quality and Value

Quality means doing it right when no one is looking.

—Henry Ford

Improving safety, quality, and value are the cornerstones of healthcare transformation. Although there are many ways in which quality and value are defined and measured, healthcare organizations (HCOs) must adopt and internalize their own definitions of quality in order to create quality goals, objectives, and targets that are meaningful and relevant to the organization and, more importantly, the patients they serve. The adage, "You can't improve what you can't measure," applies to healthcare analytics; this chapter will discuss why and how quality must be defined in quantifiable terms so that data analytics can be effectively leveraged to measure, monitor, and maintain healthcare improvements.

What Is Quality?

From the patient's perspective, healthcare is often thought of in terms of quality and expressed in questions such as, "Which hospital or provider will provide me the best healthcare possible?" Because patients are concerned with receiving high-quality (and affordable) care, quality of care delivery should be of utmost importance to every HCO. Many HCOs stake their reputation on the quality of their care, and patients' lives literally depend on it. Hospitals, clinics, and providers that are deemed to be of high quality earn stellar reputations, attract patients, are successful at attracting top staff (including both clinical and research professionals), and earn more money, which can be in part reinvested into QI initiatives.

What is *quality*? Some people claim to be able to know quality when they see it when it comes to things like automobiles, clothes, and houses. But how do they "know" quality? In vehicles, the attributes that owners associate with quality range from how solidly the door closes to more quantifiable attributes such as gas mileage. For some people, the perception of quality may all be in the brand name. With regard to everyday items, most people have defined their own sets of desirable attributes and criteria for identifying quality in their favorite products and brands.

> **Tip**
>
> Quality must be defined in quantifiable terms to enable measurement, monitoring, analysis, and, most important, decision making and action.

The Institute of Medicine defines *quality* as "the degree to which health services for individuals and populations increase the likelihood of desired health outcomes and are consistent with current professional knowledge."[1] This definition implies that healthcare is expected to have a net benefit to the patient and that the measurement of quality must reflect patient satisfaction, health status and quality-of-life measures, and the patient/provider interaction and decision-making process. By this definition, the provision of care "should reflect appropriate use of the most current knowledge about scientific, clinical, technical, interpersonal, manual, cognitive, organizational, and management elements of health care."[2]

A textbook definition of *quality* provides a starting point, but it is up to HCOs to apply and adapt the sentiments contained within such a definition to their own particular needs and circumstances. Quality has many facets in healthcare, so it is necessary for every HCO to thoroughly understand and define in meaningful terms what quality is to all relevant stakeholders, including and especially patients.

Many HCOs are well-meaning when initiating QI activities but falter because quality is defined in too broad or general terms consisting of good sentiment but little substance. Applying the analytics lens early in the QI process helps to remind HCOs that quality must be defined in terms that are quantifiable—meaning they can be measured, monitored, analyzed, and acted on.

Quality

According to the Institute of Medicine, "quality" is "the degree to which health services for individuals and populations increase the likelihood of desired health outcomes and are consistent with current professional knowledge."

Defining Value in Healthcare

Common themes in healthcare quality include performing the right actions correctly and consistently while achieving outcomes that are considered to be desirable to the patient. Related to this is the concept of *value*, which means that the care provided was able to improve the patient's health and well-being, resulted in a positive experience, and, most important, achieved the desired outcomes. According to corporate strategy expert Michael Porter, "rigorous, disciplined measurement and improvement of value is the best way to drive system progress";[3] he also asserts that healthcare, even now, remains largely unmeasured and therefore misunderstood. Activities that add value to a patient's visit (known as "value-added" activities) must meet the following three criteria:[4]

1. The customer (or patient) must be willing to pay for the stated activity (or activities) being performed.
2. The activity must in some way transform the product or service being provided.
3. The activity must be completed properly on the first attempt and achieve the desired outcomes.

The concept of value-added is one way to measure how much of an activity directly contributes to an outcome versus how much is "non-value-added," or waste. Non-value-added activities are those that do not directly contribute to the outcome in a significant way except perhaps to delay it. Inefficient processes and workflows negatively impact outcomes, slow down patient flow, may cost more, and result in poor patient satisfaction.

(In some jurisdictions such as those with publicly funded healthcare insurance, patients do not pay directly for many healthcare services. In these cases, the concept of "paying" for service includes other healthcare rationing methods, including waiting. Although patients may not have to pay out-of-pocket for a service, how long they need to wait for a particular service or procedure becomes a measuring factor of value.)

Value is always defined in relation to a customer—that is, whether the customer experienced value or not. When one thinks of the "customer" in healthcare, the patient immediately comes to mind. But there are many other examples of customer relationships in healthcare; in fact, any interaction that involves some combination of healthcare provider, unit, department, or service and the exchange of information, material, and/or patients can be considered a customer relationship and examined as such. For example, the emergency department may be considered a customer of the diagnostic imaging department when emergency patients are sent for X-rays or other imaging tests.

Value = (Outcomes) / (Cost)

According to Porter, value can be quantified by the ratio of desired outcomes relative to cost (as illustrated in the previous equation).[5] This representation helps to ensure that value is measured relative to the outcomes achieved via service delivery, not simply by volume of services provided. Porter states that outcomes are condition-specific and multidimensional—that is, no single outcome can capture the results of care. Costs, according to Porter, are the sum of costs for the full cycle of care for a patient's medical condition, and are *not* the cost of individual services provided.

Also related to value is patient satisfaction. For a variety of reasons, ranging from long wait times to a doctor's perceived poor "bedside manner," all aspects related to the treatment of a patient could be done technically correct yet the patient might not be totally happy with his or her experience. Given how quickly word of bad healthcare experiences can spread on social media and negatively impact the reputation of an HCO, it is vitally important for HCOs to identify and rectify the causes of poor patient satisfaction.

Table 4.1 highlights some examples of value-added and non-value-added activities that can be found within healthcare. For example, interacting with a healthcare provider or receiving treatment may be considered adding value to a patient's experience, whereas sitting idle in a waiting room waiting to be seen or suffering through repeated blood draws due to botched testing or faulty equipment is most definitely *not* adding value.

RATIO OF VALUE-ADDED TO NON-VALUE-ADDED ACTIVITY

As a general rule of thumb, somewhere between 5 percent and 20 percent of activity in healthcare can be considered value-added, whereas the remainder is considered non-value-added.

TABLE 4.1 Examples of Value-Added and Non-Value-Added Activities in Healthcare

Role	Value-Added Activity	Non-Value-Added Activity
Diagnostic imaging technician	Performing an X-ray	Waiting for porter to deliver patient to diagnostic imaging unit
Patient	Being assessed or treated by a clinician	Waiting to be seen by a clinician
Laboratory technician	Performing a lab test	Returning a requisition that is not completed properly or adequately
Nurse	Assessing or providing treatment to a patient	Double-documenting on computer and paper

One objective of healthcare improvement activities is to maximize the time that healthcare workers spend doing value-added activities while reducing the number of barriers to efficiency that result in non-value-added activities. When developing healthcare indicators, targets, and analytics that monitor and evaluate value, include both value-added activities and non-value-added activities. Examining just one type of activity or the other will not provide a complete picture of performance. For example, one measure of performance is a patient's time with a physician (considered to be value-added). If a physician is spending more value-added time with patients but this activity is resulting in an increased time *between* patients, which may result in fewer patients being seen per day, this performance change may not have the desired net effect. Effective use of analytics can help to ensure that improvements in one aspect of quality and value do not have a negative impact on other areas.

Tip

Consider both value-added and non-value-added activities when designing analytics for quality and performance improvement.

Improving a System

HCOs fit the classic definition of "system," which is a "group of interacting, interrelated, or interdependent elements forming a complex whole."[6] Healthcare consists of many types of organizational units that range from major facilities such as hospitals to physicians' practices. Most healthcare facilities themselves consist of many departments, units, programs, services, and administrative functions within a single facility. And some HCOs consist of *many* individual facilities.

In addition to the myriad departments, services, and facilities within an HCO, it is necessary to take into account the many ways in which an HCO needs to measure quality, and how these quality measures are to be used. Even top-performing HCOs are very unlikely to achieve high quality in every aspect of their performance. And due to many dynamic environmental variables such as changing demographics, patient needs, and staffing, a high-performing HCO may experience a gradual (or sudden) deterioration in performance if its policies and workflows are not kept up to date or are not robust enough to accommodate such changes.

The complexity of healthcare demands that a robust approach to measuring quality be followed. As discussed above, it is entirely possible that "improvements" in one area of healthcare can actually negatively

FIGURE 4.1 Three Components of Healthcare Quality Measurement

impact care in another. For this reason, healthcare quality and performance must be looked at from multiple perspectives; one approach is to consider healthcare from the perspectives of structure, process, and outcomes.[7]

As Figure 4.1 illustrates, these three elements—structure, process, and outcomes—form a continuum of quality measurement. Ultimately, "process measures must be linked to outcomes if they are to be effective measures of quality."[8] Patient outcomes (and other quality measures) depend on which processes and workflows are performed, how efficient and effective they are, and how well they are performed. The structure of an HCO (that is, the management, policies, and resources) will determine the organization's ability to innovate and to adopt and sustain the most efficient and effective processes and workflows possible. Without all three types of measures, only an incomplete evaluation of quality is possible within an organization.

STRUCTURE The "structure" of healthcare includes what are considered to be relatively stable aspects: healthcare delivery, including the various tools, technologies, and other resources available; the physical environment/surroundings in which the providers of healthcare work; and the overall organizational features (such as policies and management), all of which can promote high quality and optimal performance or hinder it.

Although the extent and impact of structural elements such as "leadership" and "policies" can be challenging to quantify and link to processes and outcomes, structural elements that can be quantified can be very useful. Structural elements that fall into the latter category include:

- Number of funded intensive care unit (ICU) beds
- Specialty trained physician coverage in ICU
- Number of CT scanners and their availability

Structural information is very often used to provide context to other healthcare performance data. For example, increases in lab test turnaround times that occur during certain times of day or certain days of the week may in fact be due to structure-related issues such as a reduced number of technicians. Structure-related measures help when comparing performance between units or sites. For example, two emergency departments may see similar numbers of patients in a day and experience similar lengths of stay, but if one hospital is operating with fewer beds or more physicians, that information is important to consider.

PROCESS Processes are the various activities performed by healthcare providers and the interactions between healthcare providers and patients (and/or their family members) in the course of providing medical care to the patient. Processes are very often where HCOs begin with quality and performance improvements. There are several reasons for this. First, processes can be relatively easy to measure. Traditionally, QI activities would consist of time-and-motion studies where key time intervals in a process could be measured. These measurements would form baseline performance data, against which improved processes could be measured.

Healthcare information technology now makes the collection and analysis of time-and-motion data much more convenient. Many clinical systems (such as electronic medical records [EMRs]) capture well-documented patient trajectory data throughout a healthcare encounter. Table 4.2 provides examples of the type of data that can be used for analysis of processes likely available on EMRs and other electronic clinical systems.

> **Tip**
>
> When developing analytics for performance monitoring and QI, be sure to include relevant structure, process, and outcome measures.

TABLE 4.2 Examples of Process Data

Process	Process Data
Emergency department registration	Time of arrival at emergency department Time of registration start Time of registration completion Registration clerk name/ID
Patient X-ray	Time X-ray test requisted Type of X-ray requested Clinical provider requesting X-ray Time of porter arrival for pickup Name/ID of porter Time patient leaves department for X-ray Time of X-ray start Time of X-ray completion X-ray room used Name/ID of X-ray tech Time patient returns to department Time X-ray images available for viewing

For More Indicators

There are indicator sets published by various governmental and other healthcare-related agencies. These indicators are constantly evolving as information systems and needs of healthcare change. Please visit this book's web site, http://HealthcareAnalyticsBook.com, for links to the most current healthcare indicator sets, such as the Healthcare Effectiveness Data and Information Set.

OUTCOMES An outcome is an individual, quantifiable endpoint that is focused on the patient. Examples of types of outcomes include:

- Morbidity
- Mortality
- Readmission
- Length of stay

As the results of care, outcomes are an endpoint of a treatment or other process and typically are what is of main concern to the patient. According to Porter, health outcomes should:[9]

- Include health circumstances most relevant to patients
- Cover both near term and longer term
- Consider risk factors or initial conditions to allow for risk adjustment

When developing analytics for quality measurement, be sure that all the necessary and appropriate outcomes are considered. Keep in mind that a set of outcomes exist for any medical condition or primary preventive care. Because healthcare is complex, some outcomes may even be in conflict with one another and therefore need to be weighed against one another.

Structure, Process, and Outcomes

Consider the example of a hospital surgical unit when putting these three aspects of quality together. Elements of the structure include the number of surgeons, nurses, and operating rooms, plus the various technologies available, and administrative and medical policies under which the providers must practice. The process elements are those that measure percentage of on-time starts. Finally, examples of outcome measures include the rate of critical occurrences and the mortality rate from surgery.

When reporting structure, process, and outcome data over the same time period, be aware of the risk associated with lagging indicators. A lagging indicator is one that shows a response at some time after a situational or systemic change. For example, suppose improved hospital discharge processes result in patients getting home from hospital sooner; process indicators will show lower hospital lengths of stay shortly after implementation. Shorter hospital stays, however, may result in some patients being discharged too early who may need to return to the hospital; the recidivism rate, an outcome measure, will also show an increase, but likely after some time period, given that rates of recidivism are relatively low and would take time to manifest in the data. Because of this, the change in the outcome indicator may not be apparent until some time after the process indicator shows a change. This is why it is important to continue to monitor both process and outcome indicators after an improvement activity, to ensure that positive process changes and resultant positive outcomes are sustained, and that any hint of increased negative outcomes is detected.

Overview of Healthcare QI

Most HCOs are continually striving to improve quality out of both desire to become better and necessity (because quality is a constantly moving target). The environment in which HCOs operate is in a continual state of flux, with many issues that must be faced, including:

- External challenges (such as regulatory changes and financing issues);
- Internal challenges (including human resource management);
- Changing needs of patients (due to an aging and/or increasing population); and
- Technology (that can be both practice-changing and lifesaving but may also be expensive).

This constantly changing environment requires HCOs to be always adapting, innovating, and improving, because what worked just fine yesterday may be considered irrelevant or obsolete tomorrow. But what does "improving healthcare" mean, and what does it require? And are all changes and innovations necessarily improvements? How can we tell?

Healthcare QI has been described as "better patient experience and outcomes achieved through changing provider behavior and organization through using a systematic change method and strategies."[10] Healthcare QI can also be considered as "systematic, data-guided activities designed to bring about immediate improvement in health care delivery in particular settings."[11]

What is important about healthcare QI is the focus on patient experience. After all, the patient is the primary customer of the healthcare system, and the only reason the system exists in the first place. Patients should not be viewed as passive "recipients" of healthcare but rather as individuals who can and should expect high-quality service and care. The statement above notes that healthcare improvement is brought about by "changing provider behavior and organization" and recognizes that it is the providers of healthcare that must improve their processes and activities to help ensure a better patient experience. Finally, the statement recognizes that change in provider behavior and organization requires "a systematic change method and strategies"—that the changes required do not and cannot occur without a concerted effort to identify what needs to be changed and a structured approach to bring about that change.

Using Systematic QI Methodologies

If QI requires a systematic change method, what methods are the most successful HCOs engaged in to achieve high levels of quality?

Many, if not most, successful HCOs employ an established improvement or management methodology. There are many of these approaches used in healthcare today, including Lean, Six Sigma, total quality management, constraints management, and numerous variants (such as Lean Six Sigma). Although these frameworks differ in their philosophies, tools, and methods, they are similar in that they provide a structured approach for improving quality and performance within a complex organization.

For More Information

Please visit this book's web site, http://HealthcareAnalyticsBook.com, for links to more resources and references about the QI methodologies mentioned in this book.

How Information Guides Improvement Activities

One commonality of all healthcare quality efforts is their requirement for *information* in order to be successful. Modern healthcare improvement requires accurate, timely, and readily available information through almost every phase of a quality and performance improvement initiative. The use of analytics helps to distill data into information that is relevant for a given improvement initiative and usable by QI teams to gauge effectiveness of their efforts.

One of the benefits offered by analytics is the capability to augment management reports and dashboards with deep insight into past, current, and even future performance. Some of the insight available from analytics tools includes determining if processes are in control or not (from a statistical process control perspective), determining if changes over a period are merely random variation or in fact statistically significant, and predicting what future performance might be.

One reason that some healthcare improvement initiatives fail is the lack of initial baseline assessment and ongoing evaluation and follow-up. Interestingly, there is a tendency to assume that changes introduced into healthcare processes, workflows, and systems actually will have the desired effect, and that changes in quality or performance can be monitored with the same reporting mechanisms with which performance deteriorated in the first place. This is not the case.

Analytics can help determine if changes detected in performance indicators are merely due to chance, or represent actual (and sustained) change. Changes in performance indicators (both negative and positive) need to be communicated to leaders, quality facilitators, and frontline staff in a timely manner. This timely intelligence is important so that midcourse corrections to workflows can be implemented, if necessary, or to confirm that changes are having the desired effect.

Without the relevant and rapid analysis and feedback that is possible with business intelligence and analytics, evaluations are often performed too late to allow for effective midcourse corrections. If poor performance is not detected in time, it is possible for additional poorly designed processes to become ingrained within a unit, department, program, or entire enterprise. Without a robust system in place to evaluate the impact of changes to processes, the true effect of such changes can never be known.

Tip

It is a basic tenet of QI that you can't improve what you don't measure.

Common QI Frameworks in Healthcare

Many of the current causes of healthcare inefficiency have evolved over time through the adoption of ad hoc process changes, workarounds, and decisions based on gut feeling, not evidence. In fact, many of the workarounds impeding quality today were likely at one time lauded as heroic measures demonstrating a "can-do" attitude, but now only contribute to the tangled web of inefficiency and waste.

To achieve quality and performance improvement requires careful planning, methodological change, and persistent follow-up and evaluation. The discipline required to follow a structured QI approach is one of the most challenging cultural changes for an HCO to overcome. Healthcare professionals pride themselves in being action-oriented problem solvers; such behavior, when misdirected, is how much of the inefficiency gets introduced into healthcare in the first place.

To overcome haphazard improvement efforts and stubborn barriers to improving quality, many HCOs are turning to proven QI frameworks or methodologies to provide the disciplined approach required to understand the scope of a problem, to develop and implement solutions, and to evaluate outcomes of the changes.

A QI framework provides the tools, methods, and management philosophies required to drive improvement efforts and to achieve the desired improvement goals of the organization. QI activities typically are led by an experienced facilitator, and participants include knowledgeable subject matter experts, some of whom are experienced with QI initiatives and others with no such experience. QI teams tend to be assembled for a specific project (requiring specific subject matter expertise), and disbanded as projects are completed and other teams form up for new initiatives.

There are many QI frameworks used within healthcare. Some are proprietary to an individual or corporation, some are homegrown within a HCO, and some are generally in the public domain (although some proprietary "flavors" of several public-domain methodologies exist). Many of the most common QI frameworks have their genesis in other industries, such as manufacturing and aerospace, and have since been adapted for use in healthcare.

Using quality frameworks that have been proven in other industries has allowed the healthcare practitioners of these quality methodologies to learn from what has worked well elsewhere and decide upon approaches that will likely have the greatest impact on and probability of success in healthcare. For the purposes of this book, three of the QI methodologies commonly used in healthcare today will be discussed:

1. Plan-Do-Study-Act (PDSA)
2. Lean
3. Six Sigma

See Table 4.3 for a high-level summary of these QI methodologies.

There are many considerations that HCOs account for when deciding upon which of these QI methodology to use. QI methodologies are not one-size-fits-all, and the decision of which methodology to use is situational and dependent on several factors. For example, PDSA might be well suited

TABLE 4.3 Comparing Common Improvement Methodologies

Methodology	Approach to Improvement	
PDSA	Conducting experiments and testing improvements iteratively on a local, small-scale basis.	Plan Do Study Act
Lean	Eliminating waste, improving flow, maximizing value-added and minimizing non-value-added activities.	Identify value Identify value stream Flow Pull Perfection
Six Sigma	Reducing variation and eliminating deviation in processes.	Define Measure Analyze Improve Control

for implementing a new patient scheduling process but might be inadequate for an initiative to reduce hospital-acquired infections, which may require a methodology with more analytic and process design rigor.

Many volumes have been written that cover each of these methodologies in complete detail. Within the limits of this book, only the essentials of each methodology are presented with the intent of illustrating how different methodologies can work in concert to address the problems of healthcare. This section will also discuss how analytics can be applied to improve how information is consumed by QI teams and other stakeholders working to improve healthcare quality and performance.

The following sections will look at how the PDSA, Lean, and Six Sigma improvement methodologies are used in healthcare, describe some of their key features, and discuss how analytics can play an important role in improving the capabilities of teams using these methodologies to plan better projects and to perform more in-depth and more accurate evaluations.

Plan-Do-Study-Act

PDSA is a common approach for improving processes in healthcare (and other industries). Also known as Plan-Do-Check-Act (PDCA), the basic premise is to encourage innovation by experimenting with a change in process, studying the results, and making refinements as necessary to achieve and sustain desired outcomes. PDSA is considered a staple of healthcare QI; for example, PDSA is a central tenet of the United Kingdom's National Health Service QI framework.[12]

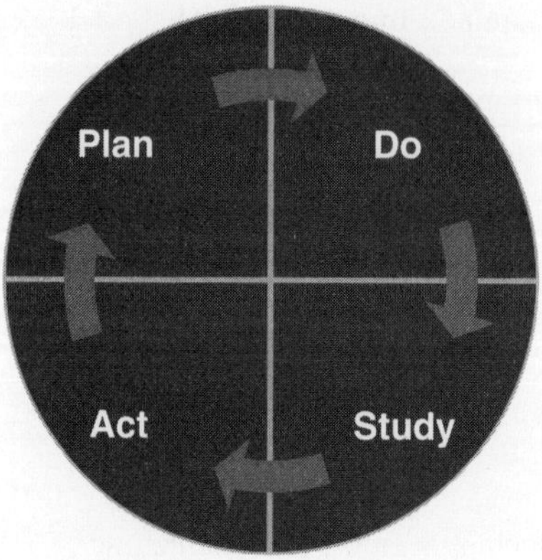

FIGURE 4.2 Plan, Do, Study, Act (PDSA) Cycle

PDSA begins, as do all QI activities, with a clearly defined goal. That is, the problem being addressed must be clearly defined, and the desired outcomes should be established as targets. Once these are in place, the PDSA cycle, as illustrated in Figure 4.2, proceeds as described next:

1. **Plan.** Start by planning the changes to a process that are to be implemented and tested.
2. **Do.** Proceed with carrying out the plan and making the desired changes to the specified process.
3. **Study.** Review the impact and outcomes of the implemented changes. What were the results of the process changes; were the anticipated outcomes achieved?
4. **Act.** Determine if the changes can be implemented as is, or if further cycles are necessary to refine the approach.

HCOs can utilize the PDSA approach as a stand-alone approach, or within other QI methodologies. For example, during Lean Rapid Improvement Events (where teams spend focused time experimenting with ways to reduce waste and inefficiency), teams may conduct several PDSA cycles throughout the event as new processes are tried, evaluated, and improved.

PLAN During the PDSA "Plan" phase, ensure that the problem is well defined and desired outcomes have been decided upon. Having a clear problem statement or project aim helps to maintain the team's focus on what is to be accomplished. To be effective, improvement aims should be framed in time-specific and measurable terms that define which specific populations of patients are going to be affected.

Appropriate metrics need to be decided upon by the time the planning phase is completed. Effective metrics are what the PDSA teams use to see if a change actually occurred. Metrics help to answer the question, "How will we know that a change is an improvement?" and the measures should be directly related to the improvement aim statement or the objective of the PDSA.

When defining the metrics for a PDSA cycle, ensure that the data used for establishing the impact either is already available or it will need to be somehow obtained. HCOs with comprehensive EMR (or other clinical systems) in place will likely be able to leverage existing data to measure performance. Organizations without the benefit of preexisting data sources will need to consider how to capture the data required. This plan to collect data needs to include who will be responsible for the data capture, how it will be captured, when it will be captured, and of course, what it is that is going to be manually captured.

> **Tip**
>
> Don't limit your PDSA (or any other QI initiative) efforts only to those areas and/or processes for which there is available electronic data. Although manual collection of data may seem anachronistic (especially when mentioned in a healthcare analytics book!), manual collection in many cases is not prohibitively cumbersome (requiring only a few data points collected each day), and may lead to real performance improvements. Process changes likely to yield significant results with a reasonable effort—"low-hanging fruit"—may be located in processes or areas of healthcare that have not undergone the sometimes intense scrutiny associated with having installed an EMR system.

DO The actual implementation of and experimentation with process changes occurs during the PDSA "Do" phase. In addition to making changes to processes and procedures, data collection and initial analysis occur during this phase. If manual data collection is required, that is done with the frequency and on the appropriate form specified in the data collection plan.

If electronic data is available, initial evaluation of this data should include checking to ensure that the metrics and reports defined and utilized for the initiative are sensitive to the changes being made in the process. In other words, determine whether the right things are being measured in the right way.

During this phase of a PDSA cycle, information can be communicated to project team members and stakeholders via project dashboards and regular reporting. Early analysis of data is critical in order to implement midcourse changes early in a project. Such midcourse corrections may be necessary if metrics and other data are not sensitive to the changes being made, or if changes being made are not having the desired effect—whether because the outcomes are not as strong as desired, or because the changes are having a negative impact.

STUDY The "Study" phase is where the bulk of the analysis occurs in a PDSA cycle. At this point in the cycle, QI teams will analyze the data in more detail to determine whether a change has occurred, and what the magnitude of the change actually is. In PDSA cycles, run charts and statistical process control charts are commonly used to monitor trends in performance and to detect changes in outcomes. It is also common to use statistical testing to detect changes in performance. For example, a *t*-test or an ANOVA might be an appropriate statistical test to detect whether a change is statistically significant (that is, whether the observed results are likely to have occurred purely by chance). In fact, both the charting and statistical approaches can be used in a complementary fashion to identify whether an improvement has indeed occurred. See Chapter 9 for a discussion of statistical and control chart principles.

ACT The last step in a PDSA cycle is "Act," where a decision is made about what to do next based on what is learned in the Study phase. There are three general outcomes of a PDSA cycle:

1. The change is successful—targets and goals have been met; no further testing required.
2. The changes are promising—process is closer to achieving goals and targets, but further revisions and experimentation are necessary.
3. The changes are not successful, and are not promising—a different approach to addressing the problem is necessary; different opportunities or approaches should be pursued.

In the event of a successful change that is meeting performance targets, the project team has identified a solution to a quality or performance issue, has utilized available data and analytics tools to determine that the changes were successful, and has achieved the desired outcomes. In the event of a successful PDSA, the work is not immediately over. To maintain momentum and ensure that the changes are sustained, the team must develop and implement a long-term process monitoring and evaluation plan. Ongoing monitoring is used to alert the HCO if process performance begins to deteriorate. If deterioration is caught early, actions can be taken to reverse it and maintain optimal performance levels.

SUMMARY OF PDSA PDSA cycles are perhaps the most commonly used QI approach in healthcare. Many nurses and other clinical providers are familiar with PDSA, having been taught it in nursing or medical school, and with many HCOs having adopted PDSA as a standard QI approach. PDSA can be a powerful tool that healthcare QI teams can use to address issues of importance. One common complaint of PDSA, however, is that PDSA cycles tend to be too localized—that is, engaging exclusively in PDSA may result in HCO fixing many little problems while still not addressing greater overall issues.

Lean

Lean is a proven QI methodology with a successful track record in healthcare. Although largely developed in other industries, and perhaps made most famous in the automobile production industry as the Toyota Production System, Lean nonetheless has been gaining ground in healthcare as a QI methodology.

Some healthcare practitioners seem to be biased against Lean because of its roots in manufacturing—that somehow by adopting Lean we are viewing healthcare as no more than an assembly line. Nothing could be further from the truth, given that Lean is focused on maximizing value for the patient and reducing inefficiencies and waste in the delivery of healthcare.

The Lean Enterprise Institute, one of the leading organizations in the promotion of Lean in healthcare, states that Lean is "a set of concepts, principles, and tools used to create and deliver the most value from the customers' perspective while consuming the fewest resources and fully utilizing the knowledge and skills of the people performing the work."[13] Another way of looking at Lean is that "Lean thinking helps to identify the least wasteful way to provide better, safer healthcare to patients—with minimal delays."[14]

At its root, Lean is a systematic process of identifying and eliminating waste and evaluating improvements. A common misconception that many healthcare professionals have of Lean, however, is that it used only to find ways of "doing more with less," that is, to streamline processes only eventually to eliminate clinical or other staff positions. This opinion tends to erect barriers, because most healthcare professionals already feel they are working as hard as they possibly can and that they already make do in less than ideal conditions and with fewer than ideal resources.

What many healthcare practitioners don't realize is that by reducing waste and inefficiencies in healthcare processes, Lean *improves* the work environment by reducing and eliminating barriers to providing safe and effective care to patients. The bottom line is that Lean helps to *reduce* the chaos and overworked feelings of healthcare providers by finding them *more* time to focus on the good work they already do and provide *more* value for the patient.

An important concept of Lean is the *value stream map* (VSM). Similar in concept to other forms of process mapping, VSMs identify both the amount of time that each step in a process takes and the amount of waiting time that occurs between steps in a process. VSMs invariably illustrate how most of the time a patient spends within a healthcare facility is actually spent waiting for the next step in a process to occur.[15] From the patient's perspective, this is wasted time and not value-added.

Lean has at its core the philosophy of identifying the least wasteful ways to provide value to patients; to support this philosophy, there are many tools associated with Lean—the benefit of its having evolved through many industries over the last several decades. The tools are commonly used by Lean practitioners to structure QI activities, to identify root causes of problems, and to develop and communicate standard work, among other tools. Although there are many tools associated with Lean, successful Lean initiatives require more than simply using a collection of tools.

The Tools of Lean

Please visit this book's web site, http://HealthcareAnalyticsBook.com, for links, resources, and references about the many Lean tools available.

The two major components of Lean in healthcare are a management system and a set of tools. Because Lean requires strong organizational support from the top on down in order to be successful, the management system exists to ensure that the corporate culture essential to Lean is in place. Lean management tools help build organizational commitment to innovation and experimentation, promote the ideals of providing value to patients, and reduce the fear of a failure in the name of learning. The Lean management system provides a framework for effectively guiding improvement activities from initial project conception and problem identification through to evaluation and sustainment while keeping the focus on providing value to the patient.

THE FIVE PRINCIPLES OF LEAN There are five key principles specific to Lean that practitioners adhere to on improvement initiatives: specify value, identify the value stream, flow, pull, and perfection.[16] These five principles help HCOs to identify and eliminate waste and efficiency within their processes, and to redesign the processes to maximize flow and value. These principles of Lean are described next from a healthcare perspective:

1. **Specify value.** Value derived from a process must always be defined from the end customer's perspective and in relation to a specific product or service. In healthcare, the primary customer is the patient, but many other customer relationships exist (such as a physician being a customer of the hospital laboratory).
2. **Identify the value stream.** Map all the steps that are required in order to deliver the product or service to the customer. For example, mapping an elective surgery value stream would involve defining all process steps (including time intervals and other critical variables) from when a decision is made to book a surgery to the time the surgery is performed.
3. **Flow.** Once a value stream has been mapped out in detail, the next step is to identify all wasteful (or non-value-adding) steps in the process such that all remaining value-adding steps flow with a minimum of interruptions, errors, and delays.
4. **Pull.** After flow is improved, it can be further enhanced by implementing a "pull" system based on patient need/demand. With a well-functioning pull system, diagnostics such as lab and imaging are always available when the patient requires these diagnostics (not at the convenience of the service provider), or when hospital admissions from emergency occur quickly after the need for admission is identified, not after some delay-inducing screening process.
5. **Perfection.** As waste and inefficiency are removed from the value stream, and as the proportion of value-added activity increases, return to the first step and continue until no waste exists.

These five principles are fundamental to the Lean approach to improving healthcare quality and performance. The iterative nature of these principles underlies the commitment that Lean requires to the ongoing pursuit of perfection, and that Lean is a journey that HCOs embark upon. The term "Lean Thinking" is used because all staff should at all times be identifying inefficiencies within their scope of work and thinking of ways to reduce or eliminate that waste.

THE EIGHT WASTES OF HEALTHCARE Always examining healthcare processes in the relentless search for waste and inefficiencies can be an extremely daunting task. To the uninitiated, even knowing where to begin can be a challenge. Because of this, the different types of waste (*muda* in Japanese) have been conveniently grouped into eight categories. These categories provide healthcare QI teams a valuable framework with which to more easily identify waste and inefficiencies within processes, and hence to identify more easily

TABLE 4.4 Summary of the Eight Wastes of Healthcare

Waste	Description
Unnecessary motion	The many physical steps needed to gather equipment, confirm instructions/orders, and organize the treatment space to care for the patient.
Unnecessary transportation	Excess movement of people (patients), supplies, forms, and information throughout a facility.
Defects and errors	Time spent doing something incorrectly, inspecting for errors, or fixing errors.
Waiting	Time spent waiting for the next event to occur or the next work activity.
Inventory	Any supply in excess of the absolute minimum requirements necessary to meet customer demand.
Processing waste	Extra effort that adds no value to the service being provided from the patient/customer point of view. Can occur when the patient is unnecessarily queried or reassessed by multiple providers.
Overproduction	Doing more than what is needed by the patient, or doing it sooner than is required.
Unused human potential	Any situation in which people are not utilized to the utmost of their skills/ability to add value to processes.

opportunities for improvement. Table 4.4 lists the eight wastes in healthcare, and provides a brief descriptive example of each.

SUMMARY OF LEAN The Lean approach of methodically identifying and removing waste from clinical processes, combined with a framework for identifying *muda* and the many tools available for problem solving and process optimization, is a very powerful toolset that many hospitals and other HCOs have used to obtain significant quality and performance improvements.

An analytics challenge associated with Lean is that data from clinical systems rarely explicitly captures value-added/non-value-added time and data associated with waste. For example, in the clinical systems I have seen, there has never been an entry field for documenting unnecessary motion. Analytics teams must work with process and subject matter experts to identify proxy measures that can be used to estimate some of these values. For example, time intervals between processes such as assessment and X-ray may be used as a proxy measure for waiting. When system data is clearly not available, it may be necessary to manually observe processes for a time to manually document critical process-related data. It is important that a lack of data never be used as an excuse to not undertake a QI initiative.

Six Sigma

Six Sigma is another QI methodology that is used in healthcare. In fact, Six Sigma is often used together with Lean to provide a rigorous QI approach. Six Sigma was originally developed in 1986 by Motorola as a set of tools and strategies for improving processes, but was arguably made famous by General Electric after it won the Malcolm Baldrige National Quality Award, one of the most prestigious awards for achieving quality, in 1988.

Whereas the goal of Lean is to eliminate waste while improving value to the customer, the approach taken by Six Sigma emphasizes the use of information (or management by facts) and statistical analyses to rigorously and routinely measure and improve an organization's performance, practices, and systems. With this approach, the goal of Six Sigma is to reduce the occurrence of defects or errors from their current level within an HCO to the Six Sigma standard of 3.4 defects or errors per million opportunities (or DPMO). To put this in perspective, some estimates are that a typical HCO has an error rate between 2,700 and 45,500 (3 and 2 sigma) errors per million opportunities.[17]

Six Sigma has many variations and has been adopted by and integrated into a wide variety of organizations in myriad industries. Although Six Sigma may vary in how it is utilized within an organization, it has several defining factors that all implementations should have in common. Most Six Sigma initiatives can be considered to have the following five elements in common:[18]

1. **Intent.** Six Sigma initiatives are undertaken with the intent to achieve significant improvement in a short time period.
2. **Strategy.** Six Sigma can be applied throughout an HCO as a corporate strategy for improvement, but can also be applied where appropriate at the tactical level on individual projects.
3. **Methodology.** Although a few Six Sigma methodologies exist, the most common is DMAIC (Define, Measure, Analyze, Improve, and Control).
4. **Tools.** The Six Sigma methodology consists of numerous tools. These fall into categories, including requirements gathering (Kano's model), statistical analysis (*t*-test and ANOVA), and experimentation. Some tools were designed for Six Sigma, while others (like most of the statistical methods) have been adopted into the methodology.
5. **Measurements.** Three of the most common measurements used in Six Sigma are DPU (defects/errors per unit), DPMO (defects per million opportunities), and Sigma level.

As mentioned above, perhaps the most common Six Sigma methodology used in healthcare is DMAIC, which stands for define, measure, analyze, improve, and control (see Figure 4.3).

FIGURE 4.3 Six Sigma DMAIC Process

The five phases of the Six Sigma DMAIC methodology constitute a structured and rigorous approach to identifying opportunities for improvement. The DMAIC methodology is described in more detail in Table 4.5.

The five stages of DMAIC are effective because they are rigorous and must be followed in the prescribed manner. Achieving Six Sigma levels of performance requires significant changes to occur in a process, and therefore Six Sigma is not something that can realistically be undertaken on a part-time basis—it takes a real commitment on the part of management and project teams to make Six Sigma work. Six Sigma is the most statistically intensive of the three methodologies discussed in this section; because of the various statistical and other analysis tools and techniques associated with it, there are training and certification programs such as Green Belt or Black Belt that enable Six Sigma practitioners to learn about and understand

TABLE 4.5 Six Sigma DMAIC Methodology

Stage	Description
Define	Clearly identify and state the problem or issue that is the focus of the QI activity, and outline the scope of the project. Determine what are the critical requirements of and key benefits to the customer. Agree on which process is to be improved, and on the plan to achieve those improvements.
Measure	Review all available data and measure the extent of the quality or performance problem (defects, errors, deviations) and obtain baseline performance information.
Analyze	Study the root cause(s) of the problem and develop potential solution alternatives based on the root cause. Tools include the Ishikawa (or fishbone) diagram for determining root causes and FMEA (failure modes and effects analysis).
Improve	During this phase, alternative processes are developed to help achieve the required outcomes. These possible alternatives are evaluated based on potential impact on the outcome, with the selected improvement demonstrating (via statistical analysis) the highest likelihood of achieving "breakthrough performance."
Control	During this phase, the project team ensures that improvements are sustained by taking ongoing measurements and conducting ongoing communications, reviews, and training on the new process.

these various tools and apply them appropriately. See Chapter 9 for a summary of several of the statistical and graphical analysis techniques that are commonly used with Six Sigma.

Working with QI Methodologies

By no means are PDSA, Lean, and Six Sigma the only improvement methodologies that are effectively used in HCOs. But these and the other methodologies all recognize one basic fact: healthcare improvement is nearly impossible without a structured, comprehensive, and robust methodology to identify and rank improvement opportunities, map out and improve processes, and evaluate outcomes. Many HCOs that are struggling with healthcare quality are doing so because they are not approaching healthcare improvement in a methodical way.

The benefit of having multiple improvement methodologies from which to choose means that HCOs can find the tool that best matches the needs of a particular type of quality or performance problem. The challenge, of course, is determining what that best fit is. The further challenge for analytics is to deliver on the information needs unique to a methodology.

It is also true that all serious improvement methodologies require data throughout the entire project life cycle—from deciding what the improvement priorities are to knowing when to turn attention to other issues. The true value of analytics is in providing the practitioners of structured QI methodologies with solid evidence and deep insight not only into *how* healthcare is performing, but *why* it is performing the way it is.

Notes

1. Kathleen N. Lohr, ed., *Medicare: A Strategy for Quality Assurance* (Washington, DC: National Academy Press, 1990), 21.
2. Ibid, 22.
3. Michael E. Porter, "What Is Value in Health Care?" *New England Journal of Medicine* 363(26)(2010): 2477–2481.
4. Mark Graban, *Lean Hospitals: Improving Quality, Patient Safety, and Employee Engagement*, 2nd ed. (Boca Raton, FL: CRC Press, 2012), 34.
5. Porter, "What Is Value in Health Care?"
6. Worldwide Business Analytics Software 2007–2011, IDC, Framingham, MA (excerpt from IDC #208699).
7. Avedis Donabedian, *Explorations in Quality Assessment and Monitoring*, vol. 1, *The Definition of Quality and Approaches to Its Assessment* (Chicago: Health Administration Press, 1980), 79–83.

8. Diane L. Kelly, *Applying Quality Management in Healthcare: A Process for Improvement* (Chicago: Health Administration Press, 2003), 6.
9. Porter, "What Is Value in Health Care?"
10. NHS Institute for Innovation and Improvement (UK), *Going Lean in the NHS*, 4.
11. Ronda G. Hughes, ed., *Patient Safety and Quality: An Evidence-Based Handbook for Nurses* (Rockville, MD: Agency for Healthcare Research and Quality, 2008), www.ncbi.nlm.nih.gov/books/NBK2682.
12. National Health Service (UK), *Quality and Service Improvement Tools—Plan, Do, Study, Act (PDSA)*, www.institute.nhs.uk/quality_and_service_improvement_tools/quality_and_service_improvement_tools/plan_do_study_act.html.
13. Graban, *Lean Hospitals: Improving Quality, Patient Safety, and Employee Engagement,* 17.
14. NHS Institute for Innovation and Improvement, *Going Lean in the NHS,* 4.
15. Graban, *Lean Hospitals: Improving Quality, Patient Safety, and Employee Engagement,* 50.
16. James P. Womack and Daniel T. Jones, *Lean Thinking: Banish Waste and Create Wealth in Your Organization* (New York: Simon & Schuster, 1996).
17. Brett E. Trusko et al., *Improving Healthcare Quality and Cost with Six Sigma* (Upper Saddle River, NJ: FT Press, 2007).
18. Ibid.

CHAPTER 5

Data Quality and Governance

It is a capital mistake to theorize before one has data.

—Sir Arthur Conan Doyle

Healthcare leaders and quality improvement (QI) teams rely on having the best possible evidence on which to base decisions and evaluate quality and performance. The best possible evidence requires effective and accurate analytical tools able to provide understanding and insight into quality and performance based on data. In other words, without good data, analytics and the evidence it provides is likely to be suspect. Having good data for analytics and QI begins with effective management of data. This chapter will focus on how IT and QI teams can work together to ensure that a data infrastructure is available to support quality and performance improvement teams with the high-quality and highly accessible analytics they need.

Data is not a static asset within a healthcare organization (HCO). People unfamiliar with how data is managed in an organization may only consider data to be something that is entered into a computer system and sits in a database until subsequently reported on for management purposes. In addition to being a very valuable asset to an HCO, however, data is in fact a very dynamic asset within an HCO. As new information systems are adopted, and analytical requirements evolve, the underlying infrastructure and management of data must also evolve. The four main activities associated with maintaining a data system that supports the needs of an HCO (or any large organization) consist of data modeling, data creating, data storage, and data usage.[1]

1. **Data modeling.** No healthcare analytics is possible without data, and no data storage is possible without a data model. A data model is a

"wayfinding tool for both business and IT professionals, which uses a set of symbols and text to precisely explain a subset of real information to improve communication within the organization and thereby lead to a more flexible and stable application environment."[2] Data models have also been described as "what ties human thinking with computer processing [and] provides a blueprint for database and application system design."[3]

2. **Data creating.** Data is created through the day-to-day operations of providing healthcare, but can also be obtained from other sources including other organizations. Data at this stage can be considered the raw material that becomes information after additional processing and analysis.
3. **Data storage.** When data is obtained or created, it must be stored in a database. Data may be reformatted or otherwise transformed to improve the efficiency of the database, or to make data more accessible to information users. With data storage comes the need for protection of the data; healthcare data must be securely stored to prevent unauthorized access and to protect the privacy of the individuals whose information is stored.
4. **Data usage.** The main purpose of creating and storage data, of course, is to use it. Analytics is one of the primary ways in which HCOs can use data to enhance decision making and to help achieve quality and performance improvement goals.

These four key activities do not, and cannot, operate in isolation; to ensure that a high-quality and secure data infrastructure is available for decision makers and other information users throughout an HCO, an effective data management culture and structure within the HCO is required.

The Need for Effective Data Management

The adoption of healthcare information technology (HIT) in the form of electronic medical records (EMRs), electronic health records (EHRs), and other clinical systems continues to expand. For example, in the United States, 69 percent of primary care physicians reported using an EHR in 2012, compared to 49 percent in 2009.[4] This increase in EHR adoption in the United States may be in part due to government incentives (such as the HITECH Act and Meaningful Use requirements), but also because of the potential benefits of improved patient care offered by HIT. Most other industrialized countries are also experiencing increases in EMR adoption—for example, Great Britain, Australia, New Zealand, the Netherlands, and Norway all report EHR adoption rates of over 90 percent.[5] Great Britain, long a leader in HIT use, is also a leader in the use of data for quality and performance improvement.

Although healthcare information systems are still in their relative infancy, they are generating large volumes of data. As the growth rate of HIT adoption continues to increase, the volume of data collected by these systems will also increase. Recent estimates are that healthcare data totaled 150 exabytes in 2011, and will continue to grow into the zetabytes and perhaps even yottabytes soon after.[6] To put that into perspective, consider that a gigabyte (GB) is 10^9 bytes, an exabyte (EB) is 10^{18} bytes, a zetabyte (ZB) is 10^{21} bytes, and a yottabyte (YB) is 10^{24} bytes. Many large healthcare networks have data volumes in the petabyte (1 PB = 10^{15} bytes) range.

While this very large and growing volume of data presents an exciting potential for use in quality and performance improvement activities, it is by no means a trivial task to ensure that this data is available, and usable, for such purposes. Fundamentally, data that is used for healthcare quality and performance improvement needs to be:

- **High quality**—to ensure that the information generated from analytics is valid and useful.
- **Well documented**—so that analysts and developers using the data are aware of its context and meaning.
- **Easily accessible**—and available in a data warehouse (or similar data store) to ensure that it is available for analysis when required.

To ensure that these three fundamentals are achieved, HCOs require strong and effective data governance strategies and structures. Organizations that do not employ strict data management and data quality policies run the risk of accumulating large quantities of data that is essentially unusable without expending great effort to clean and otherwise make it more usable. HCOs have a responsibility, as data owners, for:[7]

- **Data quality.** Determining the data quality levels required for different fields in the database, and how best to achieve those levels. Note that not all data requires the same level of quality. For example, data relating to demographics, clinical orders and observations, and billing information needs to be of the highest quality, whereas supplemental information not impacting patient care may not need to be of as high a quality.
- **Security and privacy.** The determination of who is able to access which data. Healthcare data is perhaps an individual's most private information, so maximum effort must be made to ensure that privacy is maintained at all times. Almost every conceivable analytics operation

can and should be done using anonymized data. In an instance where analytics is helping to predict an outcome for a particular patient, only the clinical provider should be unblinded to both the patient and the outcome.

- **Business rules.** The rules embedded in code that validate, map, calculate, or otherwise transform raw data into higher-quality and more useful data must be maintained and updated. Business rules are often used to calculate interval times, recode variables, and perform other transformations on raw data to make information easier to analyze.
- **Availability.** When information must be made available and when acceptable downtimes are possible. Interestingly, I have seen a shift toward the need for more round-the-clock availability of data systems and analytics. Clinical and management decision making does not stop at the end of the working day, so neither should the information required to assist with those decisions.
- **Periodicity.** How often the data needs to be updated (this can range from quarterly to monthly to near real time, depending on the needs of the system).
- **Performance**. The response time experienced by the user when accessing the system. The performance of analytical tools must be exceptionally high when supporting near-real-time clinical decision making, whereas slower performance is likely to be acceptable in non-real-time situations (such as when running reports).

As illustrated by the previous list, the responsibilities associated with ownership of healthcare data extend far beyond simply purchasing and maintaining database servers and software to house the data. These activities are essential to ensure that HCOs have high-quality data that can be utilized for quality and performance improvement, research, and management decision making, is accessible when needed, and protected from unauthorized access and usage.

Data Quality

The most important aspect of any analytics system is access to accurate, high-quality data. Before any reports are built, analyses performed, and dashboards deployed, ensuring that source data is trustworthy must be the first priority. Without data that is accurate, it is impossible to trust in the results of the many algorithms and other computations that constitute analytics. If the veracity of the raw material is called into question, then certainly the results of the computations using that raw data must also be suspect.

Accuracy and Quality Are Key

The most important aspect of any analytics infrastructure is access to accurate, high-quality data.

Without high-quality data, many quality and performance improvement projects may be negatively impacted—especially large-scale projects using a structured improvement methodology like Lean or Six Sigma. For this reason, healthcare QI specialists are important and necessary stakeholders in data quality. Improving quality and performance requires a solid understanding of previous and current performance, and an ability to detect changes in data that signal an improvement (or worsening) in performance. Having poor-quality data will likely increase the difficulty in detecting changes in performance, or lead to misinterpretation of data and incorrect conclusions.

HCOs need to determine their own data quality requirements. To assist with this determination, there are many dimensions that can be used to quantify the quality of data. The Canadian Institute for Health Information (CIHI), for example, uses the dimensions outlined in Table 5.1 for data quality.[8] The CIHI dimensions of data quality, identified by an asterisk in Table 5.1, are useful for gauging the quality and usability of a data set for use in healthcare analytics applications. In addition to the CIHI data quality dimensions, completeness, conformity, and consistency have also been identified as necessary dimensions of data quality,[9] and are also described Table 5.1.

Achieving Better Data Quality

Having good data cannot guarantee that effective analytics tools can and will be built, utilized effectively by an HCO, and result in the quality and performance improvements desired. Bad data, however, will most certainly mean that efforts to use information will be hindered due to a lack of trust or belief in the analytics and/or its results.

To begin with, how do we describe "good data"? Quality expert Joseph Juran states that "data are of high quality if they are fit for use in their intended operational, decision making, and other roles."[10] In this definition, "fit for use" means free of defects and possession of desired and necessary features. Achieving good data, however, is hard work. HCOs need to start with the source systems, and in particular the users of those source systems. In my experience, one of the best ways to improve end users' data entry is to share the analyses with them in the form of performance reports and other relevant forms that are meaningful to the individual. If end users can

TABLE 5.1 Data Quality Dimensions

Data Quality Dimension	Description
Accuracy*	Reflects how well information within (or otherwise derived from) data reflects the actual reality it is intended to measure.
Timeliness*	Reflects how recent and up to date data is at the time it is available for use in analytics. Measured from the time it was generated (or the end of the reference period to which the data pertains) to the time it is available for use.
Comparability*	Refers to the extent to which the data is uniform over time and uses standard conventions (such as common data elements or coding schemes).
Usability*	Reflects how easy it is to access, use, and understand the data.
Relevance*	Reflects how well the data meets the current and potential future analytics needs of the healthcare organization.
Completeness	Refers to how much of all potential electronic data (for example, from electronic health records, claims data, and other sources) is available for analytics.
Conformity	Reflects how well the available data conforms to expected formats (such as standardized nomenclature).
Consistency	Measures how well values agree across data sets and the extent of agreement exhibited by different data sets that are describing the same thing. This can range from the use of consistent acronyms to standard procedures by which to document patient discharge time.

* Denotes a data quality dimension identified by the Canadian Institute of Health Information.

see how the data is being put to use (and how the results can impact both their job and patient care), they may be less likely to dismiss accurate data entry as an unimportant and irritating part of their job.

Monitoring Data Quality

We have used our own analytics tools to detect poor data quality and automatically alert those people who can take corrective action. Rapid feedback dramatically increases the speed at which data quality issues are addressed.

When more direct measures were necessary to improve data quality within my own HCO, we have used our own analytics tools to encourage managers to provide coaching to staff when staff performance is not what is expected. For example, a project I was on utilized analytics tools to automatically measure the rate at which triage nurses were overriding a computerized scoring algorithm. It was found that the overrides were occurring primarily because nurses were not filling in all the required information appropriately, and the system was generating invalid results due to this data quality issue. By implementing automatic e-mail alerts to managers when the override rates were higher than desired, the managers could provide coaching or more in-depth training to staff so that they would complete all necessary data fields. This relatively simple intervention reduced the override rate of nurses using the tool from around 45 percent to around 10–15 percent, which was much more acceptable from a clinical standpoint. Furthermore, most of the overrides post-intervention were the result of real clinical disagreement with the results of the algorithm, not a result of poor data quality negatively impacting the calculations.

> **Tip**
>
> Although there are myriad possible causes of data quality problems, data quality usually begins at the source.

The best approach to improving the quality of healthcare data is to prevent data quality issues in the first place. Although there are myriad possible causes of data quality problems, data quality usually begins at the source. That is, poor data quality is most likely to be a result of the way users interact with clinical or other information systems, poorly designed user interfaces, and deficiencies in data entry validation. Less likely but still possible, poor data quality may also be the result of errors in system interface code or other instances where data is communicated between two systems.

In my experience, healthcare quality initiatives have been hindered by data quality for a number of reasons, including:

- **No data available.** Many HCOs are still not fully computerized, meaning that a lot of important data is still locked away on paper in filing cabinets. If the data needed to answer a particular question or identify a quality issue is not available to begin with, that is a blind spot that needs to be addressed. There will always be gaps in data, however—even fully computerized HCOs cannot possibly capture data on every single step of every process in care delivery.

- **Data doesn't represent workflows.** Many HCOs have had EMRs and other clinical information systems for many years. Unfortunately, processes often change more quickly (and more often) than the information systems can be updated to reflect these changes. This results in business processes becoming out of sync with the data being collected, or different meanings being attached to existing data fields. It requires commitment and effort to keep data stores up to date to reflect these changes.
- **Personal inclination.** Even if information systems accurately map to workflows, processes are well defined, and frontline staff are fully trained on the system, some staff may still choose to use the information system in an inappropriate way, which may result in the data associated with their entries being less valid. Comments such as, "Oh, I know I'm supposed to enter the data that way, but it's too many clicks, so I don't do it like that," are particularly frustrating. Obviously, frontline staff are not meant to be data collectors for QI teams, but at some point they should understand that the data being collected is used to improve care quality (and job quality) for everyone who works in the organization.
- **Data errors.** There are still plenty of good old-fashioned typos that can make analysis more challenging. For example, incorrectly spelled medications, incorrect medical record numbers, and other incorrect information can cause problems when linking data or summarizing information for analysis. Many source systems still do not employ sufficient data validation to check for the accuracy and validity of certain types of data commonly entered into the system with errors (for example, temperature, height, and weight ranges).

Overcoming Data Errors

Poor user interface design on clinical systems can be a source of poor data quality. Particularly dubious are pull-down lists that also offer the choice to enter your own data. This is where you see how creative people can get retyping information already contained on the list. For example, the Mode of Arrival field on our triage note contained an option for "Ambulance," but also had a free-text box where values for this field could be typed in. The result was that instead of having a very clean summary of how patients arrived at the emergency department, we had to contend with entries such as "arrived by ambulance," "ambulance #209," "EMS ambulance," "amblance," or simply "amb." Thankfully, the use of the free-text box was discontinued, and the data from the triage note is now much cleaner.

With growing volumes of data and increasing reliance on analytics for decision making, data quality is a major focus of research, and root causes of data errors have been studied extensively and systematically. The many possible causes of data quality problems have been grouped into 10 major causes (several of which are given in the following list, with elaboration added).[11] Addressing these root causes of poor data quality will greatly enhance the quality of data that is available for analytics.

- **Multiple data sources.** This is common in healthcare, with multiple source systems (including registration, lab, and diagnostic imaging system) storing a single patient's data; each source system may have its own data validation rules and data formats.
- **Subjective judgment in data production.** Without clear documentation and definitions of the data (both at the source *and* at time of analysis), personal interpretations of what data means impact what is recorded and how the data is eventually interpreted.
- **Security/accessibility trade-off.** If security is too tight on databases for analysis, developers may look elsewhere where data is more accessible. This is why many "rogue" copies of data are created.
- **Coded data across disciplines.** Different source systems may code data using different coding schemes (e.g., ICD-9 versus ICD-10), which may hinder comparability and compatibility if clear mappings are not available.
- **Complex data representations.** Data representing complex processes, or even simple processes that are stored iteratively, may induce errors in the extraction and analysis of the data. (Data modeling helps to alleviate this issue.)
- **Volume of data.** Large volumes of data can be challenging to work with, especially if there is limited computing power available to work with. Some desktop statistical packages can only analyze data that is in memory (as opposed to on disk), which limits the size of data that can be analyzed.
- **Changing data needs.** As the business, quality, and performance improvement needs of the organization evolve, be careful not to let these new requirements bias your understanding of the data unless the process(es) and data have, in fact, changed.

As mentioned, having accurate, high-quality data for analytics starts at the source. Analytics teams need to work together with data warehouse managers and frontline staff to ensure that all possible sources of poor data quality are identified, reduced, or eliminated. In my experience, it has been helpful for members of the analytics team to be part of system change request committees. It is likely that whenever a change to a source clinical system is required, it is because of a change in process, or because of a new process

For a comprehensive listing of data quality references and additional resources, please visit this book's web site at http://HealthcareAnalyticsBook.com.

and the need to be able to capture data from that new process. Having analytics and data warehouse team members on those change committees helps to ensure that any potential changes in data (either new fields or changes to existing data) are taken into account during change request discussions.

The full potential of healthcare analytics cannot be realized, however, if data is locked inside operational, divisional, or other information silos. One of the exciting capabilities of analytics is finding new relationships between processes and outcomes, and discovering new knowledge; this is truly possible only when data is integrated from across the enterprise. As data is integrated from multiple clinical and other systems from across the HCO, however, its management becomes an issue. How data was managed in an independent, one-off database is not suitable at all for managing data integrated from across multiple source systems. Failing to effectively manage healthcare data, across all its sources, will seriously impede the development and use of effective analytics.

Data Governance and Management

Because the quality of data is critical to quality and performance improvement activities, it is good practice to have people within the HCO who are responsible for data quality. Discussions of enterprise data quality, however, invariably raise issues of data ownership, data stewardship, and overall control of data within the organization. HCOs with very little, if any, formal data management and governance exhibit data quality management that is ad hoc and reactionary—action is taken only when it is too late and something needs to be fixed. HCOs at the opposite extreme have implemented layer upon layer of approval requirements, stewardship, and change management committees; such bureaucracy, however, can backfire and pose a risk to data quality when adhering to rules that are too strict inhibits the flexibility required to respond to changing patient care processes, changing systems, and changing analytics requirements.

Healthcare Organization Data Governance

To ensure that high-quality data is available for QI activities, HCOs must ensure that appropriate and effective data quality management processes are in place. In addition, these processes need to be enforced, and they need to provide a balance between the rigor necessary to ensure stability and the agile responsiveness required by the evolving data needs of the HCO.

According to the Data Governance Institute, data governance is "a system of decision rights and accountabilities for information-related processes, executed according to agreed-upon models which describe who can take what actions with what information, and when, under what circumstances, using what methods."[12] Data governance helps HCOs better manage and realize value from data, improve risk management associated with data, and ensure compliance with regulatory, legal, and other requirements.

The Data Governance Institute suggests a framework that organizations, including HCOs, can use to implement and maintain effective governance. A data governance framework should:

- Possess a mission.
- Define focused goals, governance metrics, and success measures.
- Outline clear data rules and definitions.
- Enable decision rights, accountabilities, and control mechanisms.
- Identify data stakeholders and data stewards.
- Establish a data governance office.
- Implement proactive, reactive, and ongoing data governance processes.

The key responsibilities of the data governance function within an HCO are to establish, enforce, and refine the policies and procedures for managing data at the enterprise level. Whether data governance is its own committee or a function of an existing body, the data governance function sets the ground rules for establishing and maintaining data quality, how and under what circumstances changes to data definitions or context can occur, and what constitutes appropriate use of healthcare data.

Based on input from the data owners, data stewards, analytics stakeholders, and business representatives, the data governance committee must create policies and procedures regarding how the data resources of an organization are managed. That is, the data governance function determines

Data Governance

Data governance is "a system of decision rights and accountabilities for information-related processes, executed according to agreed-upon models which describe who can take what actions with what information, and when, under what circumstances, using what methods."

under what circumstances the data definitions, business rules, or structure can be changed. This helps prevent an unauthorized local change to a source system causing downstream data quality issues.

The data governance committee is the ultimate authority on how data is managed throughout the enterprise. Organizations without strong and effective data governance structures will likely experience major problems as changes to processes, source systems, business rules, indicators, and even the interpretation of data start to evolve, or change dramatically, without any coordination or impact analysis. Strong data governance helps to ensure that changes ranging from a clinical process to a business rule is evaluated for impact on all other components of the data system.

The personnel structure around data governance should data owners, key stakeholders (including senior and/or executive-level representation), and data stewards from across functional areas. Finally, data governance processes need to be proactive, effective, and ongoing. One of the benefits of the data governance function is that it helps ensure that the source data, and resultant reports, analytics, and insight, are held as trustworthy and valuable within the HCO.

Benefits of Data Governance

One of the benefits of the data governance function is that it helps ensure that the source data, and resultant reports, analytics, and insight are held as trustworthy and valuable within the HCO.

A data governance committee or function within an HCO has a key role in ensuring the integrity of analytics. Decisions are being made more often within HCOs that require both real-time and non-real-time but mission-critical data. When decision makers cannot afford to be wrong, neither can the data; the trust in an HCO's data must be rock-solid. Achieving this high level of trust in data is a key objective of data governance.

I have seen the impact of poor and/or nonexistent enterprise-wide data governance within an HCO. When data quality and management are left to the business intelligence and/or analytics team to manage and "enforce" without any real authority, changes made in one place (say, for example, in a process on the front line, or on a data field in a computer system) likely will not consistently or reliably get communicated to the people responsible for the data. Very often, these changes are not discovered until it is too late and manifest as errors and unexpected results in reports, dashboards, and other analytical tools. Changes in frontline processes or in the way that source system software is used should not first show up as data quality issues in reports and dashboards because the analytics team was not notified that these changes were being implemented.

What data governance should *not* be, however, is just another layer of bureaucracy. Many HCOs have too many layers of approval required for tasks ranging from changing the design of forms on clinical systems to accessing data in a testing environment. Committees and layers of approval are not necessarily a bad thing—only when they hinder the agility of the organization to respond to actual operational needs.

Data Stewardship

As mentioned earlier, a necessary counterpart to a data governance function within the HCO is the *data steward*. Data stewardship is a necessary component of data governance to ensure high-quality and highly reliable data. The data steward is responsible for monitoring and evaluating data quality within an HCO. Specifically, the major functions associated with a data steward include:[13]

- Evaluating data quality, identifying issues, and making appropriate recommendations.
- Ensuring that any modifications to data storage and management are in line with accepted policies and procedures.
- Ensuring that data is used properly and that it is accessible.
- Helping to establish enterprise-wide standards for data quality and usage.

Within a large organization such as an HCO, the data stewardship function requires one data steward for each major data subject area or functional area.[14] In a typical HCO, this would be achieved by having assigning one data steward for each major line of business, program, and/or domain within the HCO. In a hospital for example, a data steward would be assigned for emergency medicine, surgery, cardiology, and other such functional programs.

Despite the necessity of multiple data stewards, the data stewards of each functional data set must work together and in concert with an organizational data architect to ensure that common standards and approaches are taken. This is especially important for analytics, as program and department indicators and metrics are shared throughout the organization.

The data steward works at the intersection of the business and the technology. Therefore, the data steward should have good technical skills, including knowledge of data modeling and data warehouse concepts. The data steward should also understand the business well. This is not to say that the data steward must be a clinician, but he or she must be familiar with the processes, terminology, and data required by the line of business. Finally, the data steward must possess the interpersonal and communication skills to be able to bridge the gap in discussions between technology experts and clinical and subject matter experts from the business.

The importance of effective data stewardship cannot be understated. As mentioned, accurate output from analytical systems depends absolutely on the quality of the data that serves as input. Healthcare information technology systems are still relatively immature compared to other industries, and in my experience still undergo significant changes as HCOs evolve through their adoption of HIT. Analytics teams must work very closely with data stewards (within the guidance of the data governance function) to help ensure that when computer systems must be updated or otherwise changed, any and all impacts to the data and defined business rules are understood and mitigated.

Enterprise-wide Visibility and Opportunity

Important decisions in healthcare are becoming less localized and are taking on more of an enterprise scope. Despite this, many factions within HCOs are incredibly reluctant to relinquish control of their data, or even to share it. However, as clinical systems and the data warehouses on which information is stored become more complex, the fact is that data ownership,

THE NEED FOR AGILITY AND DATA STEWARDSHIP

The capabilities of health information technology systems are improving rapidly. For example, the emergency department information system at a typical emergency department when deployed several years ago may have started as only a patient tracking system for patients within the department. Additional capabilities can be added on over time, such as clinical documentation, computerized provider order entry, and results reporting. Other changes also occur throughout the organization that must be accounted for, such as renovations and/or expansions (which require updates to locations and business rules). Other new technology, such as radio frequency identification, might also be added. The challenge is that many of these changes can, and most often do, impact the underlying data in the system. The data stewards within an HCO must be responsible for ensuring that the data, whether it be in an enterprise data warehouse or otherwise, is up to date with the latest data definitions, processes, and business rules. If any necessary changes are not communicated to the developers of analytical tools within the HCO, reporting and analytical insight will soon lose validity, and ultimately value, within the HCO.

stewardship, and management must become a shared responsibility among all data owners. The days of a department or unit owning its own standalone clinical or administrative database are numbered. HCOs must work diligently to ensure the availability and trustworthiness of the enterprise-wide data and information that decision makers require.

This shared responsibility can open up whole new opportunities for HCOs to improve transparency and break down silos that have traditionally existed and that have always erected roadblocks in the efficient flow of both patients and information. As more clinical and other data become available throughout the enterprise, the opportunities for enterprise-wide quality and performance monitoring and insight are truly exciting. Provided that the responsibilities of data governance and stewardship are taken seriously throughout the HCO, healthcare departments and programs may no longer need to work to improve quality and performance in isolation.

Notes

1. Thomas C. Redman, *Data Quality for the Information Age* (Boston: Artech House), 42–43.
2. Steve Hoberman, *Data Modeling Made Simple*, 2nd ed. (Bradley Beach, NJ: Technics Publications, 2009), 36.
3. Jack E. Myers, "Data Modeling for Healthcare Systems Integration: Use of the MetaModel," www.metadata.com/whitepapers/myers1.pdf.
4. Ken Terry, "EHR Adoption: U.S. Remains the Slow Poke," InformationWeek.com, November 15, 2012, www.informationweek.com/healthcare/electronic-medical-records/ehr-adoption-us-remains-the-slow-poke/240142152.
5. Ibid.
6. Mike Cottle et al., *Transforming Health Care through Big Data: Strategies for Leveraging Big Data in the Health Care Industry* (New York: Institute for Health Technology Transformation, 2013), http://ihealthtran.com/iHT2_BigData_2013.pdf.
7. Sid Adelman, Larissa Moss, and Majid Abai, *Data Strategy* (Upper Saddle River, NJ: Addison-Wesley, 2005), 148–151.
8. Canadian Institute for Health Information, *The CIHI Data Quality Framework*, 2009, www.cihi.ca/CIHI-ext-portal/pdf/internet/DATA_QUALITY_FRAMEWORK_2009_EN.
9. "6 Key Data Quality Dimensions," MelissaData.com, www.melissadata.com/enews/articles/1007/2.htm.
10. Joseph J. Juran and A. Blanton Godfrey, eds., *Juran's Quality Handbook*, 5th ed. (New York: McGraw Hill, 1999), 34.9.
11. Yang W. Lee et al., *Journey to Data Quality* (Cambridge, MA: MIT Press, 2006), 80.

12. Data Governance Institute, *The DGI Data Governance Framework*, www.datagovernance.com/dgi_framework.pdf.
13. Laura B. Madsen, *Healthcare Business Intelligence: A Guide to Empowering Successful Data Reporting and Analytics* (Hoboken, NJ: John Wiley & Sons, 2012), 47–54.
14. Claudia Imhoff, "Data Stewardship: Process for Achieving Data Integrity," *Data Administration Newsletter*, September 1, 1997, www.tdan.com/view-articles/4196.

CHAPTER 6

Working with Data

In God we trust. All others bring data.

—W. Edwards Deming

Data is an essential component of analytics, and working with and understanding data is a critical analytical skill. Due to its nature, healthcare data is often more complex than that in other industries. Despite this complexity, many analytical tools such as dashboards and reports use simplistic (or even incorrect) approaches to analyze and represent the data. This chapter will focus on the key concepts behind understanding and effectively utilizing data. Covered are data type common to healthcare and how to select appropriate analyses for various data types so that healthcare information analysts are able to extract the maximum information and value from collected data.

ROOKIE MISTAKES

I am sure that everyone can share a time when they were eager to "dive right into" some data, made some completely wrong assumptions about what the data meant, or what kind of data it was, and prepared a report or other analysis that was completely meaningless. The valuable lesson I have learned on these occasions is to fully understand the data and all available context prior to performing any detailed "analysis."

Data: The Raw Material of Analytics

Data is the raw material of information. Data is continuously generated as healthcare professionals such as healthcare providers, administrators, and analysts use computerized systems as part of their jobs, or enter data into databases as part of post hoc data collection efforts for research, QI, or other reasons. The data that is stored in source-system databases, however, is rarely useful in and of itself. Just like any raw material, data must be *processed* in order to become useful. This processing is how *data* starts to become *information* that is useful for understanding the operations of a healthcare organization (HCO).

Figure 6.1 illustrates the information value chain. At the beginning of the chain is data, the raw material. The data is generated by electronic medical records and other computerized tools within healthcare. The next step in the chain is analysis, the step in which data is taken from its raw database form, summarized, and transformed into a more useful format. By applying the analysis and other processing available in analytics tools, the result is information and insight that is available to clinicians, administrators, and other information users. The intent is that this information helps to trigger actions, such as by implementing process improvements or assisting in clinical decision making, which in turn leads to improved outcomes that are in line with the quality and performance goals of the HCO.

When someone who is working on a healthcare QI project asks for data, the request is in fact rarely for just data. That is, someone would normally not be asking for a dump from the database unless that person is planning to do his or her own analysis. Requests for data usually stem from the need for *information* to help understand a problem, identify issues, or evaluate outcomes. Even simple summarizations of data (including counts, averages, and other basic statistics) begin the process of turning raw data into something that is more useful—information and insight that can be used for decision making and taking action.

FIGURE 6.1 Information Value Chain

Preparing Data for Analytics

It is important to fight the urge to dive into a new data set or newly added data elements without obtaining a clear understanding of the context of the data, and how it relates to the business. When developing analytics to address a need for insight and information around a quality or performance improvement initiative or issue, requisite information that an analyst needs to know includes:

- **What the data represents.** What process, workflow, outcome, or structural component does the data correspond to?
- **How the data is stored.** What kind of storage is the data in (such as an enterprise data warehouse), how is the data physically stored on the database, and how might that storage format constrict what can be done with the data? Also, how good is the quality of the data; are there missing values that might bias analysis, and are there invalid entries that need to be cleaned and/or addressed?
- **The data type.** Regardless of how data might be physically stored in a database, what kind of data do the values represent in "real life"?
- **What can logically be done with the data.** Given the type of data and how it is stored, what kind of database and mathematical operations can be performed on the data in meaningful ways?
- **How can the data be turned into useful information** that drives decision making and enables leaders and quality stakeholders to take appropriate and necessary action?

When analysts begin working with a new data set, they should spend time on the floor (or elsewhere in the HCO) where the activity occurs that generates the data, and where the resultant analytics insight is used. This hands-on exposure helps relate data to actual situations and conditions and provides invaluable context to existing documentation and metadata.

Understanding What Data Represents

At the heart of successful quality and performance improvement in healthcare is modifying existing and creating new business and clinical processes

Lessons Learned

Whenever I work on a QI project, I see the necessity of presenting data in the context of the business processes (and see the problems that occur when that doesn't happen). Every data element in a database is conveying some information regarding a process. But the meaning of that information is uncertain without knowing its context (that is, the associated business process or workflow). Summarizing and analyzing data without the benefit of knowing the context will likely lead to inaccurate or misleading analysis results.

that reduce waste, are more effective, and reduce the likelihood of medical errors. To be useful for quality and performance improvement, data must be analyzed within the context of the processes and workflows through which it is originally generated. This section will focus on the methods for aligning data to processes and using that data as a basis for analytics.

Aligning Processes with Data

Clinical processes and workflows have been in place since the advent of modern medicine; enterprise data warehouses and clinical software applications are much more recent inventions. It is not surprising, then, that until very recently, the people primarily concerned with the processes of healthcare were not the same people whose primary concern is the data generated by those processes. Because healthcare systems are dynamic, processes are constantly changing; stewards of healthcare data are often not informed of such changes, or may not be able to keep up with the changes in processes occurring on the front line.

To provide accurate insights, analytics must use data that is representative of what is actually happing on the front lines. For this reason, analytics professionals must work very closely with business subject matter experts who are able to convey the most recent process changes and validate that the current assumptions on which analytics is based match what is occurring on the front line.

Figure 6.2 represents, at a high level, the steps necessary for a patient to be seen by an emergency department physician. Each of the steps in the process represents its own activities (such as triaging a patient), requires a specific resource (such as a registration clerk, nurse, or physician), and generates its own data (via interactions with clinical software). See Table 6.1 for a sample of the type of data that would be typically generated in a process such as the one illustrated in Figure 6.2.

In addition to knowing which process a data item is associated with, other important information to note about each data point includes:

- Who performs the activity that generates the data?
- Who enters the data element into the system (in the case an observation or similar data) or causes data to be generated (through some other interaction with a clinical system such as changing a status code)?

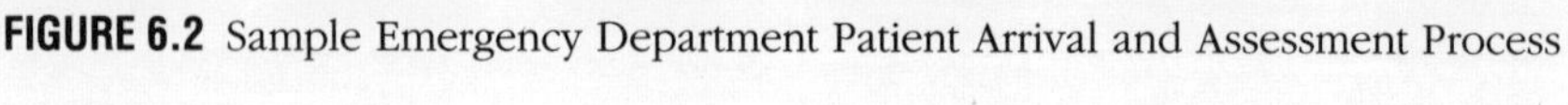

FIGURE 6.2 Sample Emergency Department Patient Arrival and Assessment Process

TABLE 6.1 Context Details of an Emergency Department Patient Arrival and Assessment Process

Process Step	Description	Data
Triage	Nurse performs a preliminary triage assessment of the patient to determine his or her presenting complaint and the urgency of the patient's condition.	Arrival time Mode of arrival (ambulance, car, etc.) Time triage started Time triage completed Triage acuity score (1 through 5) Presenting complaint Vital signs
Patient arrival	Registration clerk registers patient and collects full demographic and billing information.	Time registration started Time registration completed Full patient demographic and insurance information

- What is the trigger for the data to be stored?
- What type of data is stored (such as numeric, alphanumeric, and date/time)?
- What business and validation rules are associated with the data item?
- What data is required to provide the information and insight required to address the quality and performance goals of the organization?

Types of Data

Data can be divided into two basic types: quantitative or numeric, and qualitative or nonnumeric.[1] Quantitative data typically is obtained from observations such as temperature, blood pressure, time, and other similar data. Qualitative data, on the other hand, tends to be more descriptive in nature, and may consist of observations and opinions (entered into an electronic medical record), patients' experiences while receiving care, transcribed notes from focus groups, or researchers' notes. Quantitative data is easier to summarize and analyze statistically; qualitative data usually requires more preparation prior to analysis, but can reveal insights into quality and performance that standard quantitative analysis cannot pick up.

Improvement science identifies three types of data: classification, count, and continuous.[2] Classification and count data are sometimes collectively referred to as *attribute data*, and continuous data likewise is often referred to as *variable data*. Attributes associated with classification data are recorded as one of two classifications or categories, such as pass/fail, acceptable/

unacceptable, or admitted/nonadmitted. Count data, as would be expected, is used to document the number of occurrences of typically undesirable events or outcomes, such as number of central line infections, falls from hospital beds, critical incidents, and other occurrences related to quality and performance. Finally, continuous data is often associated with productivity or workload, such as emergency department census, X-rays performed, wait times, and other measures of performance.

Once an understanding is obtained of what the data means in "real life" (that is, how the data is mapped to processes, workflows, and other aspects of healthcare delivery), the data needs to be understood in terms of what type of data it is (once again in "real life") versus how it is stored and formatted on an electronic database. Knowing this allows analysts and developers to create meaningful analyses of the data; if the type of analysis performed on data is not appropriate, the results may in fact be nonsensical, as the following examples will illustrate.

ELECTRONIC STORAGE OF DATA People who are familiar with programming languages or databases will know that data can be *classed* in many ways based on what is being stored. In a database, for example, the data type assigned to a field (or object) typically will define four main attributes of what is to be stored in that field (or object).[3] These four main attributes (at the database level) consist of:

1. The *kind* of data being stored (for example, numeric, character, binary).
2. The *size* (or *length*) of the data being stored (for example, how many characters the field can hold).
3. The *precision* of the data (for numeric data only): the total number of digits in a number.
4. The *scale* of the data (for numeric data only): the total number of digits that fall to the right of the decimal point.

At the database level, the data type that is assigned to a field controls what kind of information can be stored in that field. This helps to ensure the integrity of data stored so that when the data is read back from the database, the software knows how to interpret the data being loaded. See Figure 6.3 for a sample screenshot from a database program illustrating various data fields and how their type is encoded.

Data types in a database ensure the integrity and management of the information stored on the database. The data type assigned to a database field also dictates what operations can be performed on the data in that field. For example, typical mathematical operations (such as multiplication and division) cannot be applied to character-type data, so multiplying a patient's name by a number (or multiplying two names together) would be

Name	Type	Length	Decimals
First Name	varchar	255	0
Last Name	varchar	255	0
Chart ID Number	varchar	8	0
Date of Birth	date	0	0
Height (cm)	int	4	0
Weight (km)	float	6	2
Acuity Score	int	3	0

FIGURE 6.3 Screenshot of Database Showing Data Fields and Data Types

an illegal operation. Databases (and analytical software) typically strongly enforce these rules so that inappropriate operations cannot be performed.

A challenge arises, however, if data is coded in a database as an inappropriate type. Attributes of data from a computer database may not always accurately relay what analysis *truly* makes sense to perform on data. For example, I have seen numeric temperature values such as 37.0 stored in text-type data fields because the programmers wanted to store the entry as "37.0 degrees Celsius" to ensure the unit of measure was captured with the temperature (even though a temperature is clearly numeric and can be treated as such). When this occurs, data type casting (that is, converting from one data type to another) and other manipulations may be necessary to allow for the desired operations to be permissible. In this case, the "degrees Celsius" would need to be stripped from the data, and the resultant values type cast to a numeric value so that graphing, summarizations, and other calculations become possible with the temperature data.

In summary, know your data and beware of treating data strictly as specified in database attributes without first knowing the context of the data, what it really means, and what data summarizations and analyses must be performed.

LEVELS OF MEASUREMENT Data is stored in a database using data types that best approximate the type of data the field represents. In Figure 6.3, for example, the "Chart ID Number" is stored as a "varchar" type, which is a field that can hold both letters and numbers. Chart numbers are typically numeric (such as 789282), but may include non-numeric characters (such as 789282–2 or AS789282), so a character format may be necessary to accommodate such non-numeric values. Also in Figure 6.3, height (in centimeters) and weight (in kilograms) are stored in numerical formats (integer and floating-point, in this instance), and the "Acuity Score" is stored as an integer.

Regardless of how data is (correctly or incorrectly) stored in a database, every observation has a "true" data type that, depending on the context and

TABLE 6.2 Classes of Data (Levels of Measurement)

Data Type	Description
Categorical (Nominal)	Non-numeric data that is placed into mutually exclusive, separate, but non-ordered categories.
Ordinal	Data that may be categorized and ranked in a numerical fashion, and for which order matters. The difference between values is not meaningful nor consistent.
Interval	Data that is measured on a scale where the difference between two values is meaningful and consistent.
Ratio	Measurement where the difference between two values is meaningful and consistent, and there is a clear definition of zero (there is none of that variable when it equals zero).

the meaning of the data, dictates what types of analysis or computation are meaningful to perform with that value. From a scientific point of view, there are four generally accepted classes of data (or levels of measurement). The four classes of data according to traditional measurement theory consist of *categorical* (or nominal), *ordinal*, *interval*, and *ratio*.[4] See Table 6.2 for a summary of these four basic levels of measurement.

CATEGORICAL AND ORDINAL DATA Any values that are mutually exclusive (in that they cannot belong to more than one category) and do not follow a specific order can be considered categorical data. An example of categorical data is a patient's gender, typically either female or male. Another example of categorical data is location or bed number. In Figure 6.4, the top set of ovals represents emergency department locations ("Resus 1," "Resus 2," "Waiting Room," etc.) and can be considered categorical in nature. These fit the criteria of categorical data because there is no implicit order and the categories are mutually exclusive.

Ordinal data is similar to categorical data in that it is groupings, except that the order of the values does matter. Consider, for example, the bottom set of ovals in Figure 6.4, which represent triage acuity scores. In the example, the triage acuity scores are on a 5-point scale (1, 2, 3, 4, 5) where 1 represents the sickest patient whereas 5 is the least sick. In this case, the order of the values implies a level of illness, but the difference in illness between a 1 and a 2 is not the same as that between a 2 and a 3, and so on. In the example, and all ordinal data, the actual differences between the numbers have no meaning except to imply an order; in this case, the acuity scale could have just as easily been A through E.

INTERVAL AND RATIO DATA Values that are mere categories or groupings are good for counting, but not very good for measuring—that is where interval

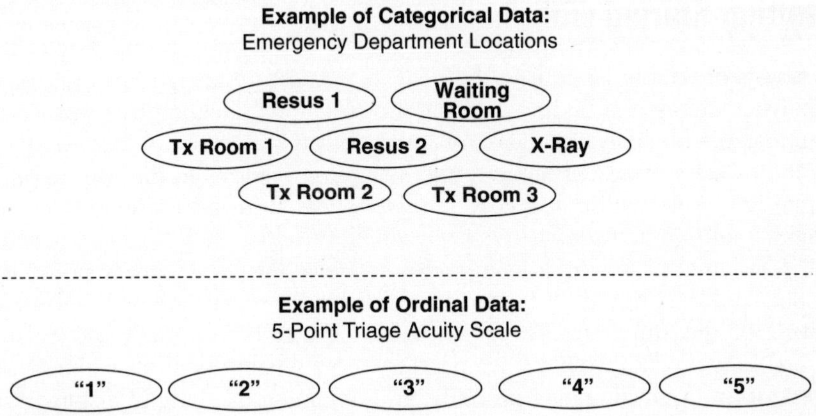

FIGURE 6.4 Illustration of Categorical and Ordinal Data

and ratio values are important. Intervals and ratios are where "real" analysis becomes possible, because the difference between any two interval or ratio values is both meaningful and consistent. The difference between interval and ratio values, however, is that there is a clear definition of zero in ratio values. Take the example of temperature (illustrated in Figure 6.5). Both Celsius and Fahrenheit temperature scales include zero degrees, but zero degrees Fahrenheit and Celsius do not represent an absence of temperature (although it might feel like it!); temperature values are regularly recorded in negative values as part of the scale. The Kelvin temperature scale, however, is considered a ratio because "absolute zero" (zero degrees K) means the total absence of temperature.

Most measurements that are taken in physical sciences, engineering, and medicine are done on a ratio scale. For example, readings for mass (pounds or kilograms), time (seconds, hours), and blood glucose (mmol/L) all start at zero, which represents an absence of that quantity.

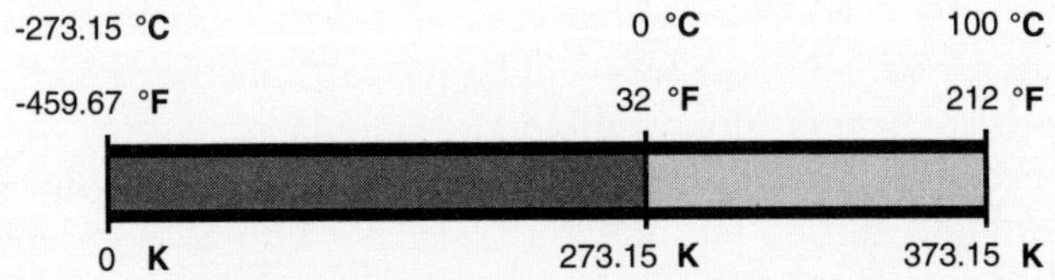

FIGURE 6.5 Illustration of Interval and Ratio Values Using Temperature as an Example

Getting Started with Analyzing Data

Analysis of data is, of course, the heart of healthcare analytics. Developing analytics strategies, building data warehouses, and managing data quality all culminate with analyzing data and communicating the results. Data analysis is the process of describing and understanding patterns in the data to generate new information and new knowledge that can be used for decision making and QI activities.

One might ask why it is important to delve into how data is stored on a database and how it is related to categorical, ordinal, interval, and ratio levels of measurement. The bottom line is that before we perform any operations on data we have, we need to know what operations make sense to perform. Analyzing data properly, and obtaining meaningful results from analytics, requires that we know what kind of data we are dealing with. If we perform operations on data that fundamentally do not make sense in relation to the type of data we're working with, then any outputs from (and inferences made based on) those analytics will be faulty.

Just looking at data in a database is not very helpful—usually "something" needs to be done with the data, such as summarizing it in some way, combining it with other data, among other possible operations. The type of information that data represents ultimately determines what computations can be performed with it.

Summarizing Data Effectively

There are many uses for data, including to evaluate the outcome of a QI project, assist in clinical decision support, or gauge the financial health of an HCO to name a few. Regardless of how data is used, the strength of and value derived from analytics is the compilation and analysis of large amounts of data and resultant synthesis of a meaningful summary or insight from which clinicians, administrators, and QI teams can base decisions and take meaningful, appropriate action.

Population versus Sample

A population is a "precise definition of all possible outcomes, measures, and values for which inferences will be made,"[5] whereas a sample is simply a representative portion of the entire population.

For example, a population might be all the patients who visited an outpatient clinic during the previous year, but only a representative and randomly selected sample would normally be chosen for mail-out satisfaction surveys.

It seems as though dashboards are becoming nearly ubiquitous throughout HCOs. This is because the visualization techniques used in well-designed dashboards provide an "at-a-glance" overview of performance. Most dashboards used in the management of healthcare require, at the very least, basic summaries of data such as count (frequency), average, or range. More sophisticated uses of information (such as are common in quality and performance improvement) may require more advanced operations to be performed with the data.

Table 6.3 is an overview of common data summary approaches along with the types of data for which each of the summaries is appropriate. As a point of clarification, when we are describing a population of patients, the term for the values describing the population is "parameters," whereas "statistics" is the term for the descriptive characteristics of a sample.

Learning Statistics

For more in-depth learning about statistics, I will defer to the many excellent statistical textbooks, web sites, and online videos that teach that subject very well. For a listing of and links to resources that provide further instruction on statistics, please visit the book's web site, http://HealthcareAnalyticsBook.com.

TABLE 6.3 Overview of Data Summaries

Summary	Description	Applies To
Count	A tally of all the values (or ranges of values) in a sample of data.	Nominal, ordinal, interval, ratio
Mode	The most commonly occurring value in a data set.	Nominal, ordinal, interval, ratio
Percentile	The value in a data set below which a specified percentage of observations fall.	Ordinal, interval, ratio
Median	The "midway" point of a ranked-order data set; the value below which 50 percent of the data elements sit. Also known as the "50th percentile."	Ordinal, interval, ratio
Minimum	The lowest value in a data set.	Ordinal, interval, ratio
Maximum	The highest value in a data set.	Ordinal, interval, ratio

(*continued*)

TABLE 6.3 *(continued)*

Summary	Description	Applies To
Mean	The arithmetic average of a data set calculated by adding all values together and dividing by the number of values.	Interval, ratio
Variance	A measure of how spread out the numbers are within a data set and is measured by a value's distance from the mean.	Interval, ratio
Standard deviation	Provides a sense of how the data is distributed around the mean and can be considered an average of each data point's distance to the mean.	Interval, ratio

COUNTING Counting data is perhaps the most simple operation that can be performed, yet it is one of the most common and useful ways to look at data. A few of the most common questions asked by healthcare managers and executives is "how much" or "how many"—"How many central line infections occurred last week?" or "How many patients are now in the waiting room?" or "How many influenza patients can we expect to see during next flu season?" Many quality and performance initiatives are concerned with *reducing* the number of something (such as medication errors, unnecessary admissions, or patients exceeding length-of-stay targets) or *increasing* the number of something (such as patients answering "excellent" on a satisfaction survey). Accurate counts are an essential component of baseline data, and can assist in profiling data for data quality management efforts.

Counts of data appear on almost every performance dashboard and management report, and can figure prominently in the development of predictive models. Two common ways to report counts of variables include *frequency distributions* and *histograms*.

FREQUENCY DISTRIBUTION Before working in depth with data, it is important to get an overall sense of what the data "looks like" to have a better idea of what statistical approaches might be appropriate. A frequency distribution is a count of occurrences of one or more of the values (or ranges of values) that are present in a sample of data.

There are many uses for frequency distributions in healthcare quality and performance improvement. These include counting (for example, the number of surgical procedures performed, by procedure code, and at a certain hospital site) and understanding the "spread" of the data, or how tightly clustered it is. For example, a tabulation of the number of surgeries performed in each of a hospital's operating theaters over a specified time period could be illustrated in a frequency distribution. Frequencies are also invaluable for identifying limitations in the data and highlighting cleaning needs. For instance, frequency distributions can be used for determining the percentage of missing values and invalid data entries in a sample of data.

A frequency distribution can display the *actual* number of observations of each value, or the *percentage* of observations. Frequency distributions are very flexible, in that they are appropriate for all types of data values (categorical, ordinal, interval, and ratio), so no other mathematical operation is required other than counting (and calculating a percentage).

See Table 6.4 for a sample frequency distribution of emergency department visits by triage level. Note that in this case, triage level is ordinal data—the order matters (ranging from 1 being the most acute to 5 being the least acute), but the difference between the numbers does not.

With the data graphing capabilities that are available in even the most basic data analysis tools, it is very rare to see a frequency distribution table without some graphic representation. Many people are able to grasp data better through visual representation, and differences in values can often be highlighted more effectively in a graphical format than can be done with a simple table.

Bar graphs and line graphs are two very common ways to visualize frequency data. See Figure 6.6 for a bar graph of the frequency distribution shown in Table 6.4. Notice how the graph clearly shows the large number of visits triaged as 3 and 4 compared to other triage scores. If the triage scale is such that 1 is the most acute and 5 is the least acute, then it is clear by Figure 6.6 that the emergency department represented in the graph sees many more patients that are mid-to-low acuity than highly acute patients.

HISTOGRAM Sometimes a detailed picture of how data is distributed throughout its range is necessary to answer questions such as: Do the values cluster around some single value? Are there many outliers? and What is the overall "shape" of the data? To help answer these questions, a histogram is used. A histogram is a specialized form of graph that is used to display

TABLE 6.4 Sample Frequency Distribution (Emergency Department Visits by Triage Level)

Triage Level	Visits (*n*)	Percent (%)
1	364	0.80%
2	5,888	13.02%
3	17,907	39.58%
4	20,177	44.60%
5	904	2.00%

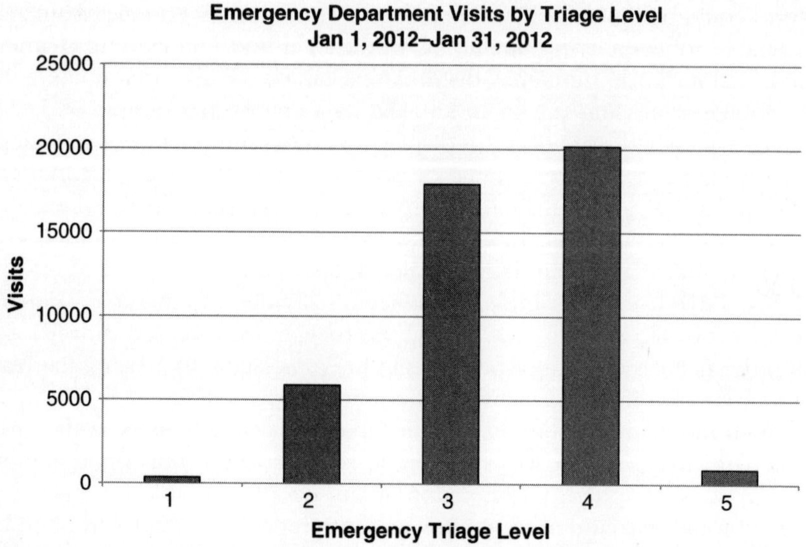

FIGURE 6.6 Frequency Distribution of Emergency Department Visits by Triage Level

the distribution of a set of data over its range (or sometimes a portion of the range). More formally, a histogram is an estimate of the probability distribution of a continuous variable (that is, a variable for which any value is possible within the limits of the variable's range).

See Figure 6.7 for a sample histogram drawn from emergency department lengths of stay. A histogram is constructed by placing a series of adjacent bars over discrete intervals in a range of data; the height of each bar represents the frequency of observations within that particular interval. A histogram can be made more or less detailed by changing the size of the bin that each bar represents. From the histogram in Figure 6.7, it is possible to see that the majority of lengths of stay fall roughly between 0 and 5 hours, and that there are a number of outliers that stay up to 24 hours. The main difference between the histograms in Figure 6.7(A) and Figure 6.7(B) is that (B) is divided into 30-minute intervals compared to 60-minute intervals in (A). In summary, a histogram can be used:

- When data are numerical.
- To observe the shape of the distribution of data.
- To determine the extent to which outliers exist in the data.

Knowing the shape of a distribution can reveal important details about the data and the processes from which the data was generated.[6] For

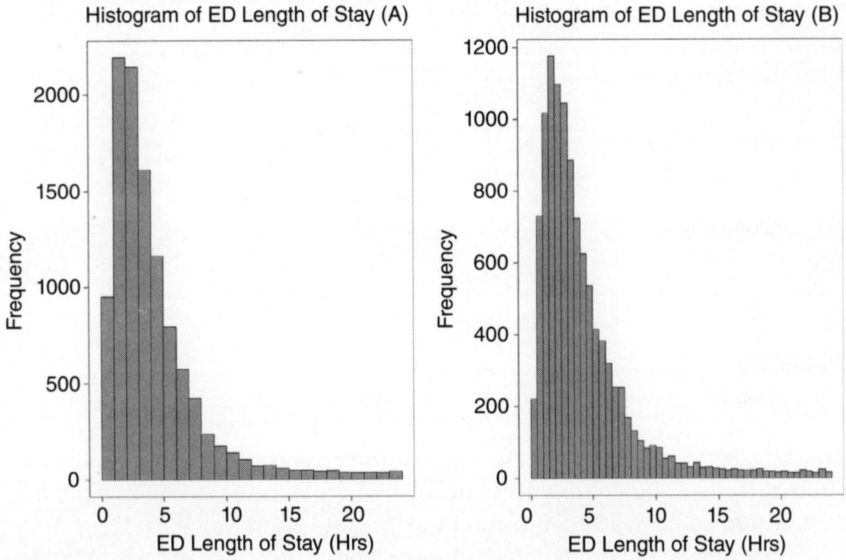

FIGURE 6.7 Histogram of Emergency Department (ED) Length-of-Stay Values

example, a shape that resembles the normal distribution or "bell curve," in which data points are as likely to fall on one side of the curve as the other, suggests that the underlying process may be in control, exhibiting expected natural variation. Some statistical tests can only be performed on a data set that is normally distributed. A skewed distribution is asymmetrical, leaning to the right or to the left with the tail stretching away, because some natural limit prevents outcomes on one side. For example, histograms of length of stay (such as Figure 6.7) are very often skewed to the right (meaning the tail stretches to the right) because lengths of stay cannot be less than 0. Another common distribution observed in a histogram is bimodal, which shows two distinct peaks. A bimodal distribution suggests that the sample may not be homogeneous, and perhaps is drawn from two populations. For example, a histogram for lengths of stay that included both admitted and nonadmitted emergency department patients may exhibit a bimodal tendency, with one peak occurring for the shorter lengths of stay for nonadmitted patients and another peak from the lengths of stay of admitted patients.

Central Tendency

When you look at values associated with a quantitative variable (such as length of stay), the values are not usually spread evenly across the range of possible values, but tend to cluster or group around some central value.

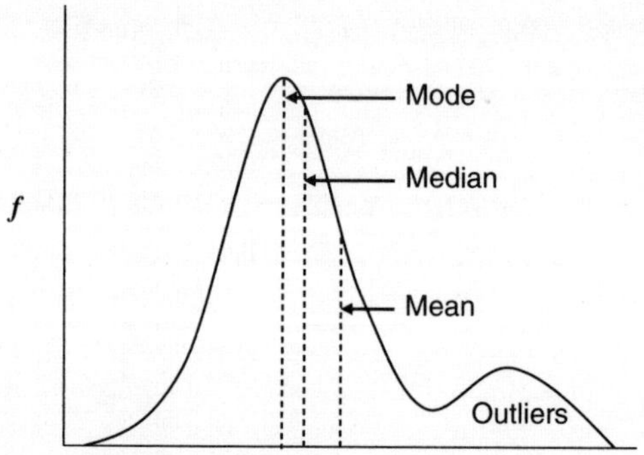

FIGURE 6.8 Measures of Central Tendency

This is called *central tendency*. A measure of central tendency, then, is an attempt to describe data as accurately as possible, using a single value that best describes how data tends to cluster around some value.

The three most common measures of central tendency are the *mean* (or average), the *median*, and the *mode*. When a healthcare administrator or QI team member asks for a summary of a set of data, one of these (or typically both the mean and median) is usually what is implied. See Figure 6.8 for an example of how the measures of central tendency may fall on a fictional distribution of data.

The average (or mean) is probably one of the most commonly used methods to summarize data, but it may also at times be misused. In essence, the average is calculated by summing up all the values of a variable in a set of data and dividing by the total number of observations. Average is a standard calculation on nearly every software tool that manages or manipulates data, so is typically the default summary of data. There are a few key points to remember when using averages. First, not all seemingly numeric data can be averaged; average is only appropriate for ratio and interval data (such as time, weight, temperature, and other physical observations). If a 5-point triage scale is in use, it would never make sense to say, "Our average triage acuity score was 3.4 today." (An alternative, however, would be to say, "Over 50 percent of our cases were triaged at level 3 or higher.")

Another issue with mean is that it is susceptible to outliers. If all observations in a data set tend to cluster around the same set of values, then average may be an accurate representation of that clustering. The average, however, can be skewed by small numbers of observations at extreme ends of the range of values. For example, if the typical hospital stay is between two and three days, the average of all observations can be skewed upward by even relatively few numbers of patients with extreme lengths of stay (say 30 days or more). See, for example, in Figure 6.8 that there is a group of outliers in the upper value ranges of the *x* axis, and as a result the mean is skewed to the right (that is, it is made to be larger).

There are other ways to summarize data either in conjunction with or instead of mean if the data is likely affected by outliers or is not a ratio or interval type. The alternative is to use the median (and percentile values). In essence, a *percentile* is the particular value in a set of data below which a certain percentage of the observations in a data set are located. For example, in a sample set of data, the 25th percentile is the value below which 25 percent of the values fall. Likewise, the 90th percentile is the value in the set that 90 percent of the samples lie below. The median is a specific instance of a percentile—it is the name given to the 50th percentile; in a data set, half of the observations of a particular variable will be below the median value, and the other half above it. In Figure 6.8, the median is much closer to the main clustering of observed values than is the mean due to the effect of the outliers. Figure 6.8 also illustrates the mode, which is the value in the data set that occurs the most frequently. Interestingly, I have never been asked for the mode of a data set directly, but rather I get asked for "mode-like" information, such as "What is the triage acuity with which most patients present," "What time of day do we see the most patients walk in the door," and "What is the most commonly ordered diagnostic test."

Median and percentiles are valuable measures of central tendency in healthcare because they are not impacted by extreme outliers in a data set. In addition, median and percentiles can be calculated for ordinal, interval, and ratio data types. (They do not apply to categorical data because there is no implied order in the categories.)

The Big Picture

It is seldom a good idea to report complex healthcare performance parameters as a single value. For example, what does an average hospital length of stay of 4.9 days really mean? Judging from that number alone, it can mean anything from almost all patients staying nearly exactly five days to half of the patients staying less than one day and the other half of patients staying 10 days. While neither of these scenarios is particularly likely, it is impossible to discern what the true distribution of patient lengths of stay looks like from a single value.

Given the current capabilities of even relatively inexpensive analytical tools (not to mention some exceptional capabilities in open-source software), there is no excuse for not presenting information in a comprehensive manner that provides a more complete picture of quality and performance within the HCO. Just as it would be absurd for a pilot to navigate a plane based on "average airspeed" or "median altitude," it is now up to HCOs to guide clinical, administrative, and QI decision making with data that is more

TABLE 6.5 Summary of Three Months of Emergency Department Length-of-Stay Data

Statistic	Value (hours)
Average	4.86
Median	3.25
Maximum	23.97
25th percentile	1.88
75th percentile	5.68
90th percentile	10.37

comprehensively and accurately summarized (and in ways that make the data easier to understand).

Consider a data set containing three months of visit data for a midsized emergency department during which time there were 11,472 visits. Providing just a few basic statistics can help to provide a more complete picture than a single statistic alone; when combined with a graph, the result is even more helpful. The three-month performance of our midsized emergency department can be summarized in Table 6.5.

In Table 6.5, the average length of stay (LOS) is 4.86 hours whereas the median LOS is 3.25 hours. Table 6.5 also indicates that 75 percent of the visits had an LOS of 5.68 hours or less, and 90 percent of the LOS values were at 10.37 hours or less. What do these basic statistics tell us about the LOS data? Since the median is the midpoint of the data (or the 50th percentile) and the average at 4.86 hours is 1.61 hours *greater* than the median, with the value at the 90th percentile (10.37 hours) being almost twice that of the 75th percentile, those differences tell us that the data, in some way, is skewed. (If the data was tightly clustered around the mean, there would be very little difference between the mean and the median.) Judging from the values alone, it is possible to determine that although 75 percent of the visits experience an LOS of 5.68 hours or less, 25 percent are in fact *greater* than 5.68 hours and 10 percent are greater than 10.37 hours. While these values when used in concert provide a better overview of LOS performance than a single statistic (such as average) used alone, there is nothing really "actionable" in this data, and there are no real clues as to where to begin looking for opportunities for improvement.

When the statistics in Table 6.5 are combined with an appropriate visualization of the LOS data (such as a histogram) as in Figure 6.9, the picture becomes more complete. With the visualization, users of the information can see that indeed the majority of emergency department visits are between 0 and 6 hours, but also that there are considerable numbers of

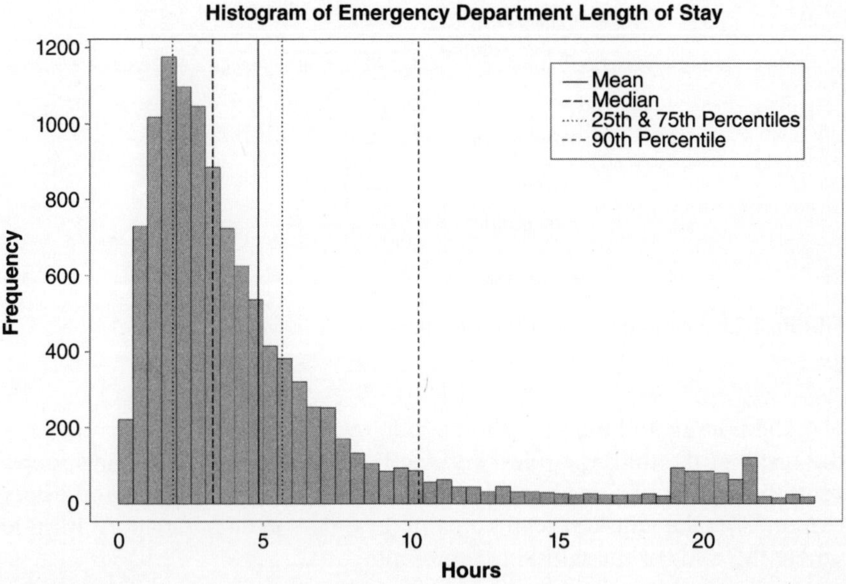

FIGURE 6.9 Histogram of Emergency Department Length of Stay with Measures of Central Tendency

visits between 6 and 24 hours. One thing that the data in Table 6.5 did not indicate is the small cluster of outliers around the 20-hour mark. Whether this group of outliers around 20 hours is indeed an issue and worthy of further investigation will require additional analysis of the data. The point is, however, that without a more thorough summarization of the data (using multiple statistics and appropriate visualization), this potential opportunity for improvement might not have been noticed.

Another very useful way to summarize data is to use a *box-and-whisker plot*. Box-and-whisker plots present a very concise summary of the overall distribution of a given variable within a data set.[7] Figure 6.10 is an example of a box-and-whisker plot; in a single graphical element, the box-and-whisker plot illustrates:

1. **Lower extreme**—the smallest value of the variable.
2. **First quartile**—the value below which 25 percent of the observations are situated.
3. **Median—**the value below which half of the observations are situated.
4. **Third quartile—**the value below which 75 percent of the observations are situated.
5. **Upper extreme**—the largest value of the variable.
6. **Outliers**—any data that is not included between the whiskers.

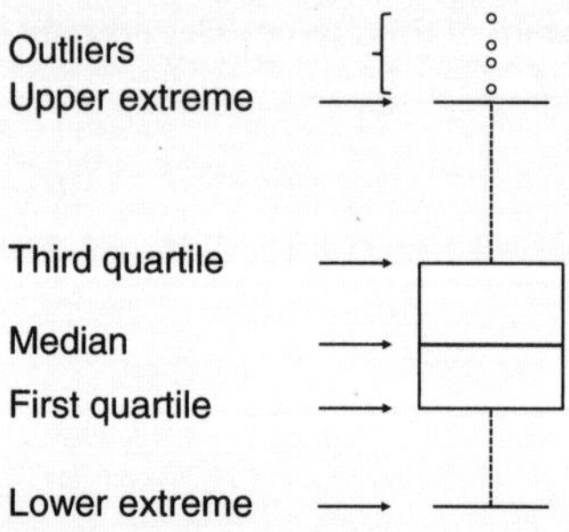

FIGURE 6.10 Example Box-and-Whisker Plot

The bottom and the top of the box in this type of plot always represent the first and the third quartiles, and the band within the box always represents the median. There are some variations in the way the lower and upper extremes, or the whiskers, can be plotted. Some common variations include where the ends of the whiskers represent:

- One standard deviation above and below the mean of the data.
- 1.5 times the interquartile range.
- The minimum and maximum of all data in the data set.

In fact, the whiskers of a box-and-whisker plot can represent almost any range that suits the particular needs of an analysis as long as the specified range is clearly labeled on the plot. When data exists that does not fall within the specified range of the whiskers, it is customary to individually plot those outlier data points using small circles.

Box-and-whisker plots are helpful to compare the distributions between two or more groups to help determine what, if any, differences in performance or quality may exist as exhibited by variations in their data. For example, even though two subgroups of data may exhibit similar characteristics (such as mean or median), a box-and-whisker plot helps to determine the presence of any outliers in any of the groups, and how the overall spreads in the data compare. Figure 6.11 illustrates emergency department LOS data graphed in a box-and-whisker plot broken down by acuity level. In Figure 6.11, it is possible to see how the different subgroups (triage acuity level) differ in their medians and spread, suggesting that these patient subgroups follow different trajectories during their emergency department stay.

Scatter plots are used to determine if there is a correlation or relationship between two variables.[8] For example, Figure 6.12 is a scatter plot with emergency department time "waiting to be seen" (WTBS) by a physician on

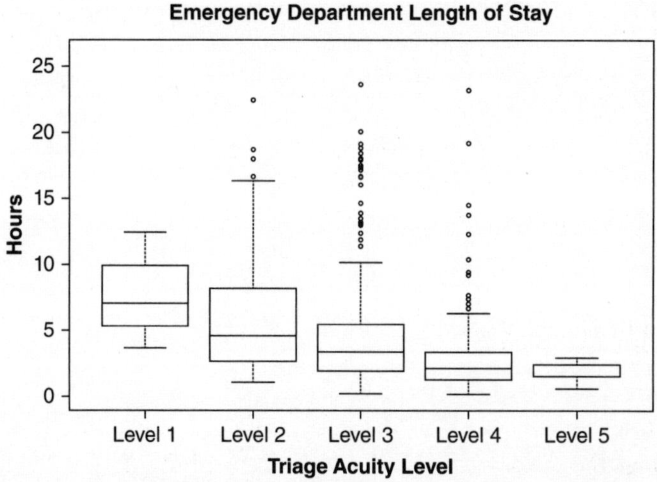

FIGURE 6.11 Box-and-Whisker Plot of Emergency Department Length-of-Stay Data Broken Down by Triage Acuity

the *x* axis and "left without being seen" (LWBS) on the *y* axis. By plotting the two variables against each other on the graph, it is possible to see the direction and strength of their relationship (if any). Figure 6.12 shows that there is a positive, but somewhat weak, and generally linear correlation between WTBS and LWBS when daily averages of LWBS and WTBS were compared; this makes intuitive sense, since the longer people need to wait for a doctor in the ED, the more they are likely to leave and seek treatment elsewhere. The more defined the trend is on the graph, the stronger the relationship (either positive or negative); the more scattered the plotted values are, the weaker the relationship.

Scatter plots are often the starting point for more advanced analytics. Scatter plots often may provide a clue that a relationship between two (or more) variables does exist and that it may be possible to model that relationship and use it for predictive purposes.

Data summarized in ways similar to those described in this section is more complete, more useful, and more likely to provide actionable insight than a single statistic or high-level summary, yet does not require significantly more statistical literacy on the part of the consumers of the information.

I am not advocating that every dashboard, report, and other analytical tool must be loaded with as much context and information as possible; this would indeed lead to information overload. The purpose of these examples is merely to illustrate that because many quality and performance problems in healthcare are complex, the more ways that a problem or issue can

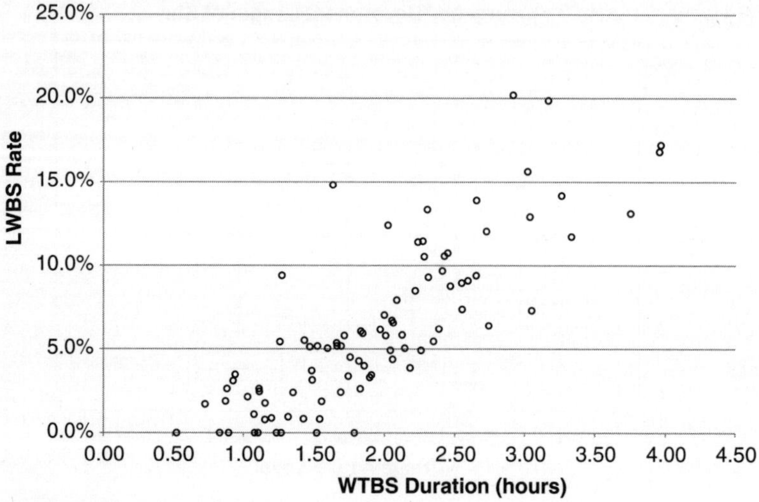

FIGURE 6.12 Scatter Plot of Left without Being Seen Rates and Emergency Department Length of Stay

be broken down and analyzed, the more likely it is that opportunities for improvement will be identified and that changes in quality and performance can be detected and evaluated. That is, after all, what I believe healthcare analytics is really about.

Summary

In my experience developing analytics for quality and performance improvement, I have rarely needed to rely on much more than these descriptive statistics to effectively communicate and identify process bottlenecks, performance changes, and overall quality. I believe it is much more important to focus on getting the data right, and focus on getting the right metrics that truly indicate the performance of the organization, than using complex statistics to overcome poor data quality and/or looking for a signal in the noise when there is no real signal in the first place. I have seen many analysts bend over backwards trying to use statistics to look for a change in performance when in fact the data was not good enough to answer the question that was being asked. Statistical analysis should never be a substitute for good data, for well-defined metrics, and should never be used to look for something that is not there.

Notes

1. Lloyd P. Provost and Sandra K. Murray, *The Health Care Data Guide: Learning from Data for Improvement* (San Francisco: Jossey-Bass, 2011), Kindle ed., location 1431.
2. Ibid., locations 1480–1481.
3. Microsoft Developer Network (MSDN), “Data Types (Database Engine),” http://msdn.microsoft.com/en-us/library/ms187594(v=sql.105).aspx.
4. Provost and Murray, *The Health Care Data Guide*, location 1496.
5. Glenn J. Myatt, *Making Sense of Data: A Practical Guide to Exploratory Data Analysis and Data Mining* (Hoboken, NJ: John Wiley & Sons, 2007), Kindle ed., location 641.
6. ASQ, “Typical Histogram Shapes and What They Mean,” http://asq.org/learn-about-quality/data-collection-analysis-tools/overview/histogram2.html.
7. Thomas H. Wannacott and Ronald J. Wonnacott, *Introductory Statistics*, 5th ed. (New York: John Wiley & Sons, 1990), 29.
8. Ibid., 478.

CHAPTER 7

Developing and Using Effective Indicators

What's measured improves.

—Peter F. Drucker

Healthcare organizations (HCOs) have more data available to them than ever before. Raw data is rarely useful, however, for healthcare quality and performance improvement. To begin with, there is now often *too much* data generated through all the activities and systems within healthcare to use effectively. Indicators provide convenient performance snapshots of processes, financial measures, and outcomes critical to the quality and performance goals of the HCO. This chapter will discuss the importance of indicators in quality and performance improvement, and how to create or choose indicators that are most effective for the requirements of your HCO.

Measures, Metrics, and Indicators

There is a saying that "you can't improve what you can't measure." While this may not be strictly true—I have seen HCO undergo tremendous improvement via the foresight and vision of remarkable leaders—bringing about change in healthcare requires measurement of processes and workflows and effective representation of those measurements.

As a result of the increasing volumes of available data and the abundance of analysis tools, many different reports, dashboards, and other information requests are being generated for decision making. Even though HCOs are experiencing a proliferation of dashboards and other information tools, many are still struggling to improve their quality, performance,

HOW TO MAKE MEASURES MORE USEFUL

There is some thinking that the development of metrics and indicators is the sole domain of the business or QI teams. It is vital that analytics teams are aware of how to develop effective indicators, however, because it is they who bring indicators to life. They need to know not only how to analyze data but also how to put that data into context. When asked for metrics and measures, analytics teams should know that the analysis is only part of the solution; every indicator should be presented with appropriate ranges and targets. If this information is not available for inclusion with the indictor on a dashboard, report, or other analytical application, analytics teams should approach the requestor of the information for that context. Without that context, the information gets buried in just another report that does not assist the HCO in making decisions or achieving its quality goals.

and competitiveness. It is clear, then, that having data, producing more reports, and developing more dashboards is not the only answer.

Rather than simply collecting more data, healthcare leaders need information grouped and summarized in logical ways that let them know how their organization is performing. The usual starting point is to define measures, metrics, and indicators that are representative parameters for examining the performance of the organization. These three terms are commonly (but incorrectly) used interchangeably. Although there is by no means universal agreement as to the *exact* definition of the terms, the definitions below are sufficient to convey how the terms differ in meaning, and how those differences relate to the measurement of healthcare.

Tip

Rather than simply collecting more data, healthcare leaders need information grouped and summarized in logical ways that let them know how their organization is performing.

Measure. The term "measure" (when used as a noun) in healthcare typically refers to a quantitative value representing some aspect of patient care, and may (or may not) be linked to specific performance and QI initiatives. Typically, measures have not been processed (except for perhaps being

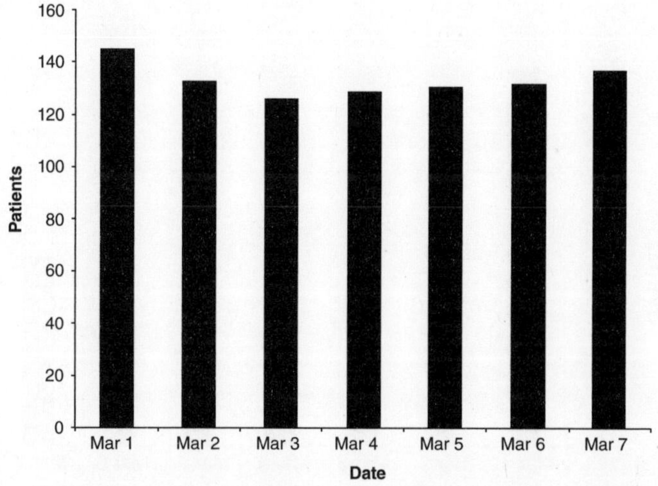

FIGURE 7.1 Sample Graph of a Measure (Number of Patients Triaged)

grouped in some logical manner) and may include variables such as time (such as hours waiting), counts (such as patients), and other similar data. Since almost any quantitative value can be considered a measure, I like to consider measures as the raw data that forms the basis for further analysis.

Figure 7.1 illustrates a measure—simply the number of patients who have been triaged in the emergency department over a seven-day period. This information is "nice to know," in that it provides some context as to the busyness of the emergency department over that time period; however, it doesn't provide any additional information about the performance of the department.

Metric. A metric is some aspect of healthcare quality or performance to which a quantitative value is attributed for purposes of monitoring and evaluation. I consider metrics to be measures with more focus and purpose. Metrics typically specify a given point of time or a time period. Metrics can be situational (for example, they may be relevant only for a special purpose or project), but can also measure performance longitudinally, as long as the metric is relevant to some aspect of quality or performance that the HCO needs to monitor. Examples of metrics used in healthcare improvement include time (such as length of stay), number of patients seen by a physician per shift, number of medication errors, and other important descriptors of quality and performance.

Figure 7.2 illustrates a metric, in this case the percentage of patients whose triage scores were overridden by the triage nurse from what was suggested by the computer's triage algorithm. I would consider this a metric, because it ties directly to a process within the department (the triage

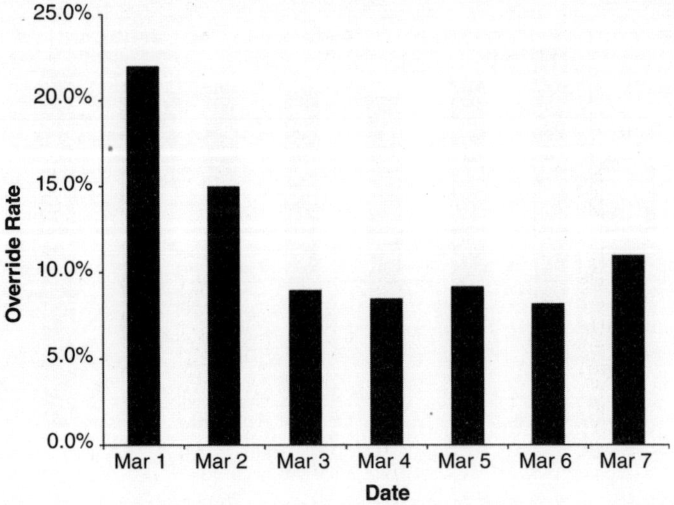

FIGURE 7.2 Sample Graph of a Metric (Triage Override Rate, March 1, 2013, to March 7, 2013)

of patients) and it relates to quality (too frequently overriding triage scores may present a clinical and legal risk, and may suggest that the computerized triage algorithms need adjusting). The purpose of monitoring this metric is to minimize clinical and legal risk and to ensure clinical quality.

In this case, we can see that March 1 and 2 had higher override rates than the other seven days, but the chart tells us little else. A few things are missing from this metric that would make it really useful: some indication of what a good (or acceptable) override rate is—the target—and how current performance measures up against previous (or baseline) performance. Without this additional context, it is difficult to know if any corrective action is necessary, and if so, what action to take.

Indicator. A metric without context may be insufficient for making decisions—it is merely "a number," and having too many metrics may actually contribute to information overload and impede decision making. Indictors, then, are metrics that are more useful for driving business decisions, because indicators have *context* assigned to them. See Figure 7.3 for the graph of a sample indicator. Some of the most important pieces of contextual information that separates an indicator from a metric is having an acceptable range and target assigned to the indicator, which is necessary to

- Identify whether current performance is "good" or "bad,"
- Determine how far away performance is from reaching its performance target, and

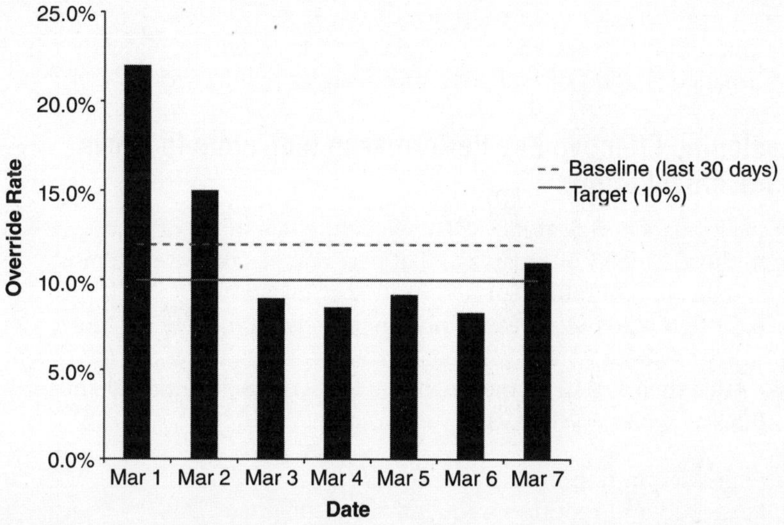

FIGURE 7.3 Sample Graph of an Indicator (Triage Override Rate, with Baseline and Target, March 1, 2013, to March 7, 2013)

- Tell whether performance is trending toward meeting the target (or staying within target range) or if it is trending away from the target (or trending toward becoming out of the target range).

The triage override rate metric becomes a true indicator and trigger for action once we add the baseline performance (so that we can compare current performance over past performance, in this case, over the last 30 days) and the target (which is what would be considered an acceptable rate of triage override). With the two new pieces of information, we can see in Figure 7.3 that, over all, performance over the last seven days was better than the baseline for five out of seven days, and that performance was within the target range for four out of seven days. It is possible that March 2 and 7 are outside the target range due to random variation, but March 1 appears to stand out. This could, for example, trigger the nurse manager to see who was triaging that day—perhaps one or more of the triage nurses is inexperienced and needs a refresher on the triage tool. Note how important the target information is: if the acceptable range for override rates was 20 percent (not 10 percent), then likely no corrective action would need to be taken at all.

To keep focus on the measures that matter, performance dashboards should be populated with indicators. Indicators are preferable on dashboards and performance reports because they relate to a particular process or other component of the healthcare business. When using indicators with an appropriate visualization approach (such as a line or bar graph), not only can trends be spotted, but also the associated targets highlight whether performance is good or bad, and improving or getting worse.

Developing Effective Key Performance Indicators to Focus Improvement Efforts

Key performance indicators (KPIs) are defined as "a set of measures focusing on those aspects of organizational performance that are the most critical for the current and future success of the organization."[1]

Although many executives and other decision makers may have different opinions about what constitutes "critical for the success of the organization," KPI expert David Parmenter has identified the five main characteristics of KPIs that work for successful organizations:[2]

1. Expressed in nonfinancial measures.
2. Measured and reported frequently (typically daily, 24/7).
3. Acted upon by senior management (including chief executive officer) and key decision makers (to ensure that the KPI can make a difference).
4. All staff understand both the measure and the particular corrective action required (so that all know their part in improving quality and performance).
5. Ties responsibility of performance and action to the individual or team (so that no KPI and accompanying corrective action goes unassigned).

Despite their obvious value to managing an organization, KPIs are claimed by some people to be "dead." These claims are made on the basis that with so much data now available to some HCOs on nearly every aspect of their clinical and operational performance, insight on any aspect of performance is now merely a click away and thus does not need to be boiled down to a handful of indicators. While this point may be true, HCOs can focus on only a few areas of improvement at a time. Indicators are absolutely necessary for organizations to stay focused on the issues and actions that matter the most at a given period of time. As priorities of the HCO change, new indicators will emerge and older, less relevant ones will be deemphasized. In this way, the key priorities of the organization can always stay in focus with the proper indicators selected.

Tip

Indicators help organizations stay focused on the issues and actions that matter the most at a specific period of time.

It is important to have indicators, but if they are not measuring the right things, then it's likely improvement efforts will falter. In healthcare, there are literally hundreds, if not thousands, of parameters that could be monitored. How can an HCO choose which parameters to follow and turn them into relevant, effective indicators?

A common acronym that is used to help guide the development of indicators is SMART. That is, well-formed indicators that can be used to identify bottlenecks and other quality issues and to drive decision making should, whenever possible, be:

- Specific
- Measurable
- Actionable
- Relevant
- Time-bound

Specific. It must be clear exactly what it is the indicator is measuring, and what the defined acceptable ranges and targets are. The indicator must describe a unique, distinguishable component of the business (such as process or workflow). A poor example is "length of stay," which is generic and doesn't indicate what it is that we're measuring the length of stay of. A better example would be "length of stay for emergency department patients who are not eventually admitted to hospital." The acceptable ranges and targets associated with indicators must also be specific. For example, an emergency department length of stay of less than four hours for 95 percent of patients is a specific target. The more specific indicators are, the better they are at discerning changes in performance.

Measurable. Even though an indicator may be very specific, it may not be measurable. This may be because no data can be obtained to calculate the indicator value, or that the data is incomplete and inaccurate. There is no point in creating an indicator, even if it is vital to the business, if sufficient data is not available. For example, tracking the number of times an electronic chart is corrected might be an important indicator of data and/or clinical quality, but if that data is not available in audit data, then it's necessary to refocus efforts on developing indicators that can actually be measured.

Actionable. "Actionable" is a commonly used word, but what does it mean? As an example, the fuel indicator on a vehicle's dashboard is actionable because when the indicator gets too close to the empty mark, it is obvious when to take action (and what action to take)—the driver must fill up with fuel or risk running out of gas. Ideally, healthcare indicators should also be similarly actionable in that the performance trends they monitor identify when action is needed. For example, if a real-time indicator suggests that a patient is at high risk for falls, then the appropriate falls-prevention protocol can be activated to prevent that occurrence within the department.

Relevant. The problem with information is that sometimes there's just too much of it. It takes a lot of effort to turn around the performance of an HCO, and QI teams can only focus on a few problems at a time. Bombarding teams, management, and executives with too much extraneous information can actually complicate the decision-making process. Indicators should be chosen for their importance to the effective operations of the HCO and their relevance to the goals and objectives of QI projects.

Time-bound. When appropriate, indicators and their associated targets should be time-bound. That is, the indicator should specify what time period the indicator covers (daily, weekly, monthly), and the target should also indicate what time frame the indicator is aiming for (e.g., within one week, one month, etc.). For example, if the rate of central line infections is an indicator of interest, a relevant time frame and target date must also be defined when measuring and reporting the data.

Aligning Indicators with Data and Processes

The section in Chapter 6 titled "Aligning Processes with Data" discusses the importance of aligning data with business processes so that important contextual background (such as business rules) can be incorporated into analytics. Indicators must also be in alignment—with both data and processes. Indicators must align with one or more data points, since, after all, indicators are a summarization of performance based on data.

The reason that metrics and indicators must maintain alignment with both data and processes is because any changes in processes that are being monitored by indicators may in fact violate basic assumptions of the indicator's calculations. In other words, process changes may result in changes to data that in turn *incorrectly* impact the calculation of indicators.

An important case in point comes from my own experience. Prior to implementing electronic clinical documentation, we would use data from our emergency department information system to calculate the length of stay of a patient as the time the patient was originally registered in the system prior to triage to the time the patient was removed from the tracking

MORE ABOUT INDICATORS

Please visit this book's web site, http://HealthcareAnalyticsBook.com, for additional examples of indicators and for resources about the creation of effective healthcare performance indicators.

board. The rationale for using removal from tracking board as the endpoint of the visit was that the manually inputted discharge time was the time a disposition decision was made (i.e., when the physician decided the patient could leave), *not* the actual time the patient left the department. The time the patient was removed from the board, on the other hand, was the time the patient actually vacated the bed, so we felt this was a better indication of length of stay.

It turned out that after the implementation of electronic clinical documentation, a process was devised to keep patients on the tracking board longer by placing them in a special temporary location, as a visual cue to remind care providers to complete their documentation. Within two weeks of the change in system and process, the average length of stay for the department increased by 0.6 hours, with some patients having two or more hours tacked onto the end of their visit even though they were no longer in the department.

In this case, it was the change in process that prompted my team to review the data, which uncovered the issue of extended length-of-stay values. One of the solutions was to modify the length-of-stay calculations performed during the Extraction/Transformation/Load process to account for the extra time patient names were kept on the tracking board in the special temporary location. It is easy to see how, without a clear understanding of how process impacts data, a calculation as basic as length of stay can be corrupted. And because length of stay is fundamental to many key indicators of emergency department patient flow, the basic decision-making value of these indicators would have been severely compromised had this relatively simple process change, which really has nothing to do with actual patient care, not been detected early on.

Given the number of processes and associated data elements that make up the delivery of healthcare, staying on top of changes to data, process, and indicators is not a trivial task. This is another argument for analytics teams to be in close proximity to the business and to the people who are intimately familiar with processes and how they evolve over time. This connection is crucial—without a close connection between process experts and analytics experts, it is exceedingly difficult to maintain the close connection necessary between data, process, and indicators in decision making and performance improvement.

Using Indicators to Guide Healthcare Improvement Activities

With an endless potential array of quality metrics and indicators, how do healthcare executives, unit managers, QI professionals, and analytics developers know what information is important and necessary for making the right decisions? With so many facets of healthcare, and with so many possible indicators to develop, it can be challenging to choose which indicators to focus on.

Two of the most important qualities of indicators are that they are *relevant* and *actionable*. In other words, indicators must be useful for understanding the most pressing quality and performance issues facing an HCO, should identify what needs to be done to mitigate those quality and process issues, and ultimately should trigger appropriate action when certain conditions arise.

Relevant indicators are aligned with the goals and objectives of the HCO, and can be defined for two major levels—*strategic* and *tactical*. Figure 7.4 illustrates that the metrics, indicators, and associated targets that drive analytics can be defined from a top-down perspective for indicators that are in alignment with the strategic goals and objectives of the organization, and from a bottom-up perspective to meet tactical-level requirements. Figure 7.4 also highlights that the "voice of the customer" (especially the patient) is crucial for defining metrics and indicators at the tactical level and used for specific quality and performance improvement initiatives.

Strategic goals are the quality goals and objectives for the entire organization, and specify the overall performance levels that the HCO aspires to achieve. These strategic goals typically are based on published best practices and what the HCO feels it needs to achieve. Alignment of indicators is necessary so that the goals and objectives are communicated (and being adhered to) throughout the organization. Dashboards, reports, and other analytics that provide focus to the key indicators are an excellent method of communicating these important goals and targets throughout the organization.

Focusing *only* on strategic goals and targets, however, may not provide enough information for use at the unit, department, or similar level. In my experience, the most productive and innovative QI activities occur at the *tactical* level, that is, at or near the front line where the activities associated with providing healthcare are actually performed. For frontline decision making and QI efforts, a complementary set of metrics and indicators (or submetrics and subindicators) can be developed for use at the tactical level. Frontline improvement activities use tactical-level indicators to monitor and evaluate performance during and after improvements have been made.

<table>
<tr><td>Strategic Level</td><td colspan="6">Strategic Objectives</td></tr>
<tr><td>Analytics</td><td colspan="2">Metrics</td><td colspan="2">Indicators</td><td colspan="2">Targets</td></tr>
<tr><td>Tactical Level</td><td colspan="3">Tactical Objectives</td><td colspan="3">Voice of the Customer</td></tr>
</table>

FIGURE 7.4 Aligning Indicators with Strategic and Tactical Objectives

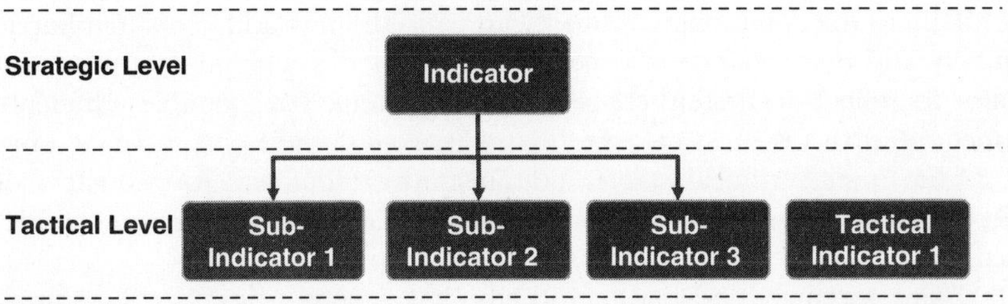

FIGURE 7.5 Hierarchy of Strategic-Level Indicators and Tactical-Level Indicators and Subindicators

Tactical-level indicators are based on the needs of specific QI activities (and perhaps remain relevant only during the span of a project and its evaluation period) and exist at the tactical level where most of the actual improvement activities are performed. Subindicators at the tactical level break down a strategic-level indicator into more detail that is relevant to a performance improvement project. Improvement projects may also have their own specific relevant indicators; these are not necessarily related to strategic-level indicators but are important for understanding performance and ongoing evaluation related to a specific improvement project. This hierarchy is illustrated in Figure 7.5.

Selecting Appropriate Indicators

With literally hundreds of data elements being generated on some modern EMR systems, it is important to differentiate which of this data is important to analyze and report on for the purposes of improving healthcare, and which should be set aside until needed at another time. It is likely that only some of the data available is relevant to the current quality and improvement performance goals of an HCO, and even less is directly actionable.

Yet with so much data available for analysis, the temptation is to create numerous indicators and to build a collection of dashboards to display them all. Creating too many different dashboards and reports risk causing an increase in information overload and loss of focus on improvement goals, which is counterproductive to the goal of improving the healthcare system.

When healthcare is under pressure, it is important to provide management and QI teams with the key pieces of information they need to focus on the most important problems and to make appropriate, timely decisions. The use of indicators to guide healthcare improvement activities often falls into one of two extremes: using a *single or too few* indicators to reflect the performance of a department, program, or facility, or the other extreme, which is using *too many* indicators.

Due to the complexity of healthcare, and the myriad factors that impact quality and performance, it is nearly impossible for a single metric or indicator to reflect accurately changes to the system. For example, efficiently functioning HCOs must measure many aspects of their performance, ranging from quality clinical care to administrative efficiency, to evaluate their performance, detect any problem areas, and take any necessary corrective action.

Using too many indicators (and who hasn't seen a dashboard crammed with every indicator possible?) serves only to confuse decision making. In the same manner that a pilot will focus on about six key instruments throughout most of a flight (with supplemental information being provided by other instruments), the critical indicators derived from approaches such as Lean and Six Sigma can guide decision making on the part of the HCO and result in real healthcare improvement.

HCOs need to be able to monitor many aspects of their performance to ensure that performance is attained and/or sustained at the desired levels. One way to make effective use of indicators is to bundle them into three groups: *outcome*, *process*, and *balancing*,[3] as outlined in Table 7.1. Outcome and process indicators are aligned with the healthcare elements of process and outcome described in Chapter 4.

Process and outcome indicators are typically what are monitored from an organizational standpoint and during QI activities. Including a variety of measure types in performance reports and dashboards is necessary to

TABLE 7.1 Outcome, Process, and Balancing Indicators

Indicator Type	Description
Outcome	Measures overall system performance, and includes the voice of the patient (or customer) and the results of improvement initiatives. Examples: percentage of unplanned emergency revisits, percentage of patients experiencing adverse outcomes.
Process	Measures how well key components (processes, workflows, steps) are performing. Examples: percentage of patients receiving rt-PA within the appropriate window, percentage of patients with chest pain having EKGs taken and read within 10 minutes of arrival.
Balancing	Provides a look at the system as a whole as processes and outcomes are improved, and may help identify unintended consequences. Examples: changes to staff workload as improvements are implemented, staff satisfaction.

obtain a comprehensive understanding of an organization's performance and the impact of improvement activities. Focusing on too many of one type of measure (such as outcomes), or even one particular outcome (such as length of stay) may lead to tunnel vision and an inability to spot any quality and performance issues in areas that are not being closely monitored. Likewise, having too many of any type of indicator will result in lack of focus. For any given improvement project, having between three to eight of the balancing measures is recommended.[4] This is a manageable number of indicators for decision makers and QI teams, and using all three types of indicators will enable a broader approach to monitoring the success of an improvement initiative.

Notes

1. David Parmenter, *Key Performance Indicators: Developing, Implementing, and Using Winning KPIs* (Hoboken, NJ: John Wiley & Sons, 2007), 3.
2. Ibid., 5.
3. Lloyd P. Provost and Sandra K. Murray, *The Health Care Data Guide: Learning from Data for Improvement* (San Francisco: Jossey-Bass, 2011), Kindle ed., locations 1326–29.
4. Ibid.

CHAPTER 8

Leveraging Analytics in Quality Improvement Activities

Knowing is not enough, we must act.

—Johann Wolfgang von Goethe

Data and information alone are not sufficient to achieve transformation in healthcare. Information and insight need to operate within a framework or methodology for quality and performance improvement decision making. Such a framework is necessary to identify priorities for improvement and evaluating outcomes. This chapter will focus on how to leverage analytics within a quality improvement (QI) environment to assist the healthcare organization (HCO) in achieving its quality and performance goals.

Moving from Analytics Insight to Healthcare Improvement

When used in concert with QI methodologies such as PDSA, Lean, or Six Sigma, analytics helps to identify the most pressing quality issues facing the HCO based on needs defined by patient safety, the quality goals of the HCO, national standards, and legislative requirements. These improvement methodologies leverage the insights gained from analytics, within their respective structured approaches, to develop interventions and solutions for healthcare quality and performance issues and evaluate outcomes to ensure the long-term sustainability of improvements.

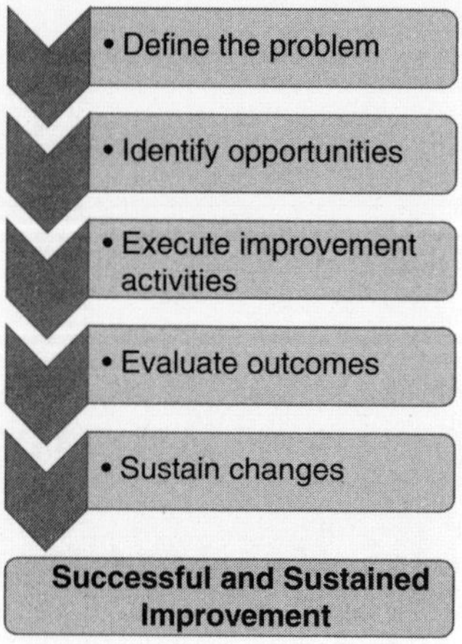

FIGURE 8.1 Five Quality Improvement Phases

To gain maximum value from analytics, QI projects need to be able to:

- Retrieve and analyze baseline data to document current performance and/or quality measures against which to compare future performance;
- Utilize or develop well-defined performance indicators (PIs) that accurately reflect the processes, procedures, policies, or treatments being changed; and
- Perform ongoing evaluation and reporting of relevant PIs to quantify the impact of implemented changes and to identify if further revisions to processes or policies are required.

Chapter 4 outlines the necessity of clearly defining what quality means in the context of the HCO, and also provides an overview of several common QI methodologies, such as PDSA, Lean, and Six Sigma. Regardless of which methodology is chosen, analytics can be incorporated at many decision and analysis points throughout a QI project, and in most decision-making processes within the HCO. This chapter will focus on the key role that analytics plays throughout quality and performance improvement initiatives. Following are five phases of a QI project during which analytics can be leveraged to help move from analytics insight to healthcare innovation and improvement. The five phases are illustrated in Figure 8.1 and described in more detail here.

Analytics is important in almost every phase of healthcare quality and performance improvement. Regardless of the QI framework chosen, the analytics needs of QI initiatives depend on:

- The phase of the initiative;
- Who is using analytics;

- What information and insight is required; and
- How that insight and information is being used.

Accurate information is necessary to understand the scope of the problem(s), identify the best possible solutions, evaluate those solutions once implemented, and monitor ongoing performance to help ensure that the improvements have been sustained.

The quality and performance problems that HCOs endeavor to address should, where possible, be in alignment with the quality and performance goals of the organization as stated in its quality and performance strategy. Those quality and performance goals serve as a kind of "true north" for keeping the organization on track as competing interests and requirements detract from strategic improvements. On occasion, problems will emerge that are not strictly aligned with the quality strategy but are nonetheless necessary to deal with. Because HCOs may have limited resources for undertaking multiple projects, the competing priorities need to be ranked in some way so that the highest-priority issues come first. Depending on the HCO's needs, the importance of problems can be ranked in different ways; three common bases for ranking issues facing an HCO are:

1. **Clinical.** Clinical concerns are perhaps the most important reason to undertake an improvement project. An HCO's clinical performance directly impacts the satisfaction and safety of patients whose care has been entrusted to the HCO. Clinically related improvement initiatives have as their goal to reduce adverse clinical outcomes and to ensure that patient care is delivered as per best practice guidelines. An example of an opportunity with a clinical focus is working on emergency department processes for stroke patients so that they receive the recommended imaging tests and medications within the proper window to minimize the loss of brain tissue.
2. **Financial.** As HCOs strive to become more financially healthy, financial considerations are likely to be a priority when selecting improvement initiatives. In this case, the costs of inefficiency, errors, or simply of doing business are likely to factor highly. For example, a healthcare payer may realize that doctors at a certain hospital are ordering more, expensive diagnostics than at other, similar hospitals. In this case, the payer would work with the hospital in question to identify new processes, guidelines, procedures, and even training to reduce these unnecessary diagnostics and associated costs.
3. **Regulatory/legislative.** Another prime driver of improvement activities is regulatory and legislative changes and/or incentives. For example, the U.S. Centers for Medicare and Medicaid Services introduced an incentive program rewarding qualifying HCOs and providers for

implementing or upgrading electronic medical records and demonstrating meaningful use.[1] This incentive program resulted in many HCOs and providers updating their processes and policies around the use of this technology in order to qualify for the incentive payment.

When classifying problems into each group listed previously (or other types of issues not listed here), HCOs can calculate the cost (whether measured in financial, clinical outcomes, or other terms) of poor quality and performance and begin to estimate the potential value or benefit of addressing their root causes. Those with higher associated costs and/or greatest potential benefit or value are considered higher-priority than those with lower associated costs. Using this type of ranking rationale helps organizations to become more transparent and quantitative in their decision making so that a decision to address one or a few problems over others can be quantitatively supported.

Analytics in the Problem Definition Stage

Once a problem has been identified and selected as a priority for the organization to address, the first step is to start with a clear and detailed description of the quality or performance problem (or other issue) that must be improved. The important considerations of this step are:

- What are the goals/objectives to which this problem relates?
- What are the relevant indicators and metrics?
- What baseline data is available, and what data will be available moving forward for monitoring and evaluation?

One of the first steps is to quantify and measure the magnitude of the problem. The problem should relate to the strategic quality and performance improvement objectives of the organization and/or the tactical-level improvement goals of units, departments, and programs, and wherever possible be described and quantified in terms of the appropriate metrics and indicators. The results of this process help to filter all the possible metrics and indicators, based on possibly hundreds of available data points, down to the critical few indicators required for the success of a quality and performance improvement project.

The information-gathering and benchmarking phase typically sees QI team members obtaining data regarding the issue in question. Once metrics and indicators are decided upon, critical to any QI initiative is effective baseline performance information. Useful baseline information, however, is more than just the collection of historical data. Baseline performance is a quantitative description of some aspect of the HCO's performance measured

Baseline Data

Baseline performance data is a quantitative description of some aspect of the organization's performance measured prior to undertaking an improvement initiative.

prior to the undertaking of an improvement initiative. (If no quantitative data is available, a qualitative description is sometimes helpful.) An accurate baseline is necessary for determining whether any actual change in performance has taken place, and what the magnitude of that change is.

Every QI project will require baseline data. In fact, baseline performance data is helpful in the everyday operations of the HCO. Baseline data can put current performance in perspective; for example, are the number of visits, lengths of stay, admission rates, or bed turnaround times today better or worse than typical? This has an important impact on dashboards and other similar tools, where baseline quality and performance information can add very valuable context to current real-time performance values.

In some cases, baseline data may not be available (for example, with the opening of a new unit or clinic, or with the adoption of a brand-new technology). In these cases, baseline data should be established as soon as possible into the improvement activity in order to gauge performance changes. The information gathered in this phase of the QI process is typically more static and historical in nature, may require some basic statistics to tease out actual performance values, and can be visualized in various types of statistical process control (SPC) charts to determine how "in control" a process is.

Knowing the true magnitude of a change requires both an accurate starting point and ending point. For example, almost any medical procedure performed on patients at a healthcare facility requires a complete baseline (including height, weight, lab results, and diagnostic imaging as necessary)—no healthcare provider would even consider performing a procedure without knowing as much about the patient as possible. Yet healthcare QI projects are undertaken too often without the benefit of clearly knowing current and/or historical performance, and this is why many of those projects fail.

Tip

Baseline data should be based on and measured in the exact same way as the indicators developed for the QI project.

Baseline data should be based on and measured in the exact same way as the indicators developed for the QI project. In order to ensure that baseline data is a true measure of existing performance, the following considerations should be made:

- **Data source.** Wherever possible, the source of baseline data should be the same as that used for ongoing measurement and evaluation; if the sources of data are different (for example, before and after the implementation of a new system), differences in the way data were recorded, processes were interpreted, and data was analyzed must be taken into account or there is a risk of performing an invalid comparison and perhaps reaching inaccurate conclusions.
- **Data quality.** If baseline data is drawn from legacy systems, or even collected from paper sources, data quality may be an issue. Ensure that the quality of baseline data is as high as possible prior to performing any analysis or comparisons.
- **Time period.** Baseline data must cover a long enough time to be an accurate reflection of performance, and must be recent enough to be a valid comparison. If baseline data is too old or does not cover a sufficient time period, processes, performance, and quality may have changed since the time encompassed by the baseline data.
- **Indicators.** Comparisons with baseline data work best if the baseline data is analyzed and reported using the same indicators that will be used moving forward for monitoring and evaluation.

Data used for the baseline should be reliable—it should be trusted as a true measure of performance, as future performance will be compared against this. If no data is available, it may be obtained manually (for example, via chart reviews), but this may have implications for what indicators are chosen for the actual improvement initiatives.

Manually Collected Data

Just because data is collected manually doesn't mean that it must always live on paper; results of audits and other manual checks can be stored electronically and made available for analysis. Several business intelligence tools will allow users to import data from external spreadsheets into existing frameworks. In my experience, we have successfully integrated external data, such as from process audits, that was collected manually into our BI tools, and used that data as part of analysis of data collected from clinical systems.

When reporting baseline data, one important consideration is how to aggregate the data. For example, when looking at a year's worth of baseline data, the temptation might be to group the data by month. When grouping by month, however, it is possible that certain details are being lost that might be helpful to determine if a change is in fact occurring.

Consider Chart "A" in Figure 8.2, in which average clinic patient length-of-stay data is grouped by month over a 12-month period. During that time, the performance of the clinic appears to be relatively static. Chart "B" hints at a slightly different story—aggregating the data by week instead of month shows that midway through the baseline data, variation in the data seems to have decreased. A decrease in variation in performance is considered to be a step toward improvement. So even though on a monthly scale performance may appear to be static, when looked at through a weekly lens, it can be

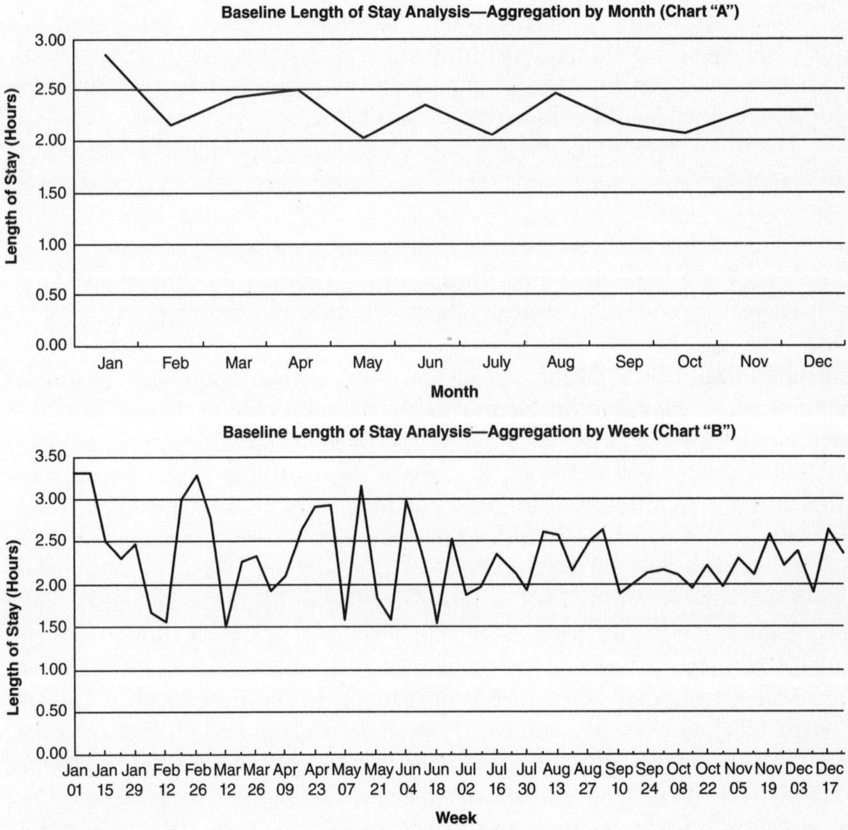

FIGURE 8.2 Baseline Data Showing a Change in Performance When Aggregated Differently

suggested that some improvement has already started to take place. The reverse is true as well; if baseline data shows increasing variability in a set of data, it is possible that capacity to perform at expected levels is deteriorating.

Using Analytics to Identify Improvement Opportunities

Once a problem has been identified and quantified, the next step is to identify improvement opportunities—that is, what steps an HCO can take to achieve the desired outcomes and levels of performance. To achieve these improvements requires specific actions and interventions on the part of QI teams. Of course, not all identified opportunities and resultant improvement activities will have the same impact, so HCOs need to establish ranking criteria with which to rank, evaluate, and select opportunities. At the problem definition stage, a cost (in financial, clinical, or other terms) associated with the quality or performance problem would have been calculated. The cost of actual improvement efforts can be compared to the cost of the problem, and a decision can be made to proceed with specific improvement initiatives that will have the greatest impact and require the least resources and effort—in other words, achieve maximum value.

The three steps in identifying and selecting improvement opportunities are as follows:

1. Determining likely root cause(s) of quality/performance problems.
2. Identifying possible countermeasures to address root causes.
3. Estimating countermeasure impact and effort to achieve goals.

DETERMINING ROOT CAUSE Healthcare QI teams often fall victim to addressing *symptoms* of problems, not the actual problems themselves. This will likely only result in the introduction of a workaround, not a solution to the problem. For example, if a medication cabinet in an observation area is regularly understocked, the "solution" may be for a healthcare aide or other staff member to raid (for lack of a better term) a medication cabinet of another area of the department. This not only results in additional inefficiency by requiring staff to move unnecessarily, but it may also cause problems downstream with other staff who rely on medications from the raided cabinet.

True QI requires healthcare professionals to move beyond "who" and "what" into "why" errors, defects, or waste occur. For real change to occur, we must change from being a blaming culture and into a solution-finding culture in healthcare by moving beyond responding to symptoms and start addressing actual root causes of problems.

Because blaming seems to come more naturally than finding root causes, there are tools that can be employed within QI methodologies to help find

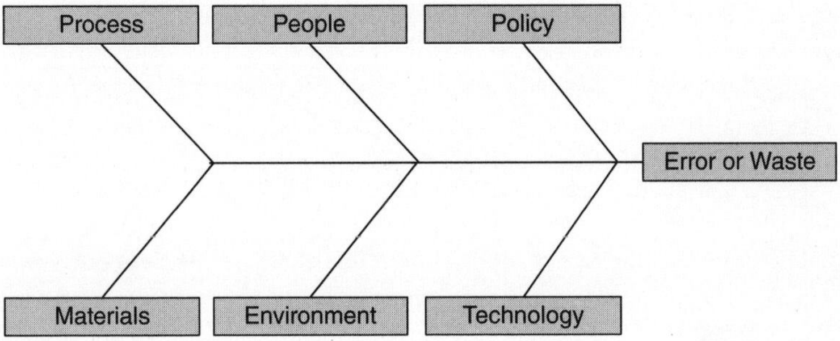

FIGURE 8.3 Sample Ishikawa (Fishbone) Diagram Used for Identifying Causes of Problems, Errors, or Waste

root causes. One approach to identify root causes using an Ishikawa (or fishbone) diagram, as illustrated in Figure 8.3. A problem, error, or waste is identified and all possible causes for it are listed under various categories. (Typically, the categories are process, people, policy, materials, environment, and technology, although variations exist and oftentimes the categories are changed to fit the particular problem under investigation.)

Once possible root causes are identified, the contribution of each root cause can be mapped in a Pareto chart (see Figure 8.4). Pareto charts are very useful to highlight the most important contributing factors to a problem or issue. The main components of a Pareto chart are the identified causes of a quality or performance problem, vertical bars to represent the number (or percentage) of times the problem occurred as a result of that cause, and a line plotting the cumulative frequency of the causes (which should add up to 100 percent).

Suppose an emergency department has implemented a new computerized triage tool and is experiencing an unacceptably high rate of triage overrides, which occur when the triage nurse does not agree with the triage score determined by the algorithm in the triage tool. During an investigation into the root causes of the overrides, triage nurses are asked to identify the reason they overrode the computer. The nurses identify five key issues that caused them to enter a score other than what the algorithm determined:

1. Too many clicks on the form; nurses are bypassing certain form fields to save time.
2. The design of the triage form is confusing, and triage nurses are missing important fields on the form.
3. Triage nurses do not feel they received enough training.
4. Triage is too busy in general to complete the form properly.
5. Some triage staff don't trust the algorithms.

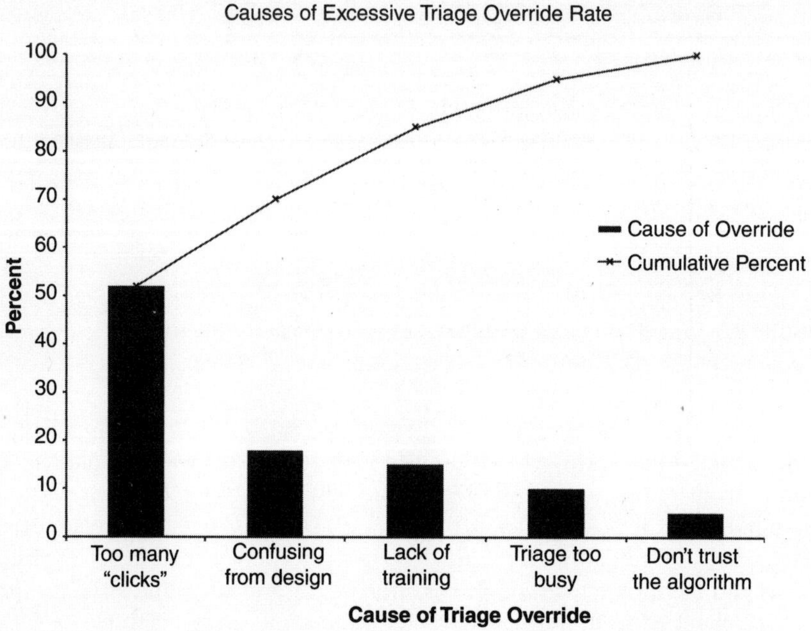

FIGURE 8.4 Sample Pareto Chart Used to Determine Important Contributing Factors to Quality Problems

These five causes of triage overrides are then plotted on a Pareto chart (see Figure 8.4). By looking at the chart, the QI team is able to determine that approximately 70 percent of overrides are the result of two main issues: too many clicks, and confusing form design. With this information, the QI team can be reasonably sure that a significant percent of overrides can be prevented by addressing these two issues, which in fact would bundle nicely into a single triage form improvement project.

Analyzing the root causes of problems in a quantitative manner such as a Pareto chart can provide QI teams the insight they require to make a transparent, evidence-informed choice on which QI initiatives to undertake.

ESTIMATING IMPACT AND EFFORT There may be some process changes that HCOs can make that would result in a large impact to the department or HCO but would require relatively little effort. Is there a way that we can quantify these high-impact changes? Consider Figure 8.5, which illustrates an impact/effort grid that can be used to help select QI projects. I have yet to encounter an HCO that has unlimited resources to dedicate to QI projects. Because of this, even though there may be many opportunities and needs for improvement, only a few projects are feasible to undertake at any one time.

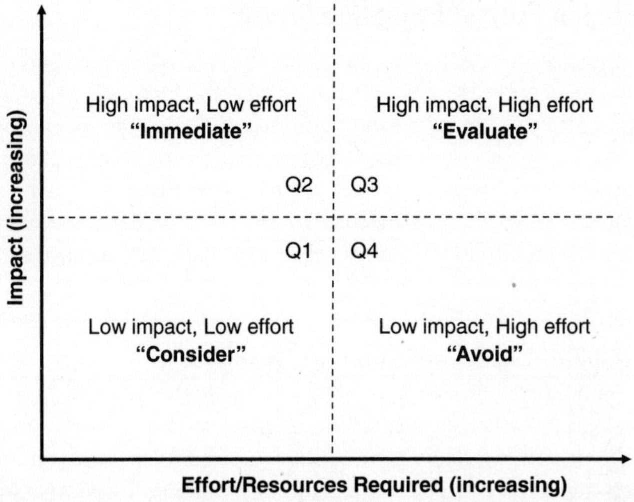

FIGURE 8.5 Sample Impact/Effort Grid for Selecting Quality Improvement Projects

The impact/effort grid helps QI teams map projects according to estimated impact (that is, how much change or benefit can be expected) and what the anticipated effort to achieve that change might be. Projects that fall into quadrant 2 (high impact, low effort) are generally favored by HCOs, as these represent potential game changers, where big wins are possible with relatively little effort. Projects falling into quadrant 4 (low impact, high effort) should be avoided, as they can be a major drain on HCO resources and QI team morale, without any definite long-term positive impact on quality. Projects that fall into quadrant 1 (low impact, low effort) can be considered, but may detract resources from other projects that may have a bigger impact. Quadrant 3 projects, those that are high impact and high effort, should be evaluated carefully to determine whether the potential benefit of the project is worth the time and resources applied to achieve that benefit.

Analytics can be very helpful when mapping projects on an impact/effort grid, especially if relevant, detailed, and high-quality baseline data is available. For example, the anticipated impact of a project can be estimated by examining baseline levels of performance against anticipated targets, or, better yet, by looking at comparable performance metrics for other programs or sites that are performing better.

Estimating the impact of a change can be challenging; without any quantitative basis, impact estimates are little more than a mere guess. Various analytical approaches, including regression modeling and other predictive approaches, as well as simulation, can be helpful in better quantifying the effect of a change. See Chapter 11 for a discussion of various advanced analytics approaches.

Analytics in the Project Execution Phase

Executing improvement activities involves finding new ways of doing the required work to achieve the desired improvements (innovation), working with staff to implement the changes (intervention), and examining interim results to make any midcourse corrections (experimentation). During project execution, QI teams use analytics to closely monitor the processes that have been changed (or that have been impacted by changes to equipment, layout, or staffing levels, for example) to quantify differences in performance and quality.

Innovation and Experimentation in Healthcare

All change in healthcare should be treated as an experiment. If the results are positive, adopt (and continue to tweak) the changes. If the results are negative, reject the changes or identify what additional changes must be made to obtain the desired results.

During the execution phase, quality teams require detailed data with a rapid turnaround to make quick adjustments to their efforts to maximize the amount of positive change (or to mitigate any negative effects the changes might have introduced). This sees a shift in the type of analytics required. During this phase, QI teams will be much more directed in the information they are seeking. The QI teams are likely dissecting existing processes and workflows and developing new processes. Depending on the methodology used and the time frame of the initiative, the QI teams will likely be changing the actual workflows and processes that staff members are performing. It is therefore likely that QI teams will require data that is closer to real-time, and much more specific to the desired processes. As processes and workflows are changed, QI teams will need to be able to see if the changes have actually led to a change in performance.

QI projects (especially ones that employ a PDSA methodology) usually begin with small-scale, localized changes as part of an initial evaluation. During the execution phase of quality group initiative, the data requirements of the team become very specific. QI teams will often break down processes into very minute detail, and will seek available metrics to measure the performance of these process components. For that reason, data and utilization requirements on QI projects are different from higher-level monitoring.

Using indicators that are monitored at a departmental or organizational level may not be sufficiently granular to detect a localized change over a period of time. For example, a new process resulting in a reduction in

TEXTBOOKRUSH
Your Online Campus Bookstore

0 000143 597911

Order 002-0144807-6713002
Order Date 1/8/2015
***Invoice* 118501 - 622**
BOUND PRINTED MATTER
AmazonCom

Ship To: Laurie Bladen
3085 Slavik RD
Coldwater, OH 45828

Bill To:Laurie Bladen
3085 Slavik RD
Coldwater, OH 45828

Send Service Inquiries To:
TextbookRush.com
help@textbookrush.com

ISBN	SKU	Item	Qty	Price	Price x Qty
1118519698 BN 360(0)	38902139 30-12-15-24	HEALTHCARE ANALYTICS FOR QUALITY AND PERFORMANCE IMPROVEMENT / STROME, TREVOR L.	1	$41.98	$41.98

Subtotal: $41.98
Tax: $0.00
Shipping: $3.99
Total: $45.97

hospital discharge times achieved over several days within a single unit may not even register on a more global indicator. For this reason, the output of analytics for a quality or performance improvement project in this stage should be:

- Relevant to the process or other change that is subject of the improvement effort.
- Focused locally on the department, unit, or other region where the change occurred.
- Available in near real time (or "short cycle") to allow for rapid adjustments.
- Presented in appropriate formats (such as run charts or statistical process control [SPC] charts) to evaluate both variability in the data and the magnitude of change in performance. (Remember that a reduction in process variability is a key step toward improvement.)

It is possible, and indeed likely, that a lot of information during this phase will not be available from existing sources. Don't be surprised if some required data is not even available in computerized form. For example, many improvement initiatives rely on audit data (that may not be available in electronic medical records or other systems) such as:

- Number of times a computer system (e.g., RIS/PACS) is not available (on downtime).
- Number of times a new process was followed correctly (as defined in standard work).
- Number of times a medical admission form was not completed properly.

Just because information may not be easily obtained or currently available does not mean that it is not important; in fact, very often these process components are overlooked. There are a few options to obtain this information. One option is to manually collect the data on audit forms placed throughout the unit and compile it in something like a spreadsheet. Although this may seem like a lot of work, often there is no other way to obtain such information. What may be possible is to link this manually collected and entered data to your current BI platform so that it can be integrated into existing dashboards or other performance reports for use by the team.

Using Analytics to Evaluate Outcomes and Maintain Sustainability

After the project execution phase and a change in performance or quality has been successfully implemented and tested on a smaller scale, the project team naturally will deploy the improvement throughout other applicable areas within the HCO. Once the project has been deployed, continued monitoring and evaluation are necessary to ensure that the desired changes in quality and performance are occurring on the new, larger scale.

There are several possible approaches for evaluating the impact of an improvement project. For example, the team might want to compare quality or performance before and after the implementation of a new process or other innovation to determine if a change occurred, and what the magnitude of that change was. Or they may compare the impact of two different changes to determine which has the greater magnitude. For example, a department manager may wish to evaluate the impact of a new type of staff member (such as nurse practitioner or physician assistant) and compare baseline department performance to performance since the new role was added to determine the overall impact.

Once the desired changes are in place, analytics can be used to quantify the impact of the changes based on the initial indicators, and comparisons with benchmarks can be used to gauge progress toward meeting the designated targets. There are many ways to monitor performance—usually in

PROCESSES VERSUS OUTCOMES

When working on quality and performance improvement, there may be a tendency to focus on indicators relating to patient flow (interval times, lengths of stay, etc.). It is important to not lose sight of the indicators that are truly important—those that relate to patient outcomes. The bias toward patient flow indicators may be related to what is most conveniently obtained from electronic medical records systems. However, nobody would argue that a shorter length of stay is a benefit to the patient when that same patient is readmitted to hospital a few days later. Having said that, it is also *not* acceptable to keep a patient in hospital or in the emergency department longer than necessary simply to prevent a possible readmission (when the risk of readmission for a particular patient is not even quantified).

One of the goals of quality and performance improvement initiatives must be to balance the overall flow of an organization with the outcomes that are important to the patient. This is where the concept of value comes into play: How can HCOs maximize the value to patients (outcomes) while improving quality, efficiency, and safety? If value is increased, the likely outcome will be happier and healthier patients and HCOs that are more efficient and more profitable.

the form of performance dashboards or other reports. SPC charts are, once again, a very valuable tool to monitor the ongoing performance relating to changes being made. Just as is necessary during the project execution phase, evaluation results must be available quickly enough to take meaningful corrective action if necessary.

Sustaining Changes and Improvements

Careful analysis and redesign of healthcare processes can be successful at improving quality and performance. Without looking at the right data, or analyzing it correctly, it may be difficult to evaluate the impact of a change. And when a change does occur, it is less likely to be sustained without ongoing monitoring and corrective action.

Healthcare QI projects typically start off with a flourish, but all too often end with a whimper. This is because the excitement generated with a new project, new opportunities, and great expectations elevates QI teams with a feeling that anything is possible. This enthusiasm usually dies down by the end of a project, when team members look to other problems to address.

It is important not to lose sight of improvements that are made, so performance must continually be monitored to ensure that things don't revert to previous (undesired) levels of quality or performance.

This final stage is critical for QI initiatives, because sustainability is in fact one of the most challenging objectives to achieve. Many initiatives appear initially successful, but the desired performance begins to tail off after a few weeks or a few months. Monitoring during this phase must allow QI teams (and the HCO's leadership) to monitor ongoing performance of the improved processes. The actual metrics being followed during this phase may be fewer in number than during the execution phase, but the metrics chosen for monitoring and evaluation must be the most relevant to the performance desired. In addition to a performance dashboard highlighting the key indicators of a newly implemented improvement initiative, regular reports and automatic alerts that are e-mailed to key stakeholders draw the attention of QI team members when performance begins to deteriorate or otherwise deviate from desired parameters.

IMPROVING RETURN ON INVESTMENT

Many information technology (IT) projects are initiated, implemented, and deployed without ever defining or measuring the return on investment (ROI); and when an ROI is claimed, the values are often unclear at best and dubious at worst. In other words, many HCOs are unclear as to what value many of their IT solutions in fact provide. Of course, analytics is not an exclusively IT undertaking (and should in fact be a strong partnership between the business and IT). But the sole purpose of BI and analytics within an HCO is to improve quality and performance. That would imply, then, that an ROI is in fact necessary—if no measurable improvement occurs, there is no return on investment.

The ROI of healthcare analytics should not be measured in terms of outputs of the system. For example, the number of reports, analytical applications, predictive models, and other analytical products is not a valid measure of ROI, since there is no indication of the value of these efforts. (In fact, it may be argued that more reports actually means less value!)

There are other types of value generated through analytics, such as in the areas of research and education. For example, the analytics teams that I work with have provided much value to clinical research efforts. The analytics infrastructure has made the extraction and analysis of data for research projects much more efficient; much data for research can be extracted and analyzed in the span of several hours with the tools now available (as opposed to the days and weeks necessary before much of the clinical data was available electronically). So ROI can be measured in terms of increased productivity in addition to real money saved.

Of course, quality and performance improvements cannot be entirely attributed to the use of analytics, but such metrics do provide a compelling measure of return on investment for QI efforts as a whole.

Note

1. Centers for Medicare and Medicaid Services, "EHR Incentive Programs," www.cms.gov/Regulations-and-Guidance/Legislation/EHRIncentivePrograms/index.html.

CHAPTER 9

Basic Statistical Methods and Control Chart Principles

If your experiment needs a statistician, you need a better experiment.

—Ernest Rutherford

There are complementary methods to measure the impact of a change or innovation on quality and performance—statistically and using control charts. Statistical methods to determine changes in performance rely on the performance of statistical tests to determine if changes in quality, performance, or other metrics are "statistically significant." Graphical approaches, on the other hand, use specialized charts known as statistical process control (SPC) charts (and specific rules to aid the interpretation of those graphs) to determine if a change in quality or performance is in fact occurring. This chapter discusses how both of these methods can be employed for quality and performance improvement.

Statistical Methods for Detecting Changes in Quality or Performance

I chose the epigraph at the start of this chapter rather tongue-in-cheek. My intent with the quotation isn't to say that statistics (and statisticians) should be avoided, but rather that the job of analytics professionals (including statisticians) is to make statistics more *accessible* and easily understood to all users of information through the use of the right tools in addressing the right problems (those of the quality and performance issues of the organization).

Statistics offers a wide range of methods with which to analyze quality and performance data. In this section, it is my intention only to introduce some basic statistical tests and terminology as they pertain to quality and performance improvement projects. I strongly encourage the reader to explore additional resources for more in-depth coverage of additional statistical topics.

Analytics is comprised of the tools, techniques, and systems necessary for obtaining deeper insight into the performance of an organization. Statistics is but one of those tools—an important tool to be sure, but not the only tool. I often say that analytics for healthcare quality improvement (QI) projects does not require *fancy* statistics, but rather *appropriate* statistics. A large part of the discussion in this book is about ensuring that high-quality data is available, that it is compiled into relevant indicators, and that it is made available to QI teams using structured methodologies. I have seen many analysis efforts become derailed because an analyst was overly concerned with applying complex statistical analysis, when this level of analysis was not necessary. Hopefully this section will demonstrate how statistics can be but one valuable tool in the quality and performance improvement toolbox.

Most QI methodologies do not require extensive statistical knowledge and the use of exotic statistical methods. Rather, statistical methods can best be used to identify any unusual variations in performance and to help pinpoint the causes of this variation.[1] This is more common in some methodologies (such as Six Sigma) that require more statistical analysis than others (such as Lean). Most QI projects can benefit from some basic statistical summaries such as average, median, and percentiles to report baseline information and current performance (as discussed in Chapter 6). Six Sigma delves deeper into more statistics, such as analysis of variance (ANOVA) and other tests, to either detect differences in performance or to increase the certainty of a result. In my experience, I have always tried to use statistics where appropriate and necessary to clarify and strengthen conclusions, not to search for a needle in a haystack.

If extreme statistical analyses are necessary to detect a change in performance, then a few scenarios are likely:

- The quality of data being used is poor.
- The wrong indicators were developed or used.
- There is no change in performance, or it is too small to be relevant.

Statistics are typically applied in one of two ways. *Descriptive statistics* are used to describe a large number of values or observations (representing an entire population or a sample thereof). There is a wide variety of descriptive statistics; the most commonly used ones include the mean (for example, the average weight of patients visiting a clinic) and the median (for example, length of stay [LOS] of emergency department patients). *Inferential statistics*, on the other hand, analyze a sample of data to help evaluate and draw conclusions about a population. See Chapter 6 for a discussion on measures of central tendency and the use of descriptive statistics. This section will focus more on inferential statistics used to confirm the statistical significance of a change in performance.

Hypothesis Testing

Consider a facility that was observing longer than desired lengths of hospital stay and decided to implement a new streamlined patient discharge protocol. Prior to the implementation of the protocol, three months of baseline data showed an average length of hospital stay of 4.54 days. Following the implementation of the new protocol, the results were evaluated and the three-month post-implementation average length of hospital stay was 3.56 days. See Figure 9.1 for a graph illustrating the results. The difference pre- and post-implementation was 0.98 days. QI teams needed to determine whether this difference is the result of the new protocols, or whether the protocols made no difference and the observed difference is entirely by chance.

The process of determining whether this difference in values is due to natural variation and chance or the result of the change in process is known as *hypothesis testing* and typically involves a test of *statistical significance.* Because of natural variations in performance, no two sets of randomly selected data will ever be exactly the same even if the two samples are drawn from the same population of patients. Hypothesis testing and tests of statistical significance will help to determine if any observed differences between two (or more) groups are likely due to *actual* differences in the populations being studied (the result of a process change or other intervention), or if the observed differences are due to random variation and chance.[2]

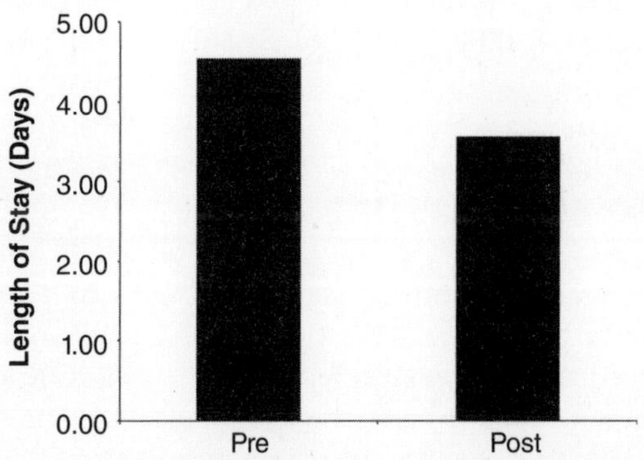

FIGURE 9.1 Sample Length of Hospital Stay before and after Implementation of New Discharge Protocols

Hypothesis testing starts with the assumption that there actually is no difference between the groups (that is, any observed differences are caused by random variation) unless there is compelling evidence to demonstrate otherwise. This is called the *null hypothesis*, and is expressed as:

$$H_0: \mu_1 = \mu_2 \text{ or } H_0: \mu_1 - \mu_2 = 0$$

The null hypothesis states that the means of data sets 1 and 2 are equivalent (that is, subtracting the mean of one data set from the mean of the other would return zero). In the case of the streamlined discharge protocol, H_0 states that there is no difference in the mean hospital LOS before and after the implementation of the new protocol—or that the new protocol had no effect on patient LOS. In the event that the null hypothesis is demonstrated to be false, the *alternative hypothesis* is then assumed to be true (that is, that the means of data sets 1 and 2 are not equal, and the differences observed between two data sets are likely *not* due to chance).

$$H_a: \mu_1 \neq \mu_1 \text{ or } H_a: \mu_1 - \mu_2 \neq 0$$

In our discharge protocol example, the alternative hypothesis is that there is a true difference in the means of discharge times measured before and after the protocol was introduced, suggesting that the new protocol *did* have an effect on patient LOS in hospital.

Comparing Performance between Two Groups

One common statistical test to evaluate situations like the pre-post evaluation of the protocol implementation is the *t*-test. The *t*-test is a statistical method that can be used to help determine if a statistical parameter (such as the mean, or average) is the same when compared between two groups (the null hypothesis) or different (the alternative hypothesis).[3]

LEARNING MORE ABOUT STATISTICS

If you are interested in learning more about the scientific and statistical basis behind hypothesis testing and statistical significance, there are many good statistical textbooks that cover these topics. I would also encourage you to review the resources listed in this chapter for more information. You can also visit this book's web site, http://HealthcareAnalyticsBook.com, for links to relevant resources.

A *t*-test can be used in two situations, depending on the number of samples. The *one-sample t*-test is used to compare one point of interest to a sample. For example, the one-sample *t*-test can be used to compare a sample's average performance to the target value of an indicator. If an emergency department's average left without being seen (LWBS) is 3.4 percent and the target LWBS rate is 2.5 percent, a one-sample *t*-test could be used to determine if the difference between actual performance and the target value is statistically significant.

A *two-sample t*-test is used to compare the performance of two groups. There are two varieties of this type of *t*-test; the best one to use depends on the two samples being tested. For example, if you are testing the hospital LOS at two different hospitals—Hospital A versus Hospital B—then the test to use is the *independent t*-test. The independent *t*-test assumes that the two populations are indeed independent, and are normally distributed. The independent *t*-test would not be appropriate in our example of the pre-post analysis of the streamlined discharge protocols. A pre-post study evaluation, also known as a *repeated measures* design, requires use of the *dependent t*-test variant.

A *t*-test can be applied to the "pre-change" and "post-change" groups in the example highlighted in Figure 9.1 to see if the difference of 0.98 days is statistically significant. Normally, statistical tests such as the *t*-test would be performed in a statistical software package or a spreadsheet with statistical capabilities. In the case of our discharge protocol example, running a dependent *t*-test on the two groups generates the following output from the statistical software used to run the test, which in this case is R:

```
t = -33.3139, df = 89, p-value < 2.2e-16
alternative hypothesis: true difference in means is not
  equal to 0
95 percent confidence interval:
 -1.0385635 -0.9216485
sample estimates:
mean of the differences
              -0.980106
```

What do these results mean? Consider if we repeated the discharge protocol pre-post test a second time and the results were similar, with a difference of 0.92 days; chances are our confidence in the results would improve, with two repeated tests demonstrating the same trend. Now, if we repeated the pre-post test 100 times and found that 95 out of these 100 times produced similar results, our confidence would be pretty high that the discharge protocols actually did decrease LOS for patients. If we repeated the test 100 times and found that the LOS of the protocol patients was shorter than nonprotocol patients for only 60 of the trials, we would be less confident in the results. Finally, if each group had the shorter LOS 50 percent of the time over 100 repetitions of the pre-post test, we would likely deem that the protocols did not result in shorter lengths of stay.

Of course, it would be extremely time consuming and expensive to repeat trials such as our discharge protocol evaluation the necessary number of times to fully gauge confidence in results. This is where statistical tests are very useful, to determine how confident we can be that any differences observed are the result of a process change, or whether the observed difference likely occurred by chance.

More formally, the statistical significance is the probability of obtaining the observed (or more extreme) results if the null hypothesis were in fact true.[4] This chance or probability is calculated on the basis that the null hypothesis is correct; the smaller this chance, the stronger the evidence against the null hypothesis. Statistical analyses such as the *t*-test provides a quantitative assessment of this confidence with the *p*-value. A common *p*-value target often used in scientific research and QI is 0.05 or less, which means that there would be less than a 5 percent chance of obtaining the observed results if the null hypothesis was true.

In the previous example, the *p*-value is estimated to be less than $2.2e^{-16}$ by the computer software, suggesting that there is an extremely small chance of observing an LOS difference of 0.98 days if there was in fact no difference between the protocol and nonprotocol groups. This small *p*-value can provide the QI team with confidence that the discharge protocols actually are making a difference in lengths of stay of patients.

Another value reported by the computer software on the example above is the 95 percent confidence interval (CI). The CI is a computed range of numbers within which the true value is expected to lie.[5] In this case, the *t*-test calculated that the 95 percent CI, or the range of values in which the difference in LOS for protocol and nonprotocol patients can be expected to lie, is most likely between −1.039 and −0.922 (with rounding). In other words, we can say there is only a 1 in 20 chance that the true difference between the groups is *not* within that range.

If the CI included zero (for example, if the CI was between −0.5 and +0.5), it would imply that "no difference" in means, or a difference of zero, was as likely as other values within the CI. Because zero is not within the CI, however, it is likely that there is in fact a true difference.

The description of the *t*-test and test of significance earlier is to provide a flavor of how tests of statistical significance can help determine whether an actual change is occurring in a process. The *t*-test is ideal for comparing two groups, but what if more than two groups need to be tested at once, or you needed to test categorical data, or if other assumptions required of the data to perform a *t*-test are not met?

Comparing Performance of More Than Two Groups

What if an analyst needs to compare the performance of more than two groups? For example, consider the case where an analyst needs to compare the hospital LOS between three different facilities for patients who undergo a coronary artery bypass graft (CABG) procedure. Table 9.1 illustrates sample CABG patient LOS for three different facilities—A, B, and C. What would be the best approach to determine if there is a statistically significant difference between groups, or if the differences observed are simply the result of random variation?

The first instinct might be to perform pairwise comparisons—that is, compare A to B, A to C, and B to C using standard *t*-tests. This approach has two drawbacks. First, as the number of groups to compare grows, the number of pairwise comparisons that are required becomes unwieldy very quickly; after just seven groups, the number of comparisons required would be 21. Technically, we can get computers to run multiple *t*-tests quite simply, so the number of comparisons is not really a concern. However, as more *t*-tests are performed, the risk of obtaining a statistically significant difference *purely by chance* increases. Although there are corrections (such as the Bonferroni correction) that can be made for this when performing multiple tests (such as *t*-tests) on the same set of data, other statistical options are available.

In this case, and other cases when the *t*-test is not appropriate to use, there are other tests that can be used. The ANOVA (*an*alysis *o*f *va*riance) test is helpful when you need to compare more than two samples to each other to determine whether any of the sample means is statistically different from the other sample means.[6] A *one-way* ANOVA is valid if the groups are independent (as three sites would be), the data is normally distributed, and the variance in the populations is similar. Without going into the formulas, ANOVA works by comparing the variance *within* each group with the variance *between* the groups, and comparing the ratio of the within-group and between-group variance; the ratio is known as the *F-statistic*. If the variation between groups is much higher than the variation within groups, and the F-statistic exceeds a critical value, then a difference observed between the groups can be considered statistically significant. (Note that the critical F-statistic value can be looked up on a specially designed table of critical values, but more often than not, this will be performed by computer.)

TABLE 9.1 Sample Hospital LOS for CABG Patients for Three Sites

Facility	Hospital Length of Stay (days) for CABG Patients
Hospital A	8.5
Hospital B	9.8
Hospital C	8.9

Comparing Observations of Normal and Ordinal Values

What if the data that needs to be compared between two (or more) groups is nominal or ordinal, that is, data for which a mean cannot be generated for a test like a *t*-test or an ANOVA? A *chi-square test* is useful for determining if there is in fact a relationship between two categorical variables,[7] and would be appropriate in this situation. Rather than comparing a statistic such as the mean of two or more groups, the chi-square sums the squared differences observed and expected frequency of observations within each category.[8]

The different scenarios for which you may consider using the different types of ANOVA tests include:

- **One-way between groups.** Use the one-way between-groups ANOVA when the performance of three or more groups needs to be compared (as in the above example).
- **One-way repeated measures.** When performance has been measured a few times (for example, prior to a QI project, during the execution of the QI project, and after the QI project), the one-way repeated measures ANOVA can test for a statistically significant change in performance.
- **Two-way between groups.** This is used when looking for more complex interactions. For example, if comparing hospital LOS for CABG procedures, QI teams may be interested in understanding the interaction between whether the site is a teaching hospital or community hospital, and the overall hospital LOS.
- **Two-way repeated measures.** This is similar to the one-way repeated measure, but includes an interaction effect (for example, if you wanted to test whether type of X-ray had any impact on changes in the processing time of diagnostic imaging patients).

Lessons Learned

Many software packages include statistical tests built in, so it is relatively simple to perform a *t*-test, ANOVA, or other statistical test. Keep in mind that although software makes it easy, applying a statistical test to a set of numbers on a spreadsheet may not achieve accurate results. Before proceeding with a statistical test, always ensure that the basic assumptions required of the test are met (for example, does the test require normally distributed data?), and that the test can provide the type of answer being sought.

Graphical Methods for Detecting Changes in Quality or Performance

Hypothesis testing and tests of statistical significance are one method of determining if any change is occurring in quality and performance within a healthcare organization (HCO). The challenge with statistical tests, however, is that most require large samples of data to be accurate, and can be cumbersome to run every time the performance or quality associated with a process needs to be measured. Another issue is that they tend to utilize aggregated data (for example, determining if the mean of two samples is statistically significant). If all analysis is done in aggregate, it is possible to lose sight of variations in the way that processes are performed and in the outcomes of those processes. One danger of solely relying on aggregate data and statistical analysis is that although *average* values of data sets might be meeting a target value, individual performance and quality may vary so widely that the inconsistency poses a risk to patient safety.

Control charts are a very common visual approach to evaluate performance and quality with associated rules to determine if a process is in control and improving (or getting worse). Graphical analysis is a highly regarded approach in healthcare QI. It has been recommended that "methods for the analysis of data should be almost exclusively graphical (always including a run order plot), with minimum of aggregation of the data before the initial graphical display."[9]

Graphical analysis of performance data provides visual evidence of the variability inherent in a process. Measuring and understanding the variation in a process is merited because it is "important to eliminate extraneous process variation wherever possible, while moving well-defined metrics toward their target values."[10]

Variation in Performance

There are many different causes of variation in performance. Causes can range from differences in the way individuals perform tasks to calibration differences in equipment. All the different causes of variation, however, can be divided into two categories:

1. **Common (or random).** These are causes of variation that are inherent in the work being performed, affect everyone who performs the work, and affects all outcomes of the process.[11] Common cause variation is generally predictable and expected and can be caused by myriad reasons ranging from complexity of patient needs to materials available. An example is the natural variations in the time it takes to triage an emergency patient; although every triage is different because each

patient presentation is unique, there is a typical range in the time it normally takes to complete a patient triage.

2. **Special (or assignable).** These are causes of variation that are *external* to the system or the work being performed, and do not occur all the time; they arise due to special circumstances.[12] An example of special-cause variation would be a nurse who takes significantly longer to triage patients than is typical. This may be caused, for example, by a nurse who is improperly trained on the use of the triage system.

Quality not only means that a process is able to meet target performance on average, but it must accomplish this within certain tolerances and consistency; that is, it must be considered *stable.* A stable process refers to one that is free of special-cause variation. The term "in control" is also used when variations in data are present and exhibit a pattern that is random.[13] (Note that "in control" does not mean an *absence* of variation, since even the best processes will demonstrate some variability.) In addition, a statistically "in control" process may still not be acceptable if the variation falls outside a range that is deemed safe or otherwise acceptable by the HCO, clinical experts, or governing bodies.

One of the tenets of process improvement is that a process must be stable before it can be improved. Strictly speaking, even the act of changing a process from one that is out of statistical control to one that is within statistical control (i.e., with reduced variability in the output of the process) can be considered an improvement.

Almost every report showing any metric will display some variability in the performance of a process. No process in healthcare is so stable that it is able to produce the same results every single time. The question is how to determine how much variability in a process is too much, and how much is acceptable. Statistical process control (SPC) is a technique that QI teams use to improve, evaluate, predict, and control process through control charts.[14] In essence, an SPC chart is the chronological time series plot of an indicator, metric, or other important variable and is used for, among other things, analyzing the occurrence of variations within a process. Many statistics can be plotted on an SPC chart, including averages, proportions, rates, or other quantities of interest.[15]

Rather than simply plotting values on a graph, one of the unique components of SPC charts is the addition of upper and lower reference thresholds, which are called *control limits.* The control limits are calculated based on the process data itself; the plotted points of data must almost always fall within the control limit boundaries, as the control limits specify the natural range of variation within the data. Points falling outside of the control limit boundaries "may indicate that all data were not produced by the same process, either because of a lack of standardization or because a change in the process may have occurred."[16] When looking for changes in performance, then, a reduction in variation and/or a deliberate and consistent shift to values near (or outside of) the control limits may signal that changes in a process are occurring.

Statistical Process Control Chart Basics

Many analytics tools with even basic visualization capabilities can be used to generate SPC and run charts. There are some stand-alone software tools (as well as plug-ins for Microsoft Excel) that can generate excellent SPC and run charts (and provide other visualization tools for quality and performance improvement). Even without dedicated SPC generation capabilities, very useful charts similar to SPC charts can be generated with the basic graphics capabilities of most analytics and business intelligence software provided that the basics of SPC charts are understood (and a little creativity is applied).

> **Tip**
>
> For a list of software tools that can be used to generate SPC and run charts, and examples on how to build them, please visit this book's web site at http://HealthcareAnalyticsBook.com.

See Figure 9.2 for a sample control chart. The important features of control charts are:

- **Data points** that represent a quality or performance indicator associated with a process (and may be a statistic such as mean or proportion).
- A **centerline (CL)** that is drawn at the mean value of the statistic.
- An **upper control limit (UCL)** and **lower control limit (LCL)**, which represent the values outside which performance of the process is considered statistically unlikely.

The centerline of a control chart is drawn at the mean ($\bar{x}$) or average value of the observations being plotted. Upper and lower control limits are typically drawn at $+3\sigma$ and -3σ (where σ is one standard deviation) from the centerline. The sample SPC chart in Figure 9.2 demonstrates a process that would generally be considered to be in control. All the data points are randomly scattered around the mean ($\bar{x} = 9.20$) and all fall within the upper control limit (UCL = CL+3σ = 9.47) and the lower control limit (LCL = CL -3σ = 8.94).

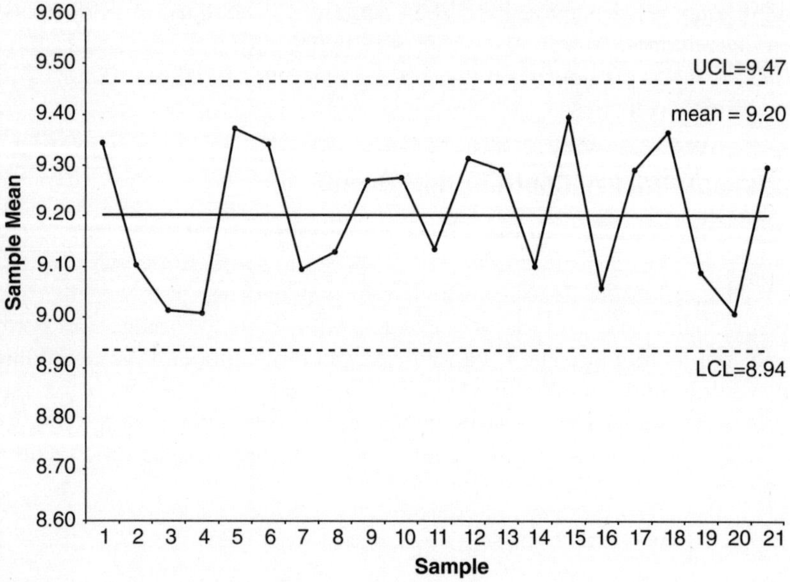

FIGURE 9.2 Sample Control Chart

When a change in process occurs as the result of a QI activity (or some other cause of change), the SPC chart can be used to monitor if a change in performance and/or outcomes has occurred. The limits of an SPC chart should be revised when the existing limits are no longer relevant or useful. When a shift in process occurs, it is helpful to reset the mean and control limit lines to better isolate the new process from the old process in the chart. If new mean and control limits are not reset, the existing mean and control limits will expand (or otherwise adjust) as new data is added to the calculations. This may make it more difficult to identify any actual change in outcomes or performance.

Figure 9.3 illustrates an updated version of the Figure 9.2 chart, this time with new data points added after a process change, and with the new mean and control limits added. With this chart, the baseline performance is shown, the time at which the new process was introduced is clearly evident, and the performance of the new process stands out from the baseline data. When the SPC chart is drawn in this way, the new performance can be evaluated not only to see if the desired target performance is being met but also to investigate the stability of the new process and whether it is in control.

Data Considerations for Statistical Process Control Charts

As mentioned earlier, when developing analytics for quality and performance improvement, it is important to use the right data, and that the

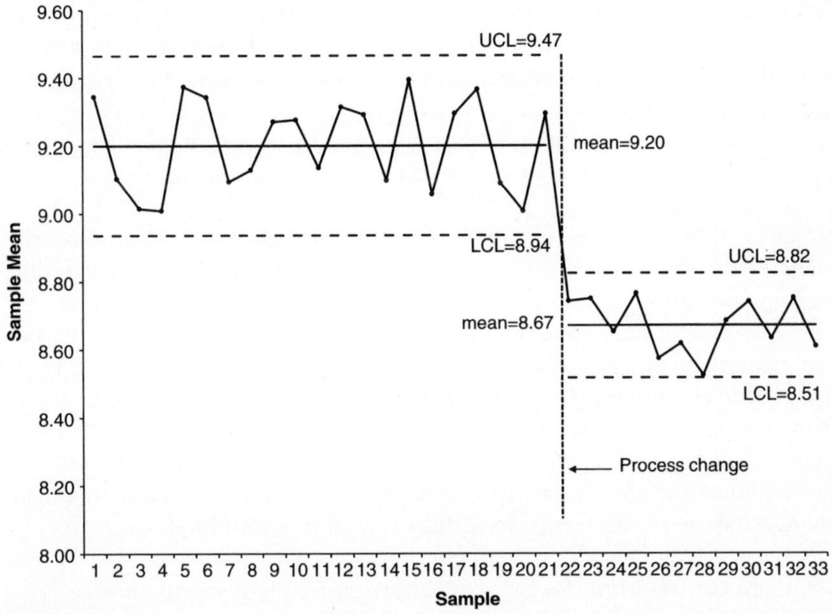

FIGURE 9.3 Sample Control Chart Highlighting Performance before and after a Change in Process

underlying assumptions of any statistical test or other tool are being met, otherwise inaccurate results are possible. SPC charts are no different; there are a few data considerations to ensure that SPC charts are accurate and that any conclusions drawn from them are valid.

When obtaining data for SPC charts, it is recommended that there be a minimum of 20 to 30 consecutive subgroups,[17] which are comprised of at least 100 consecutive observations.[18] For example, if the sample SPC chart in Figure 9.2 was evaluating the emergency department LOS for patients to be admitted, it would be ideal to plot at least 100 admissions over a period of 20 days for optimal validity of the control chart. In this example, assuming that there are at least five admissions from the emergency department every day, each subgroup would be the average LOS for admitted patients over a 20-day period. The mean for each subgroup would be plotted on the *y* axis, and each day would be plotted *in chronological order* along the *x* axis. This number of observations is necessary because, as in most evaluation methods, insufficient data may lead to inaccurate results.

Graphically Displaying the Stability of a Process

As long as the basic data requirements are met, a change in process can be quite clearly identified on an SPC chart. It takes more than simply "eyeballing" it, however, to determine a change in performance or to detect undesirable variations and trends in the data. Figure 9.4 outlines a set of rules that can be used to determine the stability of a process based on data plotted on a control chart. The rules help quality teams to interpret the process patterns on the charts, specifically to special causes of variation. Figure 9.5 is a visual representation of the rules specified in Figure 9.4.

Different patterns that manifest on control charts may signal different issues or different causes of variation. In manufacturing and other industries, many of the rules help detect problems with machinery and other manufacturing issues. Healthcare is in many ways much more complex than manufacturing, so changes in control charts may be caused by any number of reasons. For example, a single point above the UCL (or below the LCL) may indicate that a single abnormality occurred that day (with possible causes ranging from a multicasualty incident causing a surge of patients at the emergency department to a lab equipment glitch requiring all blood work to be redone).

Some of the indications in Figure 9.4 and Figure 9.5 that a significant change has occurred or a process may not be in control include:

- Eight (or more) points in a row above or below the centerline
- Four of five points between $+1\sigma$ and $+2\sigma$ (or -1σ and -2σ)
- Two of three points between $+2\sigma$ and the UCL (or -2σ and the LCL)
- Any one point above the UCL or below the LCL

When reviewing SPC charts, the important point to remember is that any time the chart stops exhibiting random variation and patterns begin to manifest in one or more of the ways described, it is an indication that *something* is causing a process to change, whether as the result of deliberate intention or due to inconsistent practices, performance, or other causes.

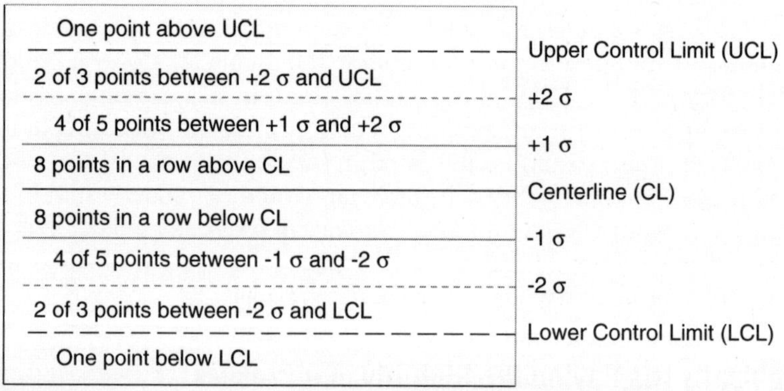

FIGURE 9.4 Detecting Stability in a Process Using Control Charts

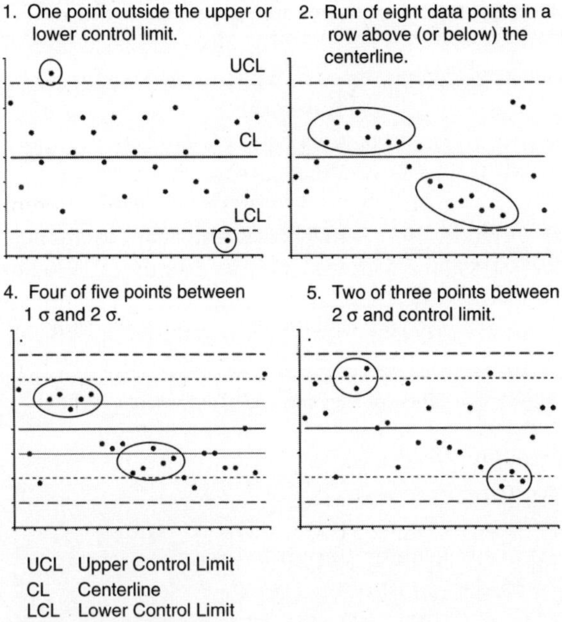
1. One point outside the upper or lower control limit.
UCL
CL
LCL
2. Run of eight data points in a row above (or below) the centerline.
3. Six consecutive points trending upwards or downwards.
4. Four of five points between 1 σ and 2 σ.
5. Two of three points between 2 σ and control limit.
UCL Upper Control Limit
CL Centerline
LCL Lower Control Limit

FIGURE 9.5 Sample SPC Chart Rule Violations

Keep in mind that even though a value is within the UCL and the LCL, it might not be acceptable from a clinical perspective. In addition to the σ and control limit values on an SPC, often a *specification limit* will be added. The specification limit is the range of values that is acceptable to the customer (or, in this case, to the patient and/or best clinical practice guidelines).

Consider, for example, an HCO that is improving its care of patients who experience a stroke. To achieve acceptable clinical standards, the HCO might identify a target duration of three hours from the time a patient experiences a stroke to the time rt-PA is administered. If rt-PA administration times for patients are plotted on an SPC, a specification limit of three hours would be added as a visual indicator. In this case, rt-PA administration times that were within the UCL (meaning within statistical control) but outside of the specification limit would still be a cause for concern. As the assessment and treatment of stroke patients was improved and variation in performance decreased, it is likely that UCL and LCL would tighten to the point where they were inside (or very close to) the specification limit.

Types of Statistical Control Charts

This chapter discusses the fundamentals of SPC charts, and there are actually several different kinds of SPC charts that can be used.

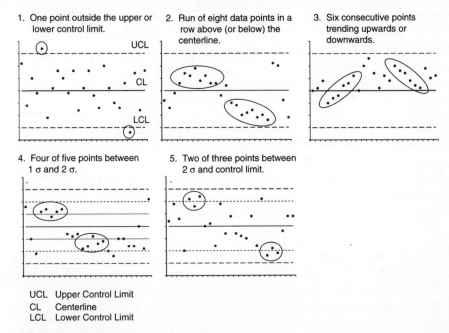

TABLE 9.2 Examples of Common Control Chart Types and How They Are Used

Data Type	Chart Type	Usage
Discrete	P-chart	Percentages
	C-chart	Counts
	U-chart	Rates
	T-chart	Time between rare events
Continuous	I-Chart (Sometimes called X-MR, where MR = moving range)	Individually measured data points
	X-Bar	Subgroups of data at the same point in time

Source: www.qihub.scot.nhs.uk/knowledge-centre/quality-improvement-tools/shewhart-control-charts.aspx.

The selection of a type of control chart depends on several factors,[19] including:

- The type of data being used (continuous versus discrete).
- Sample size available.
- What is being plotted (such as percentages, counts, rates, or time between rare events).

Table 9.2 shows a collection of common control chart types, what type of data they are appropriate for, and how they are used.

A summary of the different types of SPC charts, and a guide to selecting the best one for your particular needs, is downloadable from the book's web site at http://HealthcareAnalyticsBook.com.

Putting It Together

Critical to the development of analytics is the knowledge of who needs to use information, and how they can best make use of it. For example, QI experts working with Six Sigma and other methodologies often use SPC charts and statistical analysis in raw form to study the performance of a process and its resultant quality. In doing so, they are using SPC charts and statistics to analyze one (or a few) process changes in depth to uncover opportunities for further performance improvements and changes in quality. Healthcare executives, managers, and other healthcare leaders, who are usually concerned with the operations of an entire unit, hospital, or system, on the other hand, are not likely to benefit from SPC charts and *t*-tests outlining every performance indicator relevant to a QI activity.

Knowing who needs what kind of information is important to developing effective analytics. Analytics is able to provide deeper insight into the performance of an HCO, and is designed to make decision making easier for QI teams and healthcare leaders. Statistical analysis and SPC charts were invented long before modern analytics. The power of analytics is in the synthesis of information and insight from statistical and graphical analysis into more meaningful and easier-to-interpret formats where appropriate, and presentation of more detailed information when necessary.

Rather than simply displaying a collection of graphs and charts, dashboards and reports can be made more analytical by embedding insights gained from statistical analyses and graphical analysis. Figure 9.6 illustrates a sample dashboard for a diagnostic imaging department displaying several key performance indicators for that unit, baseline performance for the previous six months, the indicators' respective targets, the current month's performance data, the performance for the previous month, and a trendline of performance over the last eight weeks. (See Chapter 10 for a discussion on dashboard and data visualization design.)

The dashboard is a simple representation of these indicators, provides an overview of performance, and also includes embedded insight from both statistical analysis and SPC rules. Using superscript values next to the current month's data and descriptive text in the "Notes" section, the dashboard in Figure 9.6 indicates to the user that there was: (1) a statistically significant difference in performance on indicator A between last month and the current month, and (2) an SPC rule violation for indicator D. The statistically significant ($p < 0.05$) decrease in X-ray order to patient pickup times (indicator A) from the last month to the current month may suggest to QI teams and DI managers that efforts to improve processes associated with indicator A might be having a positive effect.

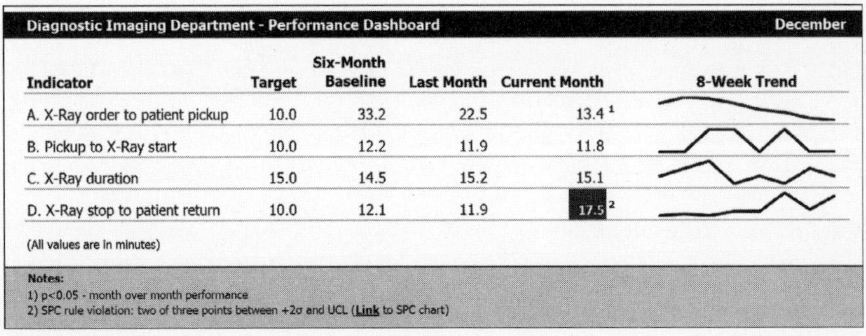
Diagnostic Imaging Department - Performance Dashboard
December
Indicator
Target
Six-Month Baseline
Last Month
Current Month
8-Week Trend
A. X-Ray order to patient pickup
10.0
33.2
22.5
13.4 1
B. Pickup to X-Ray start
10.0
12.2
11.9
11.8
C. X-Ray duration
15.0
14.5
15.2
15.1
D. X-Ray stop to patient return
10.0
12.1
11.9
17.5 2
(All values are in minutes)
Notes:
1) p<0.05 - month over month performance
2) SPC rule violation: two of three points between +2σ and UCL (Link to SPC chart)

FIGURE 9.6 Sample Dashboard Including Embedded Analytics

Although dashboards are often designed to be printed out, they are most useful when designed to be viewed on a screen (such as a computer display, smartphone, or tablet) and interacted with. Such interaction allows users to drill down into more detail (such as to view a control chart for performance indicators), select additional or other indicators to view, and even manipulate date ranges and other dashboard parameters. The example in Figure 9.6 shows that the SPC rule violation alert also includes a link to the actual SPC chart that triggered the violation, so an interested user of this dashboard would be able to launch an additional view that contains the desired additional material. The design objective is that the most important features and insight of this dashboard are immediately visible, with additional detail (links to an SPC chart) available via a simple click.

Statistical and nonstatistical approaches to evaluating quality and performance are not at odds but are entirely complementary. When used in concert, and synthesized on interactive information displays such as dashboards and other analytical tools, users of the information can quickly identify where and when performance needs to be improved, and perhaps even what actions need to be taken.

Developing effective analytical tools does require effort and expertise. Analytical teams must understand the context of the data, know control charts (and their associated performance variation rules are used), and be comfortable in enabling the basic statistical analyses required. Although the mechanics of performing the required statistical analyses and building the appropriate charts, graphs, and other data displays are possible in many analytical tools, it still requires a knowledgeable analytics team working closely in concert with quality and performance improvement experts to design concise and effective analytical information displays that provide insight about quality and performance issues, help suggest appropriate mitigation steps, and monitor ongoing results.

Notes

1. Thomas P. Ryan, *Statistical Methods for Quality Improvement, 3rd ed.* (Hoboken, NJ: John Wiley & Sons, 2011), 9.
2. Michael L. George et al., *The Lean Six Sigma Pocket Toolbook: A Quick Reference Guide to 100 Tools for Improving Speed and Quality* (New York: McGraw-Hill, 2005), 156.
3. Ibid, 161.
4. David Freedman et al., *Statistics*, 2nd ed. (New York: W.W. Norton & Company, 1991), 433–435.
5. Ibid., 348–350.

6. Thomas H. Wonnacott and Ronald J. Wonnacott, *Introductory Statistics*, 5th ed. (New York: John Wiley & Sons, 1990), 325.
7. Glenn J. Myatt, *Making Sense of Data: A Practical Guide to Exploratory Data Analysis and Data Mining* (Hoboken, NJ: John Wiley & Sons, 2007), 67.
8. George et al., *The Lean Six Sigma Pocket Toolbook*, 182.
9. Sandra Murray and Lloyd P. Provost, *The Health Care Data Guide: Learning from Data for Improvement*, Kindle ed. (Hoboken, NJ: John Wiley & Sons, 2011), location 2134.
10. Frederick W. Faltin, Ron S. Kenett, and Fabrizio Ruggeri, eds., *Statistical Methods in Healthcare*, 1st ed. (Hoboken, NJ: John Wiley & Sons, 2011), 253.
11. Gerald .J Langley, Ronald D. Moen, Kevin M. Nolan, Thomas W. Nolan, Clifford L Norman, and Lloyd P. Provost, *The Improvement Guide: A Practical Approach to Enhancing Organizational Performance*, Kindle ed. (Hoboken, NJ: John Wiley & Sons, 2009), locations 1694–1697.
12. Ibid.
13. Issa Bass, *Six Sigma Statistics with Excel and Minitab*, Kindle ed. (New York: McGraw-Hill, 2007), location 2253.
14. ASQ, "Statistical Process Control," http://asq.org/learn-about-quality/statistical-process-control/overview/overview.html.
15. Fatlin, Kenett, and Ruggeri, *Statistical Methods in Healthcare*, 254.
16. Ibid.
17. Murray and Provost, *The Health Care Data Guide,* location 3633.
18. George et al., *The Lean Six Sigma Pocket Toolbook*, 122.
19. NHSScotland Quality Improvement Hub, "Shewhart Control Charts," www.qihub.scot.nhs.uk/knowledge-centre/quality-improvement-tools/shewhart-control-charts.aspx.

CHAPTER 10

Usability and Presentation of Information

[Design is] not just what it looks like and feels like. Design is how it works.

—Steve Jobs

Besides accuracy and timeliness, usability and accessibility are two of the most important qualities of effective analytics. Software that is not easy to use, for example, only results in frustration for the end users, who will then generate countless workarounds to bypass the source of frustration. If, on the other hand, software is easy to use, people are more likely to use the tool more often and be able to focus more on the task at hand. The usability and accessibility of analytics follow very much in the same vein.

One aspect of usability is presentation and visualization of information. Not everyone who needs information and insight for decision making, however, will be directly accessing a portal or other analytical tool, or will be a "professional" analyst used to working with data in multiple formats. Therefore, making the insights generated via analytics more accessible and easy to use by applying best practices in data visualization and presentation helps to ensure that the desired message is communicated clearly and effectively.

Presentation and Visualization of Information

People cannot use information they cannot understand or make sense of. The clear and appropriate use of graphs, charts, and other data visualizations can facilitate understanding of patterns in data, enable rapid evidence-based decision making, and effectively communicate the results of an improvement initiative (especially to people who may not always work with numbers).

Tip

The clear and appropriate use of graphs, charts, and other data visualizations can facilitate the understanding of patterns in data, enable rapid evidence-based decision making, and effectively communicate the outcomes of an improvement initiative.

The inappropriate or incorrect use of data visualization, however, may cause confusion, be misleading, and, in the worst-case scenario, result in unnecessary or inappropriate actions being taken (or necessary actions not being taken). For these reasons, data presentation and visualization is so much more than simply adding "pizzazz" to numbers; data visualization is a critical tool for healthcare analytics in the transformation of healthcare quality and performance.

Tip

Data visualization is more than simply an alternative to presenting data in a table.

Data visualization serves several important quality and performance improvement functions, and is a lot more involved and useful than simply making pretty pictures out of data as an alternative to simply presenting data in tabular form. Data visualization expert Nathan Yau states, "One of the best ways to explore and try to understand a large dataset is with visualization," and that it is possible to "find stories you might never have found with just formal statistical methods."[1]

The many data visualization functions include:

- Identifying trends and signals in quality and performance data.
- Communicating goals, objectives, and targets of the healthcare organization's (HCO's) strategy.
- Sharing results of improvement activities with quality teams, managers, and other stakeholders.
- Making numerical and statistical analyses more user-friendly.

The proper visualization approaches can clearly illustrate where problems in a process or workflow exist, can demonstrate trends, and can be much more intuitive than numbers or statistics alone. One example of the importance of visualization is the graphical analysis inherent in statistical

LEARNING MORE ABOUT DATA VISUALIZATION

For more information about data visualization, including full-color examples and design hints, please visit this book's web site, http://HealthcareAnalyticsBook.com, for additional resources.

process control (SPC) charts (as discussed in Chapter 9). When properly constructed, SPC charts can highlight changes in process performance and identify the need to take corrective action.

What Is Data Visualization?

Data visualization is the process of taking the output from analytical tools and processes (which may be in a raw statistical or numeric form) and visually representing that information in ways that allow decision makers and quality improvement (QI) teams to more easily comprehend and ultimately act on that information.

There are many ways that data may be visualized. Most commonly, visualizations will include charts of various types (such as bar, column, and line charts). Charts may be used on their own, as part of a report, or as a component of a performance dashboard. There are many other ways in which information users can interact with the output of analytics systems as well. As mobile devices such as smartphones and tablets become more ubiquitous and more powerful, many healthcare decision makers are demanding that information be available via these devices. Analytics visualizations implemented on mobile devices range from simple mobile versions of desktop-type reports and dashboards to fully interactive data exploration tools that take full advantage of the unique and powerful user interface capabilities of these devices.

Presenting and Exploring Information Effectively

Up to this point in the book, significant effort has gone into ensuring that high-quality data is available for analytics, and that appropriate analysis is performed on that data to ensure meaningful results. As illustrated in

Data Visualization

Data visualization is the process of taking the output from analytical tools and processes and visually representing that information in ways that allow us to more easily comprehend and ultimately act on that information.

Chapter 6, even basic data visualization in the form of histograms, for example, can help clarify and elucidate patterns in the data that may not appear through statistics alone.

Although healthcare research and the financial management of HCOs have always relied on data and its analysis, there has recently been literally an explosion in the use of data in almost all aspects of management in nearly every industry. This is because the amount of data available is increasing, and the tools to analyze the data have been becoming more powerful and easy to use. As the computational power of information systems has grown, so has their visualization capabilities. Before the advent of high-power graphics on computers, data (and the results of calculations) was most often displayed with simple tables and low-resolution black-and-white charts. Fortunately, we are no longer forced to consume information in this way. The visualization capabilities of most analytics tools, when used effectively, can now make most information easier to understand, especially when coupled with high-resolution digital displays and color printing capabilities.

As already mentioned, visualization is not about how fancy the analysis and reporting of a particular data set can be made to look. In fact, visualizations such as charts, graphs, and other representations overloaded with too much extraneous decoration (such as multiple fonts, colors, pictures, etc.) that do not add clarity to the information being presented actually become a distraction, can make representations look amateurish, and can confuse decision makers. Graphics should serve only to focus attention on the content of the intended message to be conveyed with a visualization. Edward Tufte, a pioneer in effective data visualization, coined the term "chartjunk" for all the extraneous decorations on a graph or chart that actually take away from the message being conveyed.[2]

The starting point for all data visualizations is to determine the message that is to be conveyed by the visualization, then selecting appropriate visualization approaches (such as type of chart) that suit both the message to be conveyed and the audience for whom the message is intended. Visualizations must be selected and drafted very carefully, because they may be viewed by an audience with varied experience in the context both of the data and of the visualizations employed.

Common ways in which visualizations are used are to demonstrate a relationship between data points, show a comparison between data points, illustrate a composition of data, or show a distribution of data,[3] as well as to display a trend over time and to highlight deviation.[4] These points are discussed in the following list.

- **Relationship**—examines if a correlation exists between two or more data points, for example, to see if a relationship exists between time waiting in the waiting room and left-without-being-seen rates.

- **Comparison**—contrasts different variables, for example, the number of admissions to each of a hospital's inpatient units over the last month.
- **Composition**—portrays a complete picture of a variable, for example, a tally of the different surgical procedures performed at an outpatient surgery clinic, or a summary of the different types of lab tests ordered, during a selected reporting period.
- **Distribution**—used to study how data points are distributed throughout a data set, for example, to plot the distribution of response times to an overhead page for an EKG technician, or to examine the wait-time distribution for patients on a surgical waiting list.
- **Trend over time**—used to plot a time series of a variable, for example, the number of patient arrivals to the emergency department, or the number of coronary artery bypass surgeries performed over the last 30 days.
- **Deviation**—used to detect when values deviate from historical or baseline levels, such as when evaluating the outcomes of QI projects and needing to determine if a change in process is having an effect.

> **Tip**
>
> Visualization involves determining the message that is to be conveyed and selecting the appropriate visualization approach that suits both the message and the intended audience.

Dashboards and modern analytics software tend to rely heavily on data visualization for communication of analysis and insights. Because users of information throughout the HCO will have different levels of experience with different types of visualizations, reports and dashboards with fairly widespread distribution must be made clear enough and straightforward enough for the majority of viewers to quickly grasp the point of the visualization. Less common graphing techniques, such as the trellis chart or the box-and-whisker plot, should not distributed in reports or dashboards without a clear explanation of how to interpret such visualizations.

Information Visualization and Graphing

There are myriad ways to display information to support quality and performance improvement, and healthcare decision making in general. In its most basic format, information can be displayed in a simple data table format (the type of report that has been available now for decades). More commonly, information is expressed in a graphical format such as bar charts, scatter plots, histograms, and maps, among many others.

Finding the Right Chart Type

The challenge is not to find a chart type to convey the information to be communicated, but to pick the *right* type for the information you are presenting and the intended audience.

The data visualization capabilities of much analytics and business intelligence (BI) software, and even common spreadsheet software, are rapidly expanding. The few choices that used to be available (such as bar charts, pie charts, and line graphs with a choice of 16 colors) on such tools have now exploded into a veritable arsenal of data visualization tools ranging from box-and-whisker charts and trellis charts to "sparklines" and bullet graphs. The challenge now is not to find a chart type to convey the information to be communicated, but to pick the *right* type for the information you are presenting and its intended audience. Table 10.1 provides a suggested mapping of data visualization techniques such as scatter plot and line chart for the various types of use (such as to display a relationship in data). Keep in mind that these are not hard-and-fast rules, but merely suggestions of what graphing techniques work best for which types of messages to convey. In addition, there are many other types of information display techniques (such as bullet graphs and sparklines) that I have not included in Table 10.1; as display techniques evolve, the list of available options will continue to expand. Remember that even though software vendors may invent creative new ways to display information, always be sure to choose the chart or graph that most clearly conveys the intended message of your information display.

Refer to the book's website at http://HealthcareAnalyticsBook.com for examples of the different chart types listed here (plus several others) and how they can be used to enhance the communication of information.

TABLE 10.1 Suggested Mapping of Information Display Techniques

	Scatter	Line	Bar	Column	Pie	Data Table	SPC	Box Plot
Relationship	✓	✓				✓		
Comparison	✓	✓	✓	✓	✓	✓		
Composition			✓	✓	✓	✓		
Distribution	✓	✓		✓				✓
Trend		✓		✓		✓		
Deviation		✓	✓	✓		✓	✓	

Note that SPC refers to a statistical process control chart, and Box Plot refers to a box-and-whisker plot.

Because of the number of options now available in many tools, the appropriate selection of data visualization is more important than ever. I know that many HCOs have had the experience of developing a dashboard, scorecard, or report that was critical for decision making, only to have it rendered essentially useless due to poor design choices. Any analytics visualization that focuses on "form," such as featuring multiple "gauges," 3-D effects, and unnecessary graphics over the clear, simple, and effective communication of information is likely doomed from the start!

Consider Figure 10.1, which illustrates a chart displaying the average number of X-rays per shift for a diagnostic imaging department. To "pretty up" the chart, a picture of one of the X-ray rooms is layered in the background. To make the picture more visible, a transparency was applied to the bars, which causes them to blend into the background—a poor design choice, given that the information presented via the bars (the average number of X-rays) is the reason this chart was created in the first place! To make matters worse, the designer of this chart included a pie chart to highlight the percentage of portable X-rays performed (the dark slice) versus the non-portable X-rays (the light slice). Even though the intent of adding the image, adjusting the bars' transparency, and including the pie charts is to make the chart more "interesting" and to convey more information, the actual effect is to make the information harder to understand. The exact same information is conveyed in Figure 10.2, which is not as visually distracting, thereby allowing users of the information to make sense of it more quickly and easily. Figure 10.2 very clearly shows that, on average, the 0700–1500 shift

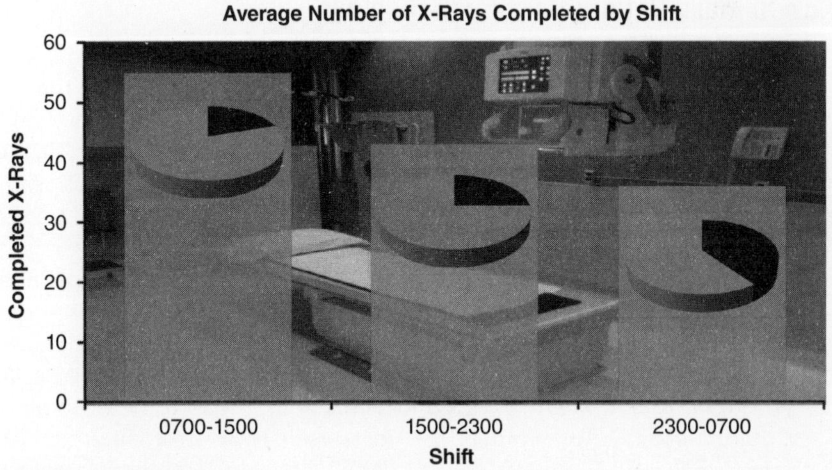

FIGURE 10.1 Sample of a Chart Exhibiting "Chartjunk"

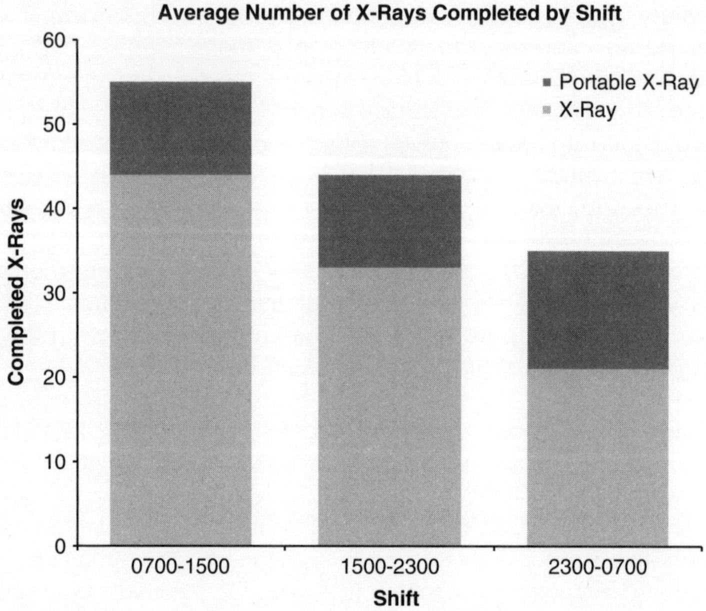

FIGURE 10.2 Sample of a Chart with "Chartjunk" Removed

performs the most X-rays, and that proportionately more portable X-rays are performed during the 2300–0700 shift.

How to Make Better Information Displays

It can be very frustrating to decision makers and other users of analytics when it is difficult to interpret or otherwise use the information that is contained on a chart. The causes of poor chart usability have been studied and grouped into types of problems that can negatively impact on the chart's ability convey the message intended.[5] A few examples of the types of problems identified are:

- **Explanation.** Some data element or other component is not explained (i.e., no definitions or descriptions are provided).
- **Discrimination.** Discrimination issues occur when items on the charts are not easily distinguished, such as charts designed for color but printed out in black and white, or symbols made too small to be readable.
- **Construction.** The layout of the chart itself is in error, such as tick marks that are incorrectly spaced, labels that are incorrect, incorrect scales, and other similar issues.

Many of these issues are illustrated in Figure 10.1. In particular, there is no explanation as to what the pie charts represent and the key information in the chart is difficult to discriminate because the bars have a transparency applied and tend to blend into the background.

In addition to the major problems to avoid that are given in the previous list, there are other tips that can greatly improve the usability of charts.[6] Some of these tips include:

- Make the data stand out (after all, it is the entire point of the chart).
- Do not clutter the data region—any additional "decoration" in the data region will detract from the overall message of the data.
- Use reference lines when appropriate.
- Strive for clarity—above everything else, the chart should be made as clear as possible so that the person looking at the chart does not need to work hard to clearly understand the message.

Don't let information presentation and visualization be the Achilles' heel of your analytics system. I have seen too many great analyses and insights ruined because somebody elected to use the default chart settings on a spreadsheet program or because somebody tried to show all the possible 3-D widgets on a single performance dashboard. A lot of time and effort goes into cleaning data, preparing metrics, designing reports, and building dashboards—spend the extra bit of time required to ensure that the intended message of a chart or other visualization is clear and that nothing in it detracts from that message.

Dashboards for Quality and Performance Improvement

The increasing pace with which decision makers and QI leaders must make decisions demands new compact methods of presenting information that enable more efficient synthesis of information and decision support. Computerized dashboards are now a very common approach with which to assemble the most important performance and quality information into a compact, accessible, and understandable format for decision makers.

Unfortunately, the term "dashboard" is perhaps one of the most abused words in data visualization today. It seems as though almost every executive, manager, and other decision maker wants a dashboard for their own particular use consisting of data that is uniquely important to them. Eager to comply, health information technology services and dashboard developers are happy to assemble a mash-up of the requested charts, tables, and gauges and deploy it, often without consideration of what other dashboards and visualizations are necessary or available.

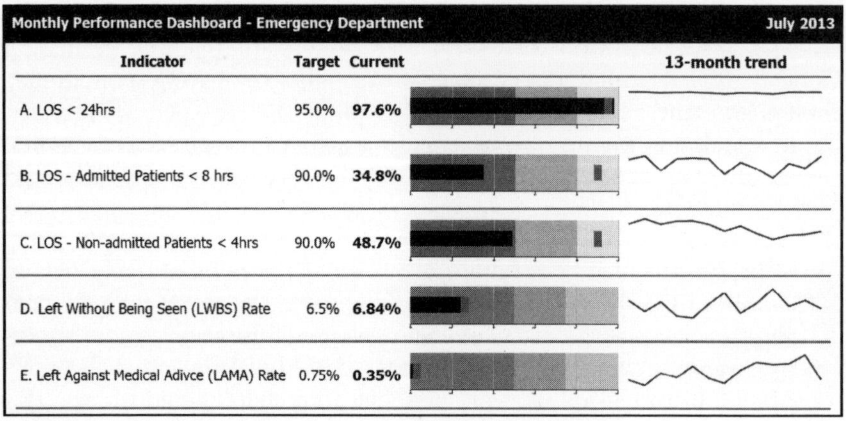
Monthly Performance Dashboard - Emergency Department
July 2013
Indicator
Target
Current
13-month trend
A. LOS < 24hrs
95.0%
97.6%
B. LOS - Admitted Patients < 8 hrs
90.0%
34.8%
C. LOS - Non-admitted Patients < 4hrs
90.0%
48.7%
D. Left Without Being Seen (LWBS) Rate
6.5%
6.84%
E. Left Against Medical Adivce (LAMA) Rate
0.75%
0.35%

FIGURE 10.3 Sample Performance Dashboard

One of the best definitions of the term *dashboard* that I've come across and use to guide my own work is from Stephen Few, who states that "a dashboard is a visual display of the most important information needed to achieve one or more objectives, consolidated and arranged on a single screen so the information can be monitored at a glance."[7] By this definition, it is important (and essential) to see that dashboards are much more than a simple collection of charts, graphs, and numbers.

Most decision makers and QI facilitators request dashboards as a tool with which to quickly assimilate information, to determine if problems exist and where those problem areas are, and to guide decision making. Although some dashboards are primarily numerical, the power of dashboards is that they are highly graphical, compact, and can often communicate insight more effectively and efficiently than numbers and text alone, or more traditional report formats.

Dashboard

"A dashboard is a visual display of the most important information needed to achieve one or more objectives, consolidated and arranged on a single screen so the information can be monitored at a glance."

Despite the promise of information clarity and superior usability offered by dashboards, many have the opposite effect and serve only to confuse the user. That is why special attention must be paid to how the information will be used, how that information will be perceived, and what design elements are most appropriate for communicating the intended message. Dashboards do not have to be cute, but they must be functional.

See Figure 10.3 for a sample dashboard that highlights five basic performance indicators for a notional emergency department. The dashboard combines numeric and graphical elements that highlight current performance and compares it against the organization's past performance. To illustrate the emergency department's performance on each indicator over a 13-month period (July 2012 through to July 2013, inclusive), the dashboard uses a graphing technique known as "sparklines," which are in essence mini–line graphs without axes or value labels. Sparklines are useful when you need to communicate previous performance trends on a dashboard but not the actual values. Intended to be condensed, data-intense, and simple in design, the purpose of sparklines is to provide a historical context of performance data; additional details can be provided in supplemental graphs or reports.[8] In this case, adding a complete line graph for each indicator would both consume valuable space on the dashboard, and be unnecessary because the trends are clearly visible without axes and labels present. The dashboard in Figure 10.3 also uses a bullet chart to illustrate the percent of cases that achieved or exceeded performance targets. Bullet charts are designed to "display a key measure, along with a comparative measure and qualitative ranges to instantly declare if the measure is good, bad, or in some other state."[9] Bullet charts consist of a series of background colors or shades that denote performance ranges such as "bad," "satisfactory," and "good." Bullet charts also include a marker that identifies the target value or comparative measure and the main bar itself that encodes the performance measure in question.

The purpose of a dashboard is to achieve one or more objectives, and therefore it should not be splattered with every indicator and data element available. This will reduce usability and perhaps lead to information overload. If dashboards are to serve for quality and performance improvement purposes, the information relayed on them must be related to this purpose. This means ensuring that true performance indicators and other measures related to QI are the sole focus of specific dashboards.

Tip

If a piece of information does not highlight a problem or impending issue, suggest a course of action, or evaluate the outcome, then the information should not be on the dashboard.

In my experience, building a special-purpose dashboard requires a focus on the specific indicators needed to monitor and evaluate a QI project. This focus in turn helps keep the QI team focused on the activities necessary to

> There are many outstanding books, web sites, and other resources on the topic of effective dashboards. For a comprehensive listing of excellent resources on the design, development, and deployment of dashboards for quality and performance improvement, please visit this book's web site at http://HealthcareAnalyticsBook.com.

achieve the project goal, since the indicators serve as a reminder of what is necessary and important. QI dashboards that serve HCO administrators can replicate key project-specific indicators to allow a visual glance of how each individual QI project is performing.

Dashboards should fit on a single screen, on the reasoning that all the information a user needs to make a decision on an issue is available at a single glance. This is an important consideration; if a dashboard spans several computer screens or several printed pages, then you've created a report. I certainly do not disparage reports; however, if the need is for a single at-a-glance collection of key information required for decision making, then stick to a single-page dashboard.

A well-designed dashboard, or a series of dashboards, can be an invaluable tool for improving quality. With the right metrics defined, proper targets identified, and necessary action triggers, a dashboard can provide true insight into the performance of an organization. It is critical, though, that as much thought and design effort go into building dashboards that truly facilitate an analytical view as went into identifying quality goals, indicators, and targets in the first place.

Dashboard Design Hints

Dashboard deployment projects seem deceptively simple, yet often result in something less than useful. In my experience, a few critical success factors are necessary to create truly useful dashboards that support decision making and taking action to improve quality and performance:

- **Focus on the indicators that are most critical to quality.** Quality dashboards should include only those indicators that are aligned with the quality goals of the organization, or are essential to the ongoing monitoring and evaluation of current improvement projects. Information not directly relevant may still be important, but probably belongs somewhere else such as a separate dashboard or supplemental report.
- **Display appropriate indicators.** When displaying indicators on dashboards, be sure to select visualization approaches that allow important

information to "pop out." For example, drawing a simple line graph of a quality indicator may not be as clear as displaying information as a deviation from a target value. Because there may be multiple indicators on a dashboard, the information necessary to make a decision must be made as salient as possible.

- **Don't be afraid to develop multiple dashboards.** Too much information crammed onto a dashboard simply to meet the one-page definition only leads to confusion and greatly decreases overall usability of the dashboard.
- **Avoid all unnecessary clutter and decoration.** Many dashboard tools are offering more and more "eye candy," such as 3-D charts and fancy gauges, yet do not provide a strong suite of tools to draw simpler but more visually effective information displays such as bar charts and line charts, and lack support for truly innovative and effective information display tools such as bullet charts.
- **Include end users in the design of dashboards.** End users must be involved in the design of dashboards, because ultimately they are the ones who will be using the information on them to make decisions. Dashboards may lack relevance and decision-making impact without the consultation of end users.
- **Make the dashboard as visually appealing as possible.** Although in previous points I have stated that the dashboard designers should avoid trying to be cute or fancy in their designs because these elements detract from information usability, dashboards should still be visually appealing (even if it's in a plain vanilla sort of way). I am sure that everyone has seen dashboards that are strikingly ugly. Even though everybody has different tastes when it comes to design, by following the design guides for data visualization listed elsewhere in this book, and using common sense, it is possible to design a dashboard that is attractive, functional, and relevant to the quality and performance initiatives it is built to support.

With the goal of keeping dashboards on-message, Stephen Few has identified a library of essential display media components for the display and/or highlighting of data on dashboards. The components identified by Few consist of graphs/charts, images, icons, drawing objects, text, and organizers.[10] The most common of these are described in the following list.

- **Graphs.** The most common display media due to the preponderance of quantitative data to be analyzed and shared, the appropriate graph or chart to be used must match the type of data being graphed and the purpose for which the information will be used.

- **Icons**. Icons are simple images with a clear meaning whose job it is to showcase certain information and highlight trends within a dashboard; simple shapes such as circles, squares, and triangles often work best and do not contribute to clutter or chartjunk when used appropriately.
- **Text**. Although by their nature dashboards are designed to be primarily graphical, text is useful for communicating information that may not be suitable for graphical representation (for example, when reporting a single stand-alone measure or value that is not compared to other values, and for labeling chart axes).
- **Images**. In some cases, an image such as a diagram or photo on a dashboard can help clarify or highlight information (for example, a unit's floor plan that indicates which rooms need cleaning), but images should never be used purely for decoration.

See the book's website at http://HealthcareAnalyticsBook.com for examples of these various media and how they can be used to enhance information displays on dashboards.

Agents and Alerts

Another factor that enhances the usability of analytics is automation. Currently, much of healthcare analytics is "self-serve" or "push." Self-serve requires users to go get the information that they need to make a decision (such as run a report, or view a dashboard), they may not be inclined to do so (because they are too busy, don't like the tools, or for any number of other reasons). Self-serve BI and analytics is ideal because it eliminates the dependency on analysts and developers to constantly run data requests; people can get what they need on their own.

Some people, however, just don't want to get information on their own, or may need to be alerted when a condition has changed. Analytics "push" may risk turning decision makers and other information users into passive recipients of information. Many busy people in healthcare prefer to get daily statistics, dashboard updates, and other information delivered into their e-mail in-box. The downside of "push" is that people may tend to tune out information deliveries (that is, reports and dashboards in their in-box)

> Real-time data systems now make it possible to create meaningful alerts that can notify decision makers when certain conditions are being met.

if it's always the same information that is received. I have seen many cases where managers, executives, and other users of information within an HCO come to rely on the push of information, and lose the ability (or sometimes the interest) to access the analytics portal and to query information sources themselves.

It is ideal when decision makers are notified when a situation warrants attention instead of being consistently flooded with information. Real-time data systems now make it possible to create meaningful alerts that can notify decision makers when certain conditions are being met or specific situations arise. When alerts are used appropriately, executives, managers, quality teams, and others can be notified of these situations using e-mail, paging, messaging, or other means. This prevents them from having to continually monitor performance dashboards, and reduces the risk of missing something important when issues do arise.

In essence, alerts (or "agents") programmed to detect certain predefined conditions or to execute certain business rules scan available real-time data, or repositories of retrospective data, for instances that violate a business rule or predefined condition. These types of agents require data that can be used to calculate the business rules, and such data must be updated frequently. The data available, and the frequency at which it is refreshed, greatly impacts the complexity of the rules that can be executed and how often they can be run.

Some of the uses that I have seen alerts employed for include:

- Identifying patients for inclusion in clinical research studies (by comparing presenting medical conditions, prior history, and other data with study inclusion requirements) and notifying researchers and/or intake nurses; and
- Alerting executives when excessive ambulance offload delays are occurring (by calculating the length of delays based on arrival time).

Although alerts can provide very timely information to executives to allow for quick action to be taken, alerts are not a solution for everything. A few things to consider are:

- People quickly become "alert fatigued"; ensure that alerts are truly the best way to induce action; otherwise, too many alerts will lead to them just being ignored.
- Send alerts to the real decision makers; if alerts are sent to delegates without decision-making authority, the alerts may not be triggering timely enough action.
- Ensure alerts are accurate; decision makers do not want to be woken at 3 a.m. because a data glitch inadvertently triggered the alert.

Providing Accessibility to and Ensuring Usability of Analytics Systems

Most BI suites offer a portal-type interface where users can navigate throughout a file structure (similar to most computer operating systems) or more intuitive and interactive web-based interface to find the reports or other information they need. This is fine so long as the number of folders, files, reports, agents, and analytic applications remains manageable and well organized. Much like on any computer, however, as the number of resources needed to be organized increases, the more difficult it is to keep the structure logical and easy to navigate. The additional challenge with an analytics or BI portal is that the navigation structure is usually somebody else's idea—or, perhaps worse, is designed by committee—and so it may not be easy to remember or may not even make any sense to the person who did not design it.

As the information needs of an HCO expand, so do their existing analytics and reporting portals. This may have a very negative impact on usability; if users need to spend a lot of time searching for the report, dashboard, or analysis that they need, they either will find some other source of information, or, more likely, will contact the analytics team to find (and execute) the report they were looking for in the first place. This second scenario is especially wasteful given that it consumes both the decision maker's *and* the analyst's time with a request that should have taken almost no time at all.

One of the ideals of BI and analytics is "self-serve," where decision makers and other users who need information from dashboards, reports, or other analytical applications can access the tools within a portal or some other repository, run the application or dashboard, and retrieve the data they require. The win-win for self-serve is that people who need information can get it when they need it, without relying on an analyst to pull it for them. The analytics professionals are thus freed to put effort into building even better self-serve tools and to work on solving more in-depth problems than simple data requests.

The two main barriers to self-serve are poorly designed portals (as described above) and reports and other tools that take a very long time to run. A few enhancements to most analytics portals can greatly improve their usability and their utilization within the HCO. A few of the enhancements I would suggest include:

- Organize the portal effectively
- Provide comprehensive documentation
- Reduce/reuse
- Minimize runtime

Organize effectively. Although everybody thinks and organizes information differently, try to organize the portal logically; for example, organize based on quality goals and other groupings of strategic interest to the organization. For example, grouping dashboards, scorecards, reports, and other analytics tools by functional area, strategic objectives, or even tactical projects would be a format that most end users of the information would understand. But I would avoid groupings that make sense only to the developer (such as grouping by request date, or by original requestor).

Provide documentation. Users need to know how the analytics portal is organized. Ensure that comprehensive documentation is available (in either downloadable form or an online "wiki" format) that clearly outlines how the portal, data warehouse, or other repository is structured; what resources and reports are available and what information they provide; and how to run available reports and tools.

Some strategies that I have seen to improve the ease of navigation through analytics portals include a web page on the opening screen that includes quick highlights (for example, a "what's new"), a frequently asked questions (FAQ) section, and quick links to the most commonly needed dashboards, scorecards, reports, and other tools.

Reduce/reuse. One of the factors that decreases usability is the sheer number of reports and other tools that are available within a repository. Chances are that not all of those are active; those that haven't been run in a year or two, or are otherwise clear, can probably be removed from the repository. Try to reduce the number of reports by consolidating; many reports within a repository are likely variations on a theme. If there are many similar reports, for example, group them into a single report but create a user interface that allows for users to select which data items they need; this will allow users to run the report and retrieve only the information they require.

Minimize runtime. Another barrier to self-serve and analytics usability is the runtime of some reports, scorecards, and other analytics tools—especially if they are running on data that is not preaggregated and in which the server must process each record individually as part of the calculations. Needless to say, there are numerous reasons analytics tools run slowly, ranging from issues with the way the report is programmed to network latency and database indexing and other optimization issues. Analytics team members may need to work with additional technical specialists (such as database administrators) to help identify root causes of slowly performing analytics and to identify solutions.

These tips represent mitigations to the most common usability issues that I have seen regarding the use of analytics and BI portals. Overall, analytics teams need to be aware that how the information is made available in portals or other means impacts the usability of that information, and should strive to develop as intuitive, clutter-free, and easy-to-navigate analytics portals as possible.

Notes

1. Nathan Yau, *Visualize This* (Hoboken, NJ: John Wiley & Sons, 2011), xvi.
2. Edward R. Tufte, *The Visual Display of Quantitative Information*, 2nd ed. (Cheshire, CT: Graphics Press, 2001), 107.
3. Alan Henry, "How to Choose the Best Chart for Your Data," Lifehacker.com, November 5, 2012, http://lifehacker.com/5909501/how-to-choose-the-best-chart-for-your-data.
4. "How to Select the Right Chart for your Data," Chandoo.com, April 19, 2010, http://chandoo.org/wp/2010/04/19/chart-selection-process.
5. William S. Cleveland, *The Elements of Graphing Data*, rev. ed. (Summit, NJ: Hobart Press, 1994).
6. Ibid.
7. Stephen Few, "Dashboard Confusion," *Intelligent Enterprise*, March 20, 2004.
8. Stephen Few, *Information Dashboard Design: The Effective Visual Communication of Data* (Sebastopol, CA: O'Reilly Media, 2006), 140.
9. Ibid., 126.
10. Ibid., 124.

CHAPTER 11

Advanced Analytics in Healthcare

The best way to predict the future is to invent it.

—Alan Kay

Analytical systems have the potential to provide healthcare leaders much more information and understanding of their organizations than simply reporting on past or current performance. In fact, just knowing what has happened is usually not enough to make transformational decisions. Healthcare decision makers must now leverage the growing volumes of data being collected by electronic medical records and other systems to gain insight into future performance and resource requirements. This is now possible by using advanced analytical tools that apply algorithms and other mathematical methods to better understand how quality and performance are likely to vary given a change in process, policy, or patient need. This chapter will discuss the tools and techniques commonly associated with data mining and "predictive analytics," identify where these algorithms can be employed within a healthcare setting, and uncover obstacles and pitfalls associated with relying on computerized prediction models.

Overview of Advanced Analytics

Because the use of data mining, text mining, and predictive algorithms is relatively new in healthcare, healthcare organizations (HCOs) are at different stages of their use of predictive and other advanced analytics. Most HCOs are likely in the early stages of using these types of analytics, while HCOs at the other end of the spectrum may be using data mining and predictive analytics in everyday clinical decision making and management.

A NOTE ON TERMINOLOGY

Although I use the terms "predictive analytics" and "advanced analytics" interchangeably at times in this chapter, "predictive analytics" refers specifically to the tools and algorithms used to analyze historical data to make an inference, or prediction, about future performance. My use of the broader term "advanced analytics" encompasses all the various analytics tools and techniques that can be used to identify patterns in and learn from healthcare databases, including those used for data mining, prediction, and other applications.

Most HCOs, however, are likely somewhere between these two extremes. This section of the book will be helpful to HCOs at all stages of adopting advanced analytics to discover new knowledge within their databases, to improve management decision making, and to better anticipate and achieve the clinical needs of patients.

Advanced analytics in general, and predictive analytics in particular, are not comprised of a singular "predictive" approach or algorithm but rather a collection of methods and techniques that must be used in concert to achieve the goal of learning from data and determining outcomes. Considered a branch of artificial intelligence, these tools and techniques build on the fundamentals of several disciplines, including computer science, computer engineering, and statistics. To be sure, predictive analytics capabilities are becoming much more accessible to analysts in many types of organizations, including healthcare. That is because several of the key factors that enable predictive analytics are now making their use more feasible. The goal of predicting outcomes, however, is not new to healthcare. The field of epidemiology, for example, has long sought both to *describe* the patterns of the occurrence of disease in populations and to *analyze* those patterns, "with the ultimate goal of judging whether a particular exposure causes or prevents disease."[1] In other words, given an exposure to a certain substance or environment, we would like to be able to predict the likelihood of an individual developing a certain outcome (i.e., disease).

Improving healthcare quality and performance is a long-term endeavor that requires information and insight to guide decision making. Simply knowing "what happened," however, is not enough to make the decisions and take the actions necessary to transform healthcare. By leveraging existing business intelligence (BI) infrastructure and systems within an organization, advanced analytics tools can help focus an HCO's improvement efforts through deep analysis of available healthcare data, identifying patterns and discovering knowledge contained within that data, determining the best opportunities

> Improving healthcare quality and performance is a long-term endeavor that requires information and insight to guide decision making.

for improvement, and evaluating the effectiveness of implemented process changes. When deployed at the point of care, advanced analytics can directly support decision making about the care of patients.

Many clinicians, administrators, and analysts are understandably excited about the promise and potential of predictive analytics and the underlying algorithms and systems that make it possible. Unfortunately the technology and the associated challenges that are inherent in using predictive analytics to enable healthcare transformation are often not well understood.

Predictive analytics uses various machine learning and statistical approaches to "characterize historical information, which then can be used to predict the nature and likelihood of future events or occurrences . . . so that we will have a chance to alter the future and prevent something bad."[2] In other words, the goal of predictive analytics is to develop and use algorithms that can analyze large volumes of data to determine trends and patterns in the past performance of an HCO, and in turn use that insight to predict future trends and patterns.

Predictive analytics has much in common with *data mining*; in fact, data mining has a strong predictive component. The two disciplines are closely related and both employ sophisticated mathematical and statistical approaches to analyze large volumes of data. Many of the analytical techniques within these two disciplines are similar, with both applying the process of analyzing large data sets in the search for useful patterns. More formally, data mining is described as "the analysis of (often large) observational data sets to find unsuspected relationships and to summarize the data in novel ways that are both understandable and useful to the data owner."[3]

Data mining is often the first step in developing predictive analytics, and comprises what is known as *data discovery*. Data mining can be used to examine data and uncover patterns that may not be previously known to or easily determined by human analysts. Predictive analytics, using many of the same algorithms as data mining, often applies patterns detected and quantified in the data by data mining efforts to make predictions regarding future performance or outcomes.

For example, data mining techniques can analyze large volumes of data looking for relationships between health conditions (for example, coronary disease or diabetes) and associated outcomes (such as hospital admissions or death) and discover within the data possible predictor variables associated with these conditions and outcomes. An analyst in turn can leverage the patterns uncovered with data mining to develop algorithms and analytical tools that can be applied to patient data to predict likely outcomes or other events directly related to the care of patients, or even determine with some accuracy proper medication doses and treatment protocols at the point of care.[4]

Applications of Advanced Analytics

Advanced analytics has potential for use in many different realms of healthcare, ranging from clinical and operations research to point-of-care clinical decision support, plus many other administrative and planning functions. Several such sample applications of advanced analytics include:

- **Clinical decision support.** This involves providing evidence to support decision making by clinicians, and has many facets including:
  - Providing real-time point-of-care information and insight;
  - Suggesting possible diagnoses given ambiguous symptoms, incomplete history, or other missing data; and
  - Predicting likely patient outcomes (e.g., admission, long stay) given the past history of a patient (and of similar patients).
- **Population health management.** Determining the most effective interventions and prevention practices for high-risk patients to prevent future adverse health events.
- **Administration and planning.** Providing the ability to peer into the future of a healthcare facility to understand likely resource requirements, including staffing levels, bed requirements, and service availability (such as diagnostic imaging).
- **Fraud prevention.** Using algorithms to detect patterns in past data consistent with likely fraudulent behavior, and applying that knowledge in real time to identify and flag suspect claims transactions and other suspicious activity *before* any money is dispensed.

Another application of advanced analytical techniques in healthcare is text mining. Electronic medical records (EMRs) often store data that is structured, numerical, historical, codified, and thus fairly easily analyzed. A significant amount of data, however, is in an unstructured format. Unstructured data is typically text-based data that is input as part of progress notes or other documentation, and is very difficult to analyze using standard methods. Unstructured data nonetheless is still a very important part of the medical record and contains significant value. Text mining algorithms are becoming more common to analyze unstructured healthcare data by converting the textual data into more structured, even numerical, formats, and rendering the information easier to analyze.[5]

Enablers of Predictive Analytics in Healthcare

Although many of the statistical methods for predictive analytics have been around for a long time, there are several key enabling factors that have paved the way for the recent advancement of predictive analytics in healthcare. These enablers include methods, data, and systems.

- **Methods.** The statistical models and algorithms used for predictive analytics are constantly evolving and improving; "classical" methods such as regression modeling are being used alongside (and in some cases replaced by) newer machine-learning algorithms.
- **Data.** The continued expansion in EMR use is providing the volumes of data necessary to develop, train, and validate statistical models and predictive algorithms without having to resort to manual data collection methods (such as chart pulls).
- **Software.** Predictive analytics capabilities are being built into more types of software, and are becoming easier to use.

METHODS Predictive analytics is itself not a single algorithm or formula, but a family or collection of methods developed from fields such as statistics, computer engineering, and computer science. Many of the statistical methods used for predictive analytics have been around since the advent of modern statistics. However, these methods traditionally were not accessible to people who did not possess some degree of training in statistics. In the not-so-distant past statistics was a bit of a dirty word that scared many people off. (Who could have guessed that by 2012 "data scientist" would be considered a "sexy" job?[6])

In addition to increasing volumes of data, and the increasing accessibility of software to perform the analysis required of advanced analytics, the analytical methods of prediction have themselves been evolving. At one time, predictive models were primarily statistical in nature (for example, based on linear or logistical regression and other statistical approaches). With the advent of computer science and related disciplines, other techniques have become available for use in predictive analytics (such as artificial neural networks and decision trees). Although such a wide array of models to choose from might at first seem dizzying, it does mean that there are more choices from which to select an approach that is appropriate for the problem (and constraints) at hand.

DATA Before healthcare information systems and accessible databases were available, the data necessary to conduct research and develop relevant models was exceedingly hard to obtain—it usually took a lot of manual effort to gather the data in the quantities required to generate statistical

Lesson Learned

Despite the increasing accessibility of the tools and data necessary for predictive analytics, don't fall into the trap of looking for a "problem" that needs a predictive analytics "solution." The need for predictive solutions will emerge as the analytics capabilities of the HCO evolve and the analytics needs of the organization are better understood.

models with any validity. Before electronic health records became widespread, it was necessary to extract data by hand from paper charts. Because pulling data this way is very labor-intensive, it was always necessary to make a trade-off between the number of records to pull (due to time and money constraints) and the statistical strength of the results given the available data. To achieve this balance, researchers would calculate how many sample records would need to be pulled in order to achieve a certain statistical power based on the assumed strength of the relationship of the variables under investigation. After all this, researchers would usually be left to work with the bare minimum number of charts and minimum amount of data required to develop and test their models.

As electronic healthcare records became more widespread in their use, the accessibility of the large amounts of data for statistical analysis and model building has been greatly enhanced; with the right data access tools, it is possible to obtain thousands of electronic record extracts based on very specific selection criteria.

TIP

Predictive analytics is a rapidly progressing field—what is state of the art as of the writing of this book may be obsolete soon after it is published. Please visit this book's web site, http://HealthcareAnalyticsBook.com, for a continually updated set of resources that point you to the most recent literature and information on developments in this field, as well as a set of links to various software tools that you can use to give advanced analytics a "test drive."

SYSTEMS There have been many recent advances in the software available with which to perform advanced analytics. For many years, specialized statistical software was used only by statisticians, researchers, and analysts primarily due to the complexity of the tools (many such tools were mainly "command line"–driven for a long time), the need to learn specialized scripting languages to get the most out of such software, and the cost, which in many cases was prohibitive.

Analytics is an emerging and rapidly growing market, so many of these barriers have been overcome, and analysts have at their disposal a much wider range of options. The variety of tools now available allows analysts to select the analytics tools that best fit their requirements *and* their budgets. Contemporary analytics tools may be stand-alone, or embedded into other products. There are several ways in which analytics capabilities can be accessed. A few examples of how advanced analytics capabilities are offered are summarized here:

- BI vendors are starting to include statistical modules in their offerings by developing their own statistical tool sets or buying out an existing statistical software tool and integrating it into their own BI suite.
- Plug-ins are available for use with popular spreadsheet software programs that can perform some of the basic predictive analytics techniques that are discussed in this chapter.
- Specialty mathematical and scientific programs contain powerful tools that help build and test predictive analytics models using a variety of approaches.
- Open-source statistical and data mining tools provide very powerful tools at a very low cost—provided that the user is willing to invest the time to learn the systems and does not need to rely on the support and training options typical of large vendors. (An open-source tool that I commonly use is R, available at www.r-project.org.)
- Specialized file and data management systems that support extremely data-intensive applications. Facebook, for example, uses Hadoop to manage its data system, which is growing by half a *petabyte*, or 500,000 gigabytes, per day.[7]

Lesson Learned

Predictive analytics capabilities can be expensive to purchase, depending on what base software is being used, and what the requirements are. If your HCO does not already have such capabilities, I recommend experimenting with a few of the less expensive options, such as open-source tools, before committing to a larger, more expensive platform. Once the need for a predictive solution is identified, you'll want to experiment with several types of models and algorithms before making a major financial commitment.

Developing and Testing Advanced Analytics

HCOs can invest significant resources and time in the development of BI and analytics solutions, including enterprise data warehouses, BI suites, selection of metrics and key performance indicators, and dashboards. Yet I find it interesting that many of these same organizations may believe that adopting predictive analytics is somehow a "plug-and-play" effort and that the software can do the algorithm development, selection, and deployment itself and subsequently operate on virtual autopilot. But just as dashboard solutions are rarely useful right out of the box and require initial customization and ongoing maintenance, predictive analytics requires significant thought and understanding to implement plus regular tweaking to maintain accurate and reliable results generation.

In a nutshell, the objective of a predictive model is to successfully use the value of one or more variables to consistently and accurately predict the value of another variable. There are two main types of predictive models: classification and regression. The term *classification* refers to when an algorithm attempts to place objects into groups based on attributes and relationships derived during the development and training process. Classification techniques are used for categorical variables (such as "yes/no," Likert scale–type data, or other such discrete data); the term *prediction*, on the other hand, occurs when an algorithm predicts an unknown (or missing) value based on a continuous-value function.[8] *Regression* models, for example, are considered suitable prediction models for data consisting of continuous, or numeric, variables (such as age, weight, height, and length of stay).[9]

For example, determining if a patient is likely suffering from influenza (as opposed to merely a cold or allergies) based on factors such as presence of high temperature, other signs/symptoms, and exposure history is an example a classification problem—that is, determining if a patient is influenza-positive based on key categorical variables. Using variables such as number of patients in the waiting room, time patients wait to be seen by a physician, and number of ambulance arrivals to predict the daily "left without being seen" rate would be an example of a regression-type prediction problem.

The Analytics Modeling Process Overview

Although predictive analytics holds potential to improve decision making and quality within healthcare, predictive analytics solutions are not trivial to implement. In fact, the important decisions in which predictive analytics is likely to be involved demand that care be taken to ensure that the problem is well defined, the data is understood and cleaned, that an appropriate algorithm or approach is selected, and, above all, that the output of predictive analytics is tested and validated. There are several widespread frameworks that aid the data mining and advanced analytics development process, including the Cross Industry Standard Process for Data Mining (CRISP-DM).[10] To help ensure the successful adoption of predictive analytics, the following steps and checkpoints based on the key points of CRISP-DM and highlighted in Figure 11.1 should typically be observed:

1. **Determine the requirements of the HCOs.** Understand and document why a predictive solution is required, and how it is going to be used.
2. **Understand, gather, and prepare the data.** Know the data to be used (i.e., what the context of the data is, how it can be used, etc.) and prepare the data for use in a predictive model.
3. **Choose and implement an appropriate model.** There are many types of predictive analytics solutions, so choose which model(s) is/are most likely to be a good fit for both the data available and the intended solutions, and then implement the model.

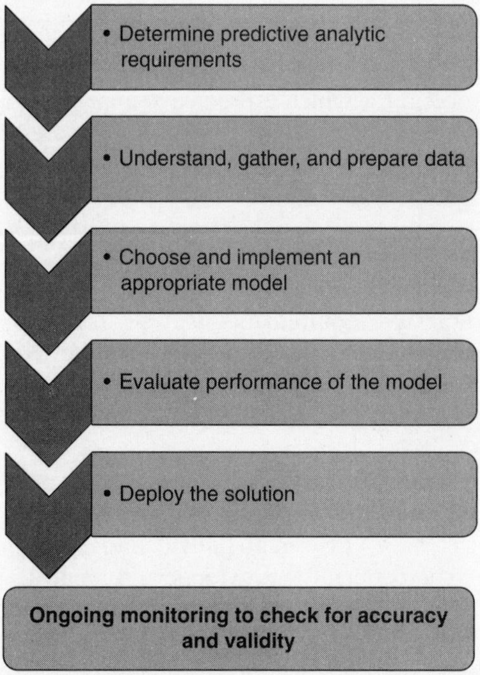
• Determine predictive analytic requirements
• Understand, gather, and prepare data
• Choose and implement an appropriate model
• Evaluate performance of the model
• Deploy the solution
Ongoing monitoring to check for accuracy and validity

FIGURE 11.1 Advanced Analytics Modeling and Deployment Process

4. **Evaluate the performance of the model(s).** Once a model (or models) has been developed, it must be evaluated to determine how accurate and suitable it is for its intended purpose.
5. **Deploy the solution.** The last step is to deploy the selected and validated model so that it can be used.

Determine the Requirements of the Healthcare Organization

As is necessary with all analytical-type projects, the first step in getting started with predictive analytics is to determine the requirements the business has for such a solution. I always find that it helps to ask, "What is the basic problem we are trying to solve?" Much like when examining processes to eliminate causes of waste and inefficiency, it is a good idea to get to the root of why a predictive analytics solution is required. Without getting to the root of the problem, it is possible that significant time and resources could be expended on implementing a predictive analytics solution that doesn't truly address the issue.

> **TIP**
>
> Always begin a predictive analytics project by determining the root cause of the problem for which a predictive analytics solution is being sought, or risk expending precious time and resources on a computer science experiment with no applicability to improving quality or performance.

It is the tendency of talented analysts to start "solutionizing" right away. Jumping past a thorough requirements analysis, however, will mean paying the price later by spending time and effort on the wrong solution (and sometimes, in fact, the wrong questions). Taking time to explore the issues and requirements will help determine:

- **Is a predictive solution necessary?** If one is *not* necessary, then don't bother wasting time and resources. To decide a true "need to have" versus a "nice to have," determine the value that the predictive solution would have to the patient, the providers, and finally to the organization as a whole. You also need to separate "research" from "operational" requirements. Much research is done without directly being implemented operationally, but adds value nonetheless. It becomes an issue of managing resources.

- **How will a predictive solution be used?** If predictive analytics is an appropriate approach to solving a clinical or other issue, the next question to ask is how the solution will be used. For example, is the solution required at the point of care in real time to assist in clinical decision making, or is it for administrative and planning purposes?
- **Is a predictive solution feasible and/or possible?** The next consideration is whether a predictive solution is feasible and/or possible given how it is intended to be used. For example, if a predictive solution is

BUILDING VERSUS ADOPTING

When a predictive solution is sought, the first instinct might be to crack open the machine-learning textbooks, fire up the data mining and predictive analytics software, and begin developing a predictive model from scratch. The effort can be very rewarding, but it can also be extremely time-consuming and resource-intensive. Before embarking on the path of from-scratch development, it is advisable to research for similar solutions that have been already developed. Algorithms developed by others and published in the literature may be just what your organization needs, or can at least form the basis for expansion or modification. Many published algorithms are likely to be peer-reviewed and -validated, which helps build confidence in the models. Sometimes it turns out that a sophisticated computer solution is not required; many published predictive models are "decision tree"–type algorithms that can be implemented electronically, but may also be applied by the clinician without using a computer.

Examples of some of these types of predictive models include:

- **Canadian C-spine rule.** This algorithm "will permit physicians to standardize care of alert, stable trauma patients, to rapidly 'clear' the cervical spine, and to be much more selective in the use of cervical spine radiography without jeopardizing patient care."[11]
- **LACE index to identify patients who are at high risk of readmission or death after hospital discharge.**[12] The LACE index uses four factors to identify the risk of death or unplanned readmission within 30 days after hospital discharge: length of stay in days for the index hospitalization (L); acuity of illness at the time of the index admission (A); Charlson comorbidity index (C); and number of emergency department visits in the six months before the index hospitalization (E).

intended to be used at the point of care for clinical decision making, it is necessary that the required data and algorithm processing are available in real time, and that a mechanism exists (also in real time) to communicate the results of the predictive tool to the provider making the clinical decision. Considerable more flexibility is possible for non-real-time solutions or for solutions that are not at the point of care. The bottom line is whether the people who need the predictive analytics will be able to obtain the desired information that is both accurate and timely enough to be of use.

Understand and Prepare Data

The foundation of an accurate and reliable predictive model is the data from which it is derived. Without accurate and reliable data, any results obtained from predictive analytics are likely to be highly suspect, because low-quality data will hinder statistical modeling and algorithm training. Following the data quality recommendations in Chapter 5 will go a long way to ensuring that there is good data for use in predictive models.

Having high-quality data is only the first step in preparing data for use in predictive models; preparing data is a crucial step in the development of predictive algorithms. Some of the steps necessary for preparing data for the development of predictive analytics algorithms include:

- **Selecting available instances.** Selecting the appropriate sample of records that contain data pertaining to the problem in question.
- **Identifying outlier data.** Removing clear outliers (as a result of data input errors, for example) from the sample data set so as not to skew the model.
- **Dealing with sparse features.** Incorporating measures to accommodate missing data in important data fields so that the model has as complete a data set as possible with which to work.
- **Converting data.** Converting data into a format that can be used within the algorithm (for example, converting alphanumeric variables to strictly numeric).

The above are just a few of the measures required to clean and prepare a data set prior for predictive modeling. Many higher-end software programs with predictive modeling capabilities may employ "wizards" or other in-software assistance that walk you through the data preparation process. If you are building predictive models from scratch (for embedding in a clinical system) or using software such as R for building models, much of the cleaning and preparation may need to be done without the help of a software wizard.

No matter how preparation of the data is done, it is a critical step in the modeling process. In all likelihood, predictive analytics will be used during clinical and administrative decision making. The time spent up front ensuring a usable data set for development and training is well worth the effort—especially if it means the difference between using faulty data versus reliable insight for clinical and administrative decisions.

Choose and Implement an Appropriate Model

As I mentioned earlier, "predictive analytics" is a very broad term, encompassing many different approaches and techniques. When first getting started, just deciding how and where to start may seem daunting. I find it valuable to maintain focus on the problem at hand to avoid getting lost in the myriad possible tools, techniques, and algorithms. When choosing a predictive approach, it is necessary to account for several key factors, including:

- **Purpose.** What problem is being addressed, and how will predictive analytics help?
- **Output required.** What information does the end user need? (Can it be a simple number, or does it need to be a full clinical recommendation?)
- **Data available.** What data is necessary to drive the model to generate the necessary output, and is that data available (either at all, or at the frequency required)?
- **Modality.** Where is the predictive model likely to be used (administratively in an office, clinically at the point of care), and does it need to be in real time (focusing on current patients or current conditions)?
- **Capabilities of the model** (including assumptions, data requirements, etc.). Is there a model that can provide the information and insight required given the previous questions and assumptions? For example, a model that returns a categorical result (i.e., "yes or no") is not appropriate if the required output is numeric (like a risk score).

Some analytics tools will scan a set of data and apply a statistical or other predictive model based on what it believes is the model that "best fits" the data. This process can help to identify and narrow down the list of possible models from which to choose. It is not advisable, however, simply to have a computer program pick a predictive algorithm for your particular problem and data set without your at least understanding the fundamentals of the particular algorithms.

When working with predictive analytics (and in fact all types of analytics), assumptions and limitations of the prospective model and the requirements of the end user must be accounted for to ensure a match and that an optimal, valid, and reliable predictive solution is developed. Even if the analytics software you are using does fit the best model with the data and the problem being solved, it is advantageous to know the basics—including the limitations, strengths, weaknesses, benefits, and drawbacks of the model, and the issues with the data—to be confident in the predictive model being selected, and to explain the reasons behind why a model was chosen.

If there are no ready-made predictive algorithms available that address the particular needs of your HCO, the option exists to develop your own predictive analytics solutions. Despite the promise that some vendors make of "plug-and-play" predictive analytics, there is a lot of work that must precede the implementation of such algorithms. And once the analytics algorithms are built, there is the continual need to monitor how well the algorithms are performing and to ensure that data or process changes haven't occurred that would invalidate the algorithms altogether.

Evaluate the Model's Performance

Because of the complexity of developing a model, it is important to test any model thoroughly and completely prior to deploying it. Once a model is built and in the testing phase, testing procedures and evaluation metrics against which to test the model will assist in an objective evaluation.[13] Extensive testing will help ensure that the model is generating appropriate output, and can be used to determine how the model will perform in the future under various conditions.

Testing a model involves determining the predictive capability of a model on an independent set of test data (where the actual results are known). Evaluating this performance is important because results of the testing will guide the ultimate selection of which prediction model to use, and will provide a sense of how well a model will perform when it is deployed.[14]

The primary factor being evaluated for a predictive test is the output variable of the model. For example, models to determine whether a patient is influenza-positive prior to receiving serology confirmation may be evaluated based on their sensitivity and specificity. That is, how well do the models perform at positively identifying patients who actually have influenza (sensitivity), and how well do they perform at ruling out those patients who do not have influenza (specificity)? The eventual model chosen would be the one that performs best on these two measures.

Another example is the testing of a model to detect hospital length of stay based on a selection of identified clinical criteria. The model that would be chosen is the one with output (estimated length of stay) most closely matched to the actual lengths of stay of patients in the testing data set.

When testing a model, it is best not to test the model on the very same data set on which it was built. The reason for this is that predictive models can be tweaked and improved to the point that they perform perfectly on their own training data, an occurrence that is known as *overfitting*.[15] This perfect performance would not be repeated for new observations, however, so testing on a new data set is necessary to observe more typical performance of the algorithm.

Deploy the Solution

Predictive analytics can take many forms that impact how it is implemented and deployed. There are many deployment possibilities based on the needs of the organization. Deploying a predictive tool is as important a step as building and testing the model. A consideration for deployment is how the predictive tool is going to be used. For example, if the predictive tool is to be used for administrative purposes, research, or non-bedside clinical work (such as analyzing diagnostic images), the use of specialized software (such as statistical modeling tools, dedicated image analysis software, or other applications) is an acceptable alternative and is probably in fact necessary. However, for use by the bedside, any predictive model should be integrated into the clinical software in use so that it is available at the point of care, or available in a mobile solution so that alerts and clinical insight generated by predictive tools are immediately available to the care provider.

It is also important to remember that predictive modeling is not simply "plug-and-play." Once a model is developed, it must be continually evaluated for performance and accuracy given that predictive analytics is likely to be used to support decision making during the provision of patient care or during other important decisions. These decisions can range from alerting home care or other services in advance to prevent a long emergency department visit due to a delayed discharge, to placing a patient in isolation due to a potential infectious risk, to providing a lifesaving medication or medical procedure. Other examples of such decision making can include:

- Determining the possible diagnosis of a patient.
- Taking preventive action to prevent queues in the waiting room.
- Providing necessary care to prevent long stays in the emergency department and preventing unnecessary admissions.

Having effective data quality and data governance measures in place is necessary to ensure that processes and data do not unexpectedly change, which would result in the performance of a predictive model becoming compromised.

Overview of Predictive Algorithms

Statistical learning is the branch of science that focuses on the development of algorithms for data mining, machine learning, and inference—the foundations of predictive analytics. Statistical learning is commonly used in many industries where computers must learn from data and make inferences or predictions of some future state. For example, in healthcare, statistical learning can be applied to predict whether a patient with certain risk factors is likely to contract a specific health condition. The same types of algorithms can be used to predict the price of a stock in six months' time based on company performance measures and economic data, or to identify the numbers in a handwritten postal or ZIP code from a digitized image.[16]

There are many different approaches, algorithms, and methods that together form the toolset of predictive analytics. Generally, the tools are broken down into *statistical modeling* and *machine learning*, based on their underlying assumptions and approaches. As mentioned previously, the selection of a model will depend on the type of data available, what assumptions exist for the models, and what the business requires of the model. The various models in this section represent several of the most commonly used models in healthcare; the fields of statistical modeling and machine learning, however, are constantly evolving, so the reader whose interest lies in these areas is encouraged to review the books and articles referenced in this chapter and to visit this book's web site, http://HealthcareAnalyticsBook.com, for links and resources related to the most recent advances in this field.

Regression Modeling

Two terms that you are likely to come across when working with statistical modeling and data analysis in general are *dependent variable* and *independent variable*. The dependent variable is the observation or outcome of interest, and is the output of a formula. An independent variable, on the other hand, is the input to a formula, and can be considered a cause (or what is tested to see if it is indeed a potential cause) of a change in the dependent variable.

One of the most common statistical approaches for predicting outcomes is *regression*. Considered to be a conceptually simple method for investigating functional relationships among variables, regression is a method used in statistical analysis to quantify the strength of a relationship between a dependent variable (such as healthcare outcomes) and one or more independent variables (such as risk factors or environmental variables).[17] Using regression, analysts work with several variables that are thought to correlate to (and possibly predict) a certain outcome, to determine if a meaningful mathematical relationship actually exists between the potential predictors and the outcome. Analysts will be looking for a relationship that can best approximate all the individual data points used as input. When linear regression is applied, for example, the relationship will take the form of a straight line. For other, more complex relationships, lines with other geometry may best represent the relationship.

Regression can be used in healthcare to better understand how factors are related in determining outcomes, and to predict outcomes of patients depending on what factors are present, and in what quantities. For example, healthcare analysts might use regression to determine and better understand the relationship between what variables contribute to unexpected readmissions to hospital after discharge. They can then use this understanding to predict which current patients in hospital might be at risk for readmission, and take preventive action to reduce the risk of a patient returning to hospital unexpectedly as a negative outcome of a hospital stay.

Just as there are many types of data to analyze, and many types of questions that need to be answered, there are several variations of regression modeling, depending on the relationship(s) you're trying to model and the data available for inclusion in the model. Several basic types of regression include *linear*, *multiple*, *multivariate*, and *logistic*, and they are detailed in Table 11.1.

There are many benefits to using regression analysis for better understanding relationships between variables and predicting outcomes. Regression algorithms are very accessible. Most dedicated statistical software can perform regression modeling with ease and, if necessary, it is even possible to perform a regression analysis with spreadsheet software.[18] I have used the open-source tool R for building regression models, and I find it a great tool for exploring predictive analytics because of its extremely low cost of adoption and extensible capabilities. For larger-scale predictive requirements using regression, dedicated BI suites may offer built-in regression and related tools. The benefit of using a solution that is integrated into an existing BI system is that it is easier to implement the predictive capabilities within an existing framework. The downside is, of course, that many of these solutions come with a hefty price tag that may be a barrier to entry for some HCOs.

TABLE 11.1 Examples of Types of Regression

Regression Type	Typical Use (and Example)
Linear	Predicts a response in single dependent variable based on a single independent variable. This type includes polynomial regression, where the relationship is modeled in the form of an *n*th-order polynomial of the single independent variable.
Multiple	Predicts a response in a single dependent variable from two (or more) independent variables.
Multivariate	Predicts a response in two (or more) dependent variables from one (or more) independent variable(s).
Logistic	Predicts a categorical response in a dependent variable from one (or more) independent variable(s).

Another benefit of regression is that it is a well-understood model and is a very common method for analysis and prediction. Regression modeling is a standard tool used by many practitioners of Six Sigma,[19] and is a staple in many clinical research and epidemiological studies. Regression is taught in some introductory and most intermediate-level statistics classes, and many professionals who work with healthcare data, if not proficient with the use of regression, have at least a passing familiarity with its basic concepts.

Because of the widespread familiarity with regression, and the number of tools with which it can be performed, regression is often the standard by which other predictive models are compared. When embarking on a predictive analytics project, a good starting point is to develop a regression model initially to determine how well the model performs (if the problem in question and data available fit the criteria for regression). If another type of model (for example, a machine-learning model) is deemed necessary, any newly developed models can be compared with the performance of the regression model, with the best-performing model being selected.

Machine Learning and Pattern Recognition

Machine-learning and pattern-recognition systems are predictive approaches that are being increasingly used within healthcare. These types of approaches are necessary when a predictive solution is required but the assumptions of more traditional approaches (such as regression) no longer hold with the problem being addressed. In all but the most trivial of cases, insights, patterns, and other knowledge contained within data sets are not obvious simply by *looking* at the data. For example, manually scanning through even a small sample of patients who contracted sepsis during their stay in a hospital ward may not reveal any clues given the many factors that may impact the occurrence of sepsis. Machine-learning algorithms provide the capability to scan *all* the cases of sepsis within a healthcare records database and determine if there are any meaningful patterns in the data, and may uncover previously unknown relationships.

Machine learning and statistics are both based heavily on mathematics, but their approaches differ. Statistical approaches tend to demand more conservative and restrictive analysis strategies, while machine-learning systems provide more flexibility. Specifically, machine-learning systems differ from statistical approaches in that they "partially adopt heuristics (in addition to mathematics) to resolve real-world problems, especially when categorical (discrete) data are being used."[20] Examples of how these types of systems are being used in healthcare include:

- Reducing instances of healthcare fraud.
- Improving disease surveillance.
- Detection of tumors and other anomalies on diagnostic images.

Although the field of machine learning is still relatively new, there are many types of machine-learning systems (and variations thereof). Three common machine-learning methods are *artificial neural networks*, *decision trees*, and *support vector machines*; these are described in Table 11.2. The selected examples in Table 11.2 do not comprise an exhaustive list; in fact, even the types of machine learning listed in Table 11.2 have different subtypes associated with them. Please visit the book's website at http://HealthcareAnalyticsBook.com for a more comprehensive, up-to-date summary of machine-learning algorithms, with links to additional resources that represent the latest developments in this important field.

There are a wide variety of machine-learning algorithms available from which to select for any given prediction or classification problem in healthcare. As is usually case, the exciting potential associated with many possible choices also creates a challenge in determining the right (or at least the best) approach to use. And the choice not only involves selecting the

TABLE 11.2 Selected Examples of Different Types of Machine Learning

Machine-Learning System	Description
Artificial neural network (ANN)	ANN is a biologically inspired mathematical model based on our understanding of how neurons in the brain function. The pattern-recognition capabilities of ANN mimic those found in biologic systems.[21] ANN is a very robust algorithm that offers high accuracy and can output discrete or real values.
Decision tree	Decision trees resemble a game of "20 questions," where "such a sequence of questions is displayed in a directed decision tree, where by convention the first or root node is displayed at the top, connected by successive (directional) links or branches to other nodes."[22] Decision tree classifiers are powerful because the results are typically easily understood (they are very similar to "standard" decision algorithms), and they can be implemented in source systems and BI software that support basic computer operations.
Support vector machine (SVM)	SVM is one of the relatively newer classification methods; it is used for both linear and nonlinear types of data and works by separating entities into mutually exclusive regions.[23] The prediction process starts with a few points (the support vectors) along the boundary area, and proceeds by transforming the data into new spaces where the separation between the classes is improved.

ADVANCED ANALYTICS IN ACTION AND SAVING MONEY

A system of four hospitals in Washington State used advanced analytics to detect and identify errant accounts and claims to realize $2 million in missed charges within a single year.[24]

best algorithm but also the best tool in which to implement and deploy the algorithm.

It is important to remember that predictive analytics in healthcare is still a relatively new field. Because of this, the tools for implementing predictive algorithms (such as the various machine learning varieties) are far from being ready to use "out of the box." Choosing and implementing a valid predictive algorithm requires a deep understanding of the problem being addressed, the data available, and the predictive algorithms likely to be employed. The best approach for introducing predictive analytics into an HCO is to develop and test several models that are likely a good fit for the problem, and determine which approach is most feasible to implement and provides the best accuracy in a "competitive evaluation" of algorithms.[25]

The relative newness and complexity of advanced analytics approaches such as machine learning should not deter any HCO from pursuing these potentially powerful tools. New uses for these approaches are always being developed and successfully implemented. If your organization proceeds incrementally with using predictive analytics, carefully matching applications with algorithms, there is a better chance that these powerful tools will be successful, even if initially only on a trial basis, within your HCO. As the capabilities of the organization grow, additional predictive tools can be developed with increased complexity as the needs of the HCO dictate and as the skills of the analytics team develop.

Notes

1. Charles H. Hennekens and Julie R. Buring, *Epidemiology in Medicine*, ed. Sherry L. Mayrent (Boston: Little, Brown, 1987), 3.
2. Colleen McCue, *Data Mining and Predictive Analysis: Intelligence Gathering and Crime Analysis* (Burlington, MA: Butterworth-Heinemann, 2006), 117.
3. David J. Hand, Heikki Mannila, and Padhraic Smyth, *Principles of Data Mining* (Cambridge, MA: MIT Press, 2001), 6.
4. Robert Nisbet, John Elder, and Gary Miner, *Handbook of Statistical Analysis and Data Mining Applications* (Burlington, MA: Elsevier, 2009), 316.

5. Ibid., 314.
6. Thomas H. Davenport and D. J. Patil, "Data Scientist: The Sexiest Job of the 21st Century," *Harvard Business Review*, October 2012, http://hbr.org/2012/10/data-scientist-the-sexiest-job-of-the-21st-century.
7. Facebook Engineering, "Under the Hood: Scheduling MapReduce Jobs More Efficiently with Corona," November 8, 2012, www.facebook.com/notes/facebook-engineering/under-the-hood-scheduling-mapreduce-jobs-more-efficiently-with-corona/10151142560538920.
8. Nisbet, Elder, and Miner, *Handbook of Statistical Analysis and Data Mining Applications*, 23.
9. Ibid.
10. Pete Chapman et al., "CRISP-DM 1.0, Step-by-Step Data Modeling Guide," www.the-modeling-agency.com/crisp-dm.pdf.
11. Canadian C-Spine Rule web site, www.ohri.ca/emerg/cdr/cspine.html.
12. Carl van Walraven et al., "Derivation and Validation of an Index to Predict Early Death or Unplanned Readmission after Discharge from Hospital to the Community," *Canadian Medical Association Journal* 182(6) (April 6, 2010): 551–557.
13. Donald E. Brown, "Introduction to Data Mining for Medical Informatics," *Clinics in Laboratory Medicine* 28 (2008): 9–35.
14. Trevor Hastie, Robert Tibshirani, and Jerome Friedman, *The Elements of Statistical Learning: Data Mining, Inference, and Prediction*, 2nd ed. (New York: Springer, 2009), 219.
15. Brown, "Introduction to Data Mining for Medical Informatics."
16. Hastie, Tibshirani, and Friedman, *The Elements of Statistical Learning*, 4.
17. Samprit Chatterjee and Ali S. Hadi, *Regression Analysis by Example*, 5th ed. (Hoboken, NJ: John Wiley & Sons), 1.
18. Conrad Carlberg, *Predictive Analytics: Microsoft Excel* (Indianapolis: Pearson Education, 2012), 4.
19. Michael L. George et al., *The Lean Six Sigma Pocket Toolbook: A Quick Reference Guide to 100 Tools for Improving Quality and Speed* (New York: McGraw-Hill, 2005), 167.
20. Illhoi Yoo et al., "Data Mining in Healthcare and Biomedicine: A Survey of the Literature," *Journal of Medical Systems* 36(4) (August 2012): 2431–2448.
21. Brown, "Introduction to Data Mining for Medical Informatics."
22. Richard O. Duda, Peter E. Hart, and David G. Stork, *Pattern Classification*, 2nd ed. (New York: John Wiley & Sons, 2001), 395.
23. Hastie, Tibshirani, and Friedman, *The Elements of Statistical Learning*, 417.
24. Eric Siegel, *Predictive Analytics: The Power to Predict Who Will Live, Click, Buy, or Die*, Kindle ed. (Hoboken, NJ: John Wiley & Sons, 2013), locations 8235–8236.
25. Nisbet, Elder, and Miner, *Handbook of Statistical Analysis and Data Mining Applications*, 316.

CHAPTER 12

Becoming an Analytical Healthcare Organization

Business intelligence and analytics excellence "is achieved when organizations have in place the strategy, people, process, and technology approaches that result in business impact, value, and effectiveness."[1] Analytics excellence, as it relates to healthcare quality improvement (QI), is when the strategies, people, processes, and technologies are applied to improvement initiatives and positively impact the quality and performance of a healthcare organization (HCO).

Being an analytical organization requires more than simply acquiring or possessing the tools and technology of analytics. To become an analytical organization, an HCO must ensure that:

1. The analytic needs of the business and stakeholders are understood;
2. The organization possesses the right analytical people and skill sets;
3. The technology infrastructure supports the analytical people and the analytical needs of the business;
4. The analytical people are deployed on the right projects and are working on activities that move the organization closer to achieving its performance and quality goals; and
5. Healthcare leaders, QI teams, and other decision makers actually use the information and insight available through analytics.

Items 1 through 4 in the list above are issues that must be addressed in the HCO's analytics strategy. (See Chapter 3 for a discussion of analytics strategies that drive healthcare improvement.) Ultimately, the analytics strategy is responsible for ensuring that the organization's analytical, business, and technology requirements are in alignment and that efforts on all fronts are focused on achieving the same goals.

Item 5 above represents a gap between analytics development and the use of analytics within the HCO, and is the most challenging step to becoming an analytical organization. Several of the reasons this is a challenge include the following barriers:

- **Resistance to change.** Healthcare leaders and decision makers are understandably very busy, and some may feel that the "old way" of decision making (replete with incomplete information and "gut feelings") is just fine. To overcome resistance to change, the value of analytics (in terms of making more effective decisions in less time) must be demonstrated by clear, tangible results.
- **Rapid business change.** Sometimes by the time an analytical tool or report is built and deployed, the precipitating crisis has passed and the HCO has moved on to other issues. To prevent this situation, analytics teams must be agile and able to respond quickly to the evolving needs of the organization. Understanding and focusing on the overall quality and performance goals of the organization (communicated via the analytics strategy) also helps analytics teams to be better prepared for the kinds of analytics the HCO will be requiring.
- **Distrust.** Perhaps the most frustrating cause of a gap in analytics utilization is distrust of the information. All it takes is two reports to show different numbers for the supposedly same metric, and executives and quality teams will be suspicious. This distrust can be rectified through strong data governance and precise data and indicator definitions. Addressing this also needs vigilance on the part of analytics teams and data stewards to ensure that all potential sources of information are in alignment and all possible sources of disparity in data are known, monitored, and mitigated when required.

The barriers identified above prevent full usability of analytics throughout the HCO, and each manifests some gap in analytics capability, whether in knowledge, skill, understanding, or technology. To further address these barriers, there are three main areas of excellence on which analytics teams must focus to achieve excellence:

1. **Technical.** Technical excellence occurs when an HCO has established an information infrastructure that allows for the smooth transfer of data from source systems into an enterprise data warehouse or other data store, the data in the data store is accurate and accessible to those who need it in a timely manner for reporting and analytics, and the analytics software and other tools are in place to meet the analytics requirements of the HCO.
2. **Professional.** Professional excellence in analytics occurs when an HCO has enough of the right professionals and the right skills to undertake

analytical activities required in the pursuit of the quality goals of the HCO.

3. **Execution.** Excellence in outcomes relies on having both technical and professional analytics excellence within the HCO. Excellence in analytics execution means that an HCO has the processes in place to deliver the right analytical capabilities and/or outputs to those who are working on actual healthcare transformation initiatives, and that the insights generated from analytics are actually used.

Of the three layers of analytics excellence above, I consider execution the most important, because that is the layer that addresses the analytics usability gap. In fact, I believe that HCOs should relentlessly pursue execution excellence (that is, actually use analytics for real-world problems), because doing so will drive the attainment of technical and professional excellence. Without execution and use of analytics throughout the organization, there will be no demand for technical and professional excellence. In extreme cases, senior management may be oblivious to the analytics needs and capabilities of the organization, thereby resulting in substandard and/or haphazardly deployed information management technologies being rolled out and poorly resourced and coordinated analytics teams left to fend for themselves. Organizations that focus too much on technical development of analytics infrastructure at the expense of execution, however, may run the risk of building the "ultimate" and likely very costly analytics solution that nobody in the organization can actually use because the focus on what actually was *required* by the organization was lost.

You do need to ensure that you always use the highest-quality data possible, and that the technical infrastructure is as robust as possible. In reality, however, no technical solution is ever going to be "perfect" (i.e., there will always be *some* data quality problems, and the technology doesn't *always* work). Furthermore, no organization is going to have the exact right mix of skills. But these issues can be overcome and evolve as analytics is used within the HCO. To ensure that your HCO does not become permanently stuck in a "build" phase, find ways to use the capabilities that already exist (and stretch those a little bit)—and continue to meet the needs of the organization while providing clear examples of how analytics demonstrates value for the organization.

Requirements to Become an Analytical Organization

Healthcare is in a state of change. HCOs can be responsible for driving necessary changes within to achieve business, quality, and performance goals, or they can be perpetually reacting to the pressures around them without really knowing the best action to take. Analytics is one of the fundamental tools that enable HCOs to achieve change.

Most of this book has focused on very tangible, quantifiable things such as data, how to manipulate data, how to demonstrate a change in performance using data, and how to turn data into information and insight that is useful to healthcare leaders and QI teams. But many HCOs have terabytes or more of data and multiple dashboards, and are making decisions, but do not seem to be achieving their performance and quality goals. Having data and dashboards alone aren't sufficient for becoming an analytical organization and achieving excellence in healthcare quality and performance. To become an analytical HCO requires:

- Strategy
- Leadership and commitment
- Focus
- Agility
- Teamwork

Strategy

As discussed at length in Chapter 3, the purpose of the analytics strategy is to guide the HCO's ability to rapidly respond to the information needs of key decision makers while maintaining a consistent direction in supporting the quality and business goals of the HCO. A solid analytics strategy will help enable the analytics team to become a strategic information resource for business improvement and not simply a purveyor of reports and data.

An analytics strategy is the starting point to help organizations achieve maximum benefit from analytics. A completed strategy will help an organization identify what it does well, what it needs to do better, where it can consolidate, and where it needs to invest. The analytics strategy should not be set in stone either; it needs to evolve as the analytics needs of the organization and its stakeholders evolve, as technology becomes better and/or less expensive, and as the state of the art in analytics itself changes. An organization should not be afraid to revisit the strategy frequently to ensure that it is up to date and that the execution of the strategy is successfully meeting all stated requirements.

Leadership and Commitment

Leadership is often the deciding factor in an analytical organization; it is, after all, the leaders within an HCO who "have a strong influence on culture and can mobilize people, money, and time to help push for more analytical decision making."[2] Although pursuing healthcare improvement through the use of QI initiatives coupled with information and insight generated from analytics seems like it would be a "slam dunk," HCOs are often resistant to that kind of change. It then takes strong leadership within the HCO to begin or continue down that road and to overcome resistance.

Key analytics-related responsibilities of leaders within the HCO are to:

- **Keep the HCO focused on strategic goals and objectives.** It is a primary job of leaders within the HCO to ensure that all QI activities align with the strategic goals of the organization, and that analytics is in alignment with those goals. Leaders also need to know when it is necessary to deviate from those stated strategic goals when unexpected, pressing issues arise. When those issues are resolved, it falls on leadership to reorient any efforts that may have been diverted back to working on strategic goals. This is where the value of quality and analytics strategies demonstrates its worth.
- **Promote and champion use of analytics throughout the HCO.** Support decision making using analytics. Support the deployment and use of analytics tools. Recognize and support the need for enterprise data structures to enhance analytics.
- **Enforce data governance policies and procedures.** Data management, regardless of the scope and scale of the data being managed, cannot be placed on autopilot. Accurate analytics requires that all aspects of data (including the process definitions from which data is derived) are constantly and consistently managed. Not all leaders will be part of governance efforts, but all should recognize and value the need for strong data governance in ensuring that high-quality data is available for reporting and analytics, and that accurate results and meaningful insights depend on having high-quality data. Effective leaders will also recognize the need for agility, and will not enforce any more layers of approval than absolutely necessary to ensure the quality of data.
- **Encourage, enable, and reward innovation and experimentation.** At the heart of healthcare improvement lies innovation. Innovation involves finding newer (and presumably better) solutions to existing problems. For example, changing processes and adding communications technology that result in decreased turnaround time for hospital inpatient beds would be an innovation. Applying analytics to solve pressing QI problems within an HCO is also innovative. HCOs that achieve their quality and performance goals usually have well-established cultures of innovation, where it is permitted and even expected that healthcare staff seek out innovative ways to improve pressing quality and performance issues. (Of course, these innovations are always being evaluated to ensure they are having the desired effect on processes and outcomes.)

- **Provide analytics teams required training and tools.** Leaders must ensure that analytics teams have the proper tools and training to perform their work effectively, and must do their best to protect the time of analytical teams to focus on work that is aligned with the strategic focus and needs of the HCO.

Focus

Commitment *and* leadership are both necessary to enable analytics teams to focus on building what is important to the organization and necessary for achieving the organization's quality and performance goals. I like to classify the type of work that analytics teams do into three categories:

1. **Strategic.** Development and analysis activities that build analytics into a strategic resource for the HCO.
2. **Tactical.** Activities that are in support of a specific quality or performance improvement project.
3. **Reactionary.** Work that is done as a result of someone's "data emergency."

Strategic activities are vitally important to the HCO, as these help to build a sustainable analytics infrastructure. Examples of sustainable analytics infrastructure include organized and intuitive analytics portals that enable self-serve access to information and insight when people require it. Overall, strategic activities are those that create a sustainable, accessible information resource that helps to identify and direct action toward organizational information needs.

Tactical activities, on the other hand, are those that are in support of actual QI initiatives. These typically involve preparing baseline data, developing project-specific dashboards, and evaluating process outcomes in detail. Tactical-type activities are an extension of the strategic activities, except they are directed at providing the information and insight that individual QI teams require.

Finally, reactionary activities are those in response to an urgent request. These types of requests can be very distracting to a team, depending on the scope of work required and how quickly it is required. These activities may be related to simple data requests, or required because of a critical incident or similar circumstance within the HCO.

It is my observation that many of the strategic-level activities that *should* be a priority for an analytics team get sidelined for reactionary activities, which is ironic, given that many strategic-level activities can actually *improve* the tools and systems available to enable designated individuals to access the information they require. One of the critical roles that leadership

H1N1 SURVEILLANCE: REACTIONARY, BUT NECESSARY

Some of the "reactionary" urgent requests are vital to the organization. For example, during the H1N1 outbreak of 2009, we were tasked with developing a surveillance report to monitor the presentations of influenza-like illness (ILI) to emergency departments. Not only was the surveillance report useful for contingency planning to deal with a potential major outbreak of H1N1-related ILI, but it provided valuable information to the government, the media, and, by extension, members of the public.

and commitment play, then, is allowing analytics teams to focus on strategic objectives that will both reduce the number of reactionary-type activities and enable analytics teams to participate more often on quality and performance improvement projects.

Agility

Analytics professionals are very highly skilled, solution-oriented, and motivated individuals coming from a variety of backgrounds, including computer science, engineering, statistics, and epidemiology (to add my own

LESSONS LEARNED: THE IMPORTANCE OF STRATEGIC GOALS

In the early days of our analytics portal, it was somewhat bloated because of development and expansion through report aggregation. As the HCO was better able to define its own quality and performance targets and to articulate its strategic priorities, we were able to focus our efforts around these targets and priorities. Some of the noticeable changes that occurred as a result of this strategic focus were that reports and dashboards featured actual performance indicators and targets, not simply counts and averages, and users of the analytics were able to identify which strategic priorities were and were not meeting expected targets. This in turn enabled decision makers to take appropriate action. As the usefulness of the analytics tools we developed increased, the number of information requests declined, allowing the team to dedicate even more time and effort to improving the usability of the analytics tools and consolidate the large body of reports into fewer but more intelligent data tools.

educational background!). The effective development, implementation, and use of analytics can be resource-intensive, involving an in-demand small group of individuals, specialized tools, and unique knowledge and skill sets.

The need for and perceived value of analytics within HCOs is increasing, and there are many different projects that compete for the same analytics skills and resources. Regardless of the size of the "analytics shop" within an HCO, whether it's a handful of analysts within a department or program or a large team within a business intelligence competency center, it will not take them very long to get bogged down in the minutiae of day-to-day data, report, information, and application requests. Within operations of a healthcare environment, it's the biggest fires, the loudest voice, or the proverbial squeaky wheel that gets the attention of resources. Unfortunately, the squeaky wheels are not necessarily the priorities that are truly important to the organization as a whole, QI in particular, or even the analytical teams themselves.

The challenge, then, is how to exactly determine what is important and should be getting the attention of the analytics team. It may be tough for analytics teams to know if they have the right tools and resources to do the jobs asked of them, and it is difficult to know what jobs to do from the realm of competing priorities. This is where an analytics strategy is necessary. The analytics strategy is essential for helping to sort and prioritize incoming requests for information.

Healthcare QI needs to be agile—that is, it must be able to respond to issues and requests as they arise. QI projects are no longer years-long efforts; time frames to achieve expected results are now measured in days and weeks. The development of analytics to address quality issues *cannot* become a barrier to the rapid initiation of QI projects. That is why analytics teams *must* understand the needs of QI teams (and in fact should work side by side).

Analytics teams must know how to take raw data and present it in a form that is quickly usable by the QI teams, and QI teams must know how to ask for information in ways that the analytics teams can respond to. It doesn't matter which types of frameworks are guiding QI efforts—Lean, Six Sigma, and others require the analytics teams and QI teams to be on the same page to bring usable analytics to the front lines.

It is unlikely that an HCO will be starting from scratch—that there are no existing QI teams and projects, and no business intelligence, analytics, or report-development resources. What is likely, however, is that the QI and analytics teams do not work closely together. In most organizations, QI teams must follow "report request" (or similarly outmoded) processes just to submit a request for a report, dashboard, or other information. QI initiatives can be highly energizing and exciting events, especially when participating in rapid improvement events or other similar activities. Nothing stifles this excitement, or otherwise inhibits innovation, more than not having the right information to make decisions or to intelligently identify issues. Even worse is when team members must go through obtuse data request procedures simply to obtain data.

When process changes are being made and evaluated in a span of hours or a few days, waiting weeks for data and other analytics is simply unacceptable. This is why I strongly advocate for analytics team members to be part of QI initiatives, or at least for there to be very strong connections between the QI and analytics teams. QI teams must know whom to talk to for the data, information, and analysis that they need. In return, the analytics team must be both aware that such improvement initiatives are happening and prepared to provide as rapid turnaround as possible. This is where a well-defined quality strategy and strong executive support for analytics is necessary, to establish and support these tight connections so that the analytics required for QI projects is available when required, and not only at the convenience of the analytics team. The need for this agility is why analytics teams cannot be encumbered with numerous data requests that detract from their ability to respond to initiatives of strategic and tactical importance.

Building Effective Analytical Teams

Throughout my career, I have seen many different types of people, with many different backgrounds, excel in healthcare analytics. I believe that it is the strong diversity of backgrounds and skills that analytics professionals possess that makes analytics indispensable for healthcare quality and performance improvement initiatives.

There are an abundance of opinions highlighting various qualities and attributes of data scientists, business intelligence professionals, and analysts. Much of the discussion, however, has centered around the math, data, or technology skills of analytics professionals. Because my focus is on the application of analytics for quality and performance improvement, the qualities I view as ideal for analytics professionals involved in these activities typically are situated within the intersection of IT, the business, and the QI activities of the HCO.

With this in mind, several of the traits I view as important for healthcare analytics professionals are as follows:

- **Natural curiosity.** As more healthcare data becomes available via the proliferation of electronic health records, there is much to be learned about the data available and in turn much to be learned from what the data tells us. Healthcare analytics professionals should be naturally curious and revel in asking "what" and "why," realizing that these questions do not expose ignorance but are truly the only way to gain full understanding of a problem.

- **Innovative mind-set.** Healthcare quality and performance improvement initiatives require a great deal of innovation to identify more efficient and effective workflows and processes. To help achieve the required levels of innovation, healthcare analytics professionals must see analytics not as "report development," but as a way to building the "information tools" necessary to solve pressing healthcare issues. They are willing, able, and excited to leverage all the technology and information available to maximum extent (whether it's experimenting and adopting new visualizations or trying novel analytical approaches). They strive for effective yet creative solutions that provide efficient access to the right information to the right people when it is needed.
- **Business focus.** Improving healthcare quality and performance requires a strong and thorough understanding of processes and workflows. Analytics to support QI initiatives must align with and provide insight into the business of providing care. This is why healthcare analytics professionals must focus on the business, striving to know the pertinent details of the healthcare domains in which they work. After all, it is these details of the business that add the necessary context to data that helps it become "information" and "insight."
- **Technological savvy.** In many ways, analytics operates at the heart of healthcare information technology, given that analytical solutions typically integrate data from multiple data sources (such as clinical and financial systems). Many systems and steps are involved in getting data from source systems into a location and format available for effective analysis. Having said that, however, experienced healthcare analytics professionals don't need to be tech jockeys (that is, they don't need to be hardcore programmers or serious database administrators). But they should be comfortable and proficient with the current and emerging technologies, such as business intelligence platforms and data cleaning, analysis, and visualization tools. This means being comfortable in using more than just a spreadsheet.
- **Team player.** Effective healthcare analytics projects depend upon having effective analytics teams. This means working well with other members of healthcare analytics and QI teams, all while respecting the differing points of view that professionals in other disciplines (such as nurses, physicians, and laboratory technologists) bring to the discussion. It also means communicating well; healthcare analytics professionals must both listen to and understand what others are saying, and articulately convey their own opinions and knowledge to others who may not be analytics experts.

Healthcare QI is now a multidisciplinary effort, involving a range of experts including clinical, administrative, technology, and process engineering professionals. Due to the different roles and teams in which healthcare analytics professionals may find themselves, a strong mix of technical, interpersonal, and analytical skills is essential to successfully operate in today's challenging healthcare environment.

Integrating Quality and Analytics Teams

I have personally seen the effects when analytics considerations are brought onto a project too late. Invariably, in these circumstances, the QI teams are not using all the possible information at their disposal, don't know whom to ask for the right information, and may not have even analyzed appropriately the data that they do have. Starting out a brand-new QI initiative without having the proper information can lead to a lot of thrashing around, indecision, and rework. Before starting any QI initiative, it is vital that the QI teams work closely with the analytics team to fully assess their analytics and information requirements so that all necessary information is at their disposal and there are no surprises later on in the project. Strong partnerships between all stakeholders in QI initiatives can help prevent statements like, "I didn't know that data was available," "I didn't know where to get that data," and "I don't know what information we need," and instead help focus all team members from all disciplines on *using* the information and insight available through analytics to improve healthcare.

Summary

Every HCO is unique and faces different challenges based on factors ranging from its patient population and their healthcare requirements to funding limitations, legislation pressures, and the makeup of clinical and administrative staff. Healthcare quality and performance improvement requires a wide range of changes, from reducing and eliminating waste and inefficiencies to analyzing processes in detail and engineering new solutions to improve patient outcomes. HCOs may begin with solving issues related to poor flow and advance to more complex patient safety and clinical outcomes issues.

HCOs that achieve their goals do so by allowing their staff to try out new and innovative ideas, to evaluate those ideas within mini-experiments, and to implement and deploy those innovations that are demonstrated to improve the way healthcare is delivered and HCOs are managed. Those same organizations utilize and rely on two of their most strategic assets—their healthcare data and the people who create insights from that data—to provide evidence-based guidance for individual improvement initiatives from inception to completion. This is the way to healthcare transformation.

Yes, healthcare QI initiatives can exist and be successful without the benefit of analytics. But analytics makes those projects much more efficient and effective. Likewise, analytics does not need to be integrated into structured QI methodologies to have a dramatic impact on operational and clinical decision making. But organizations that are striving to improve healthcare to achieve improved outcomes are more likely to succeed once their QI initiatives are fully able to leverage analytics assets and capabilities. The powerful insights possible with analytics combined with a structured approach to identifying, implementing, and evaluating improvement opportunities can greatly improve the likelihood that QI activities can achieve changes that matter and outcomes that last.

Notes

1. John Boyer et al., *Business Intelligence Strategy: A Practical Guide for Achieving BI Excellence* (Ketchum, ID: MC Press, 2010), 7.
2. Thomas H. Davenport, Jeanne G. Harris, and Robert Morison, *Analytics at Work: Smarter Decisions, Better Results* (Boston: Harvard Business School Publishing, 2010), 57.

About the Author

Trevor Strome, MSc, PMP, has nearly two decades of healthcare informatics, data management, quality improvement, and analytics experience. In his current role at the Winnipeg Regional Health Authority, Trevor leads the development and implementation of innovative analytics tools for use in healthcare quality and performance improvement initiatives for the Emergency Program. He is also assistant professor with the Department of Emergency Medicine, Faculty of Medicine, University of Manitoba, where he participates on clinical and operations research projects and lectures on statistics, informatics, and quality improvement.

Trevor completed undergraduate training in computer science and neuroscience, graduate training in epidemiology, and achieved Project Management Professional (PMP) certification and black belt level certifications in both Lean and Six Sigma. Trevor has successfully lead frontline healthcare quality improvement projects, managed teams of information technology professionals, and created award-winning healthcare analytics applications. Trevor has consulting experience in both the public and private sectors, and as a software entrepreneur has participated in the successful commercialization of software, including an emergency medical services data system launched in cooperation with the University of Alberta and other commercial partners.

In addition to this book, Trevor has coauthored three book chapters and numerous articles on various healthcare-related topics. An in-demand speaker on the topic of healthcare analytics, Trevor has shared his unique experience and insight with audiences throughout North America and around the world.

You may connect with Trevor via:

- **E-mail:** Trevor@HealthcareAnalyticsBook.com
- **Twitter:** @tstrome
- **Blog:** http://HealthcareAnalytics.info

About the Companion Web Site

Healthcare analytics is a very rapidly evolving field. State-of-the-art information published today is likely to be out of date and obsolete tomorrow. This book's companion web site, **http://HealthcareAnalyticsBook.com**, picks up where the book leaves off. In addition to downloadable forms, templates, and other documents that you can use within your own analytics practice, the site also contains links to resources, references, and other information related to the field of healthcare analytics. If you sign up for e-mail updates, you will receive a notice whenever the resource list is updated and when new downloadable material is made available. It is my commitment to you, the reader, to keep the web site updated with new material whenever advances in the field are made, so please sign up for e-mail updates and visit the site often for all the latest supplemental material available.

The **password** to the web site is **analyticsbook**.

Index